European Constitutional Law Network-Series

edited by Prof. Dr. Dr. h.c. Ingolf Pernice,
Walter Hallstein-Institute for European Constitutional Law (WHI)

Vol. 10

Ingolf Pernice | Ana Maria Guerra Martins (eds.)

Brexit and the Future of EU Politics

A Constitutional Law Perspective

Nomos

The publication of this work was supported by the Open Access Publication Fund of Humboldt-Universität zu Berlin

The Deutsche Nationalbibliothek lists this publication in the Deutsche Nationalbibliografie; detailed bibliographic data are available on the Internet at http://dnb.d-nb.de

ISBN 978-3-8487-6208-8 (Print)
978-3-7489-0324-6 (ePDF)

British Library Cataloguing-in-Publication Data
A catalogue record for this book is available from the British Library.

ISBN 978-3-8487-6208-8 (Print)
978-3-7489-0324-6 (ePDF)

Library of Congress Cataloging-in-Publication Data
Pernice, Ingolf / Guerra Martins, Ana Maria
Brexit and the Future of EU Politics
A Constitutional Law Perspective
Ingolf Pernice / Ana Maria Guerra Martins (eds.)
278 pp.
Includes bibliographic references and index.

ISBN 978-3-8487-6208-8 (Print)
978-3-7489-0324-6 (ePDF)

1st Edition 2019

Published by
Nomos Verlagsgesellschaft mbH & Co. KG
Waldseestraße 3-5 | 76530 Baden-Baden
www.nomos.de

Production of the printed version:
Nomos Verlagsgesellschaft mbH & Co. KG

Waldseestraße 3-5 | 76530 Baden-Baden

Printed and bound in Germany.

ISBN (Print): 978-3-8487-6208-8
ISBN (ePDF): 978-3-7489-0324-6

DOI: https://doi.org/10.5771/9783748903246

Introduction

Precisely one year after the UK' referendum on remaining or leaving the EU, which is the basis of Brexit, the European Constitutional Law Network (ECLN) met at the Faculty of Law of the University of Lisbon on 23 and 24 June 2017 to discuss 'Brexit – Challenge or End of EU Constitutional Law?'.

The formal inclusion of a withdrawal clause – Article 50 of the Treaty on the European Union (TEU)[1]– into the TEU through the Treaty of Lisbon opened a Pandora's box with consequences that no one could predict either before the entry into force of that Treaty or after the referendum in the UK; and even today it is difficult to fully assess the impact of the clause and, in particular, of making use of it. As the negotiations of Brexit,[2] the draft Withdrawal Agreement that ensued,[3] the successive rejections by the House of Commons,[4] and the successive decisions of the EU 27 leaders, in agreement with the UK, on the extension of the negotiations' period, first-

1 According to Article 50 TEU, any Member State may decide to withdraw from the Union in accordance with its own constitutional requirements. The Member State, which decides to leave the Union, shall notify the intention of withdrawal to the European Council. The Union shall negotiate and conclude an agreement with that Member State, which shall be concluded on behalf of the Union by the Council, by a qualified majority with the consent of the European Parliament.
The Treaties shall cease to apply to the State in question from the date of entry into force of the Withdrawal Agreement or, failing that, two years after the notification above referred, unless the European Council, in agreement with the Member State concerned, unanimously decides to extend this period.
If a State, which has withdrawn from the Union, asks to rejoin, its request shall be subject to the accession procedure.

2 The documents related to the negotiations of Brexit are available at the website https://europa.eu/newsroom/highlights/special-coverage/brexit_en (accessed 26 June 2019).

3 Draft Agreement on the withdrawal of the United Kingdom of Great Britain and Northern Ireland from the European Union and the European Atomic Energy Community, as agreed at negotiators' level on 14 November 2018, available at https://ec.europa.eu/commission/files/draft-agreement-withdrawal-united-kingdom-great-britain-and-northern-ireland-european-union-and-european-atomic-energy-community-agreed-negotiators-level-14-november-2018_en (accessed 26 June 2019).

4 The Draft Withdrawal Agreement was rejected on 15 January, 12 March and 29 March 2019.

ly, until 22 May 2019 and later on until 31 October 2019, under certain conditions,[5] have shown, the complexity of an exit process exceeds what anyone could expect, and it seems to be a challenge to overcome the political and practical obstacles that came out of that open box. Yet, in the perspective ex post, given the level and strength of the ties uniting the EU and its Member States not only economically and legally, but also politically, including social, financial and monetary matters, etc, no one should be surprised that even after three years the process is far from coming to a satisfying end.

This experience of applying Article 50 TEU in practice is perhaps the main reason why we are, currently, in a deadlock. Nobody knows what will happen in the near future. Can the UK expect a re-opening of the negotiation on the Withdrawal Agreement? After the European elections, will the UK decide for – or fall into – a "hard Brexit"; or will the government call for new elections opening new perspectives, or call for a second referendum? How many further months (or years?), if any, will the deadline of Article 50 TEU (have to) be extended? Will the EU and the UK conclude another type of agreement? If so, which one? Will the UK Parliament accept this potential new agreement? Is it still possible and feasible for the UK to remain in the EU, and if so, under what conditions? All these scenarios are for now conceivable, but, looking back to the Brexit process, some of them are more realistic than others.

As to the EU, after a rather short period, still under the impact of the referendum's shock – in which even some institutions of the EU had sustained that the Brexit should be rapid and under hard conditions in order to give an example to other Member States – since the beginning of the negotiations with the UK, its position has been characterised by serenity, precision and clarity. First, the EU accepted the decision of the UK to withdraw without making of it a drama. Second, under the political leadership of President Donald Tusk, the EU-27 has rejected the negotiation strategy by Theresa May, who demanded parallel discussions on the withdrawal and on trade. The President of the European Council insisted that the negotiations should be informed by the following principles: minimization of disruption caused by UK withdrawal; securing agreement on the rights of EU citizens living in the UK; ensuring that the UK honors its financial

5 The UK is bound to hold European Parliament elections as it is still a member of the EU, between 23 and 26 May 2019. If the UK fails to hold the elections, it will leave the EU on 1 June 2019. See European Council Decision, 11 April 2019, XT 20013/19, available at: https://www.consilium.europa.eu/media/39043/10-euco-art50-decision-en.pdf (accessed 26 June 2019).

commitments; and avoiding a hard border between Northern Ireland and Ireland. Donald Tusk stated firmly: 'These four issues are all part of the first phase of the negotiations. Once, and only once, we have achieved sufficient progress on the withdrawal, can we discuss the framework for our future relationship. Starting parallel talks on all issues at the same time, as suggested by some in the UK, will not happen'.[6] Third, contrary to one of the major fears after the UK referendum, a potential domino effect leading to the disintegration of the Union, the remaining Member States united around the strategy of the EU. In fact, the EU's 27 leaders unanimously adopted the phased strategy at the European Council meeting on 29 April 2017. Fourth, even with many obstacles, the EU has achieved to conclude a draft agreement with the UK on its withdrawal. Fifth, the EU has always left an open door for the UK to revoke the withdrawal notification and to remain in the EU. The Court of Justice of the European Union, in the case *Wightman and Others*, has confirmed that a revocation of a notice under Article 50 TEU is lawful, since its 'purpose (...) is to confirm the EU membership of the Member State concerned under terms that are unchanged as regards its status as a Member State, and that revocation brings the withdrawal procedure to an end'.[7]

Conversely, as to the UK, one has been witnessing a permanent lack of coherence and a constant dance of advances and retreats, leaving the impression that the UK was singing the music of Beatles Should I stay or should I go?, culminating in a plurality of decisions of the UK Parliament and in the Prime Minister Theresa May's request to delay Brexit twice. Even with the new Prime Minister, Boris Johnson, and his determination to go for a hard Brexit in case the EU is unwilling to reopen the negotiations on the Withdrawal Agreement – what it seems to be – it is questionalbe whether he will find support for this in Parliament. The membership of the UK to the EU, and similarly, the Brexit process were rightly qualified, by the UK Supreme Court in the *Miller* case,[8] as having constitutional implications for the UK (like for the EU), and this may explain why it attracts more public attention and binds more workforce both sides for a

6 Remarks by President Donald Tusk of 32.3.2017 on the next steps following the UK notification, available at https://www.consilium.europa.eu/en/press/press-releases/2017/03/31/tusk-remarks-meeting-muscat-malta/ (accessed 26 June 2019).

7 CJEU, judgment of 10 December 2018, Wightman and Others, C-621/18, ECLI:EU:C:2018:999, para. 75.

8 Judgment (2017) UKSC of 24 January 2017, *Miller*, paras 60, 62, 67, 68, 78, 80–82, 90, 92, 96, 100, at: https://www.supremecourt.uk/cases/docs/uksc-2016-0196-judgment.pdf (accessed 21 August 2017).

longer time as ever expected. But the process with its adverse effects on the capacities of all to tackle important other political issues cannot last without limits.

Taking into account the uncertainties and implications caused by the Brexit referendum, as well as the lasting openness of the outcome, one may ask why publishing a book on Brexit right now. The main intend of the present book is to reflect upon the Brexit process and analyse some particular issues from a constitutional perspective, with the aim to contribute to the discussion and the finding of solutions to some of the many problems raised.

From a European and constitutional law perspective, Brexit raises so many issues, however, that the contributions to this volume cannot cover all of them, and particularly cannot predict the future. Focussing on some key general questions and particularly relevant policies, the eleven substantive chapters of the book divided into three parts may give the reader a hint of how the Brexit process and its implications are seen from European constitutional law scholars outside the UK and stimulate the discussion across the channel on the future relationship between the UK and the EU.

I. As the key narrative of the UK before and after the Brexit referendum was based on the rhetoric of State sovereignty and democracy, Part I of the book is devoted to *Constitutional Issues – Basic Concepts Revisited.*

The insistence of the UK in "taking back control" over laws, borders, democracy, and money, means anything but "taking back control" over the most significant issues of UK State sovereignty and its constitutional system. Putting this decision in the hands of the people through the referendum apparently legitimates Brexit within the purest standards of democracy and protection of fundamental rights. Part I of this book will deconstruct this rhetoric.

Tom Eijsbouts, following the discourse of President Macron of 26 September 2017 at Sorbonne, proposes the development of a new notion of State sovereignty, which not only agrees with the facts of European integration instead of opposing them, but which also allows for an original conceptual development of sovereignty in the EU, concerning both the Member States and the Union itself. Analysing the way how the Euro summit came into being and got itself a permanent president, the Author concludes that this institutional development shall be faced as an exercise of European sovereignty. For Tom Eijsbouts, the European Union needs to build up an open and dynamic concept of European sovereignty, which instead of challenging national sovereignties builds upon, adds to and so strengthens the Member States' sovereignty, if it would like to prevent events such as Brexit.

Commenting Tom Eijsbouts' contribution, *Ana Maria Guerra Martins*, first, underlines how fascinating the said proposal is, but second, warns of its dangers. Above all, the introduction of the idea of sovereignty in the EU context may arise more fears and suspicion, which might well pave the way to populism, nationalism and general pessimism. Secondly, the definition of such a sovereignty would be rather difficult. Thirdly, she argues that the way how the Euro summit came into being and got itself a permanent president must be integrated in the broader context of EMU governance and, fourthly, the recent case law of the CJEU on Article 50 TEU, accepting the lawfulness of the revocation of the withdrawal notice is much more an expression of a State's sovereignty – the one of the UK – than an expression of EU sovereignty. Finally, the author does not envisage how helpful could be such an idea after the exit of the UK.

Giacinto della Cananea looks at this from another perspective: He distinguishes two main visions of the European Union, first, in order to explain and critically assess, in a second step, the options for a future relationship of the UK with the EU as a question of differentiated integration. One of these visions is close to the traditional concept of State sovereignty, the EU being 'a broad community of nation-states', the other that of an 'ever closer union' of peoples as provided in the preamble of the Union Treaties. A critical assessment of these two opposed positions leads to an analysis of the existing mechanisms of flexibility in EU law, both within the EU (e.g. the EMU, enhanced cooperation, the fiscal compact and two speed integration) and beyond the EU such as the European Economic Area, a set of bilateral agreements like in the case of Switzerland and what is called the "Schengen's mixed membership". Considering the implications for Brexit the author finds that, given the need to take account of the twin criteria of clarity and coherence a solution different from the one that exists in the context of the EEA could not be meaningfully envisaged.

Jirí Zemánek analyses the future of the protection of fundamental rights after Brexit, seeking to demonstrate that the withdrawal of the UK from a "community of destiny", which comprises three levels of protection of fundamental rights – national constitutions, European Convention on Human Rights and the EU Charter of Fundamental Rights – where the UK has, to some extent, a reserved position, would represent more than a mere withdrawal from its rights and obligations. His focus is the question to what extend the effective protection of fundamental rights of the individual is affected. As the UK plays an important role in the EU-wide dialogue on fundamental rights and their protection under the Charter of Fundamental Rights, he also points to the loss Brexit would cause in this regard.

Ingolf Pernice is looking at the different stages of the Brexit process from the perspective of democracy. Is it a challenge to, or an exercise of democracy? While the strategy to put the future membership of the UK to an advisory referendum is qualified as an exercise of democracy, and both, the procedure of Article 50 TEU and the increase of democratic awareness throughout the EU can in no way be understood as a challenge to democracy, incidences related to the preparation of the referendum as well as the interpretation of its result in the subsequent political action are found to bring about serious challenges to democracy. The author discusses the impact of open lies and targeted disinformation on democratic processes on the one side, and the way the UK Parliament has renounced to the constitutional principle of sovereignty of Parliament and brought itself into an irresponsible situation of incapability to take a positive decision, on the other side. Yet, the emergence of a new citizens' engagement, triggered by the Brexit process throughout the Member States, movements of citizens taking ownership of the EU, acting for 'remain' and calling for further developing the EU, are taken as a positive outcome of the still open Brexit process.

II. As Brexit will definitively impact on *The Future of the Internal Market and its Social Dimension*, Part II of this book addresses the effects of Brexit in the internal market, in the EU citizens' social rights and in immigration control and the future of the 'Green Border' in Ireland.

Paula Vaz Freire analyses the economic effects of Brexit in the UK and in the EU, drawing attention to the fact that the UK specialization in services, namely financial services, as well as the foreign direct investment in the UK has evolved and turned into a successful model due the UK's EU membership. The withdrawal from the EU would diminish the UK's attractiveness insofar. For the EU, as a whole, the economic effects of Brexit may be less significant, but taking into account the strategic and political importance of the UK and the contribution of the UK to the EU budget, the Brexit will also have a considerable impact on the remaining EU-27. However, from the perspective of the EU, free trade and free movement must be definitively linked, as the internal market is a global reality.

Rui Lanceiro develops a broad critical analysis of the recent CJEU case law on EU citizen's social rights, sustaining that, from *Grzelczyk* case to *Dano*, *Alimanovic* and *Garcia-Nieto* judgments, the Court has initiated a significant change in its earlier jurisprudence on non-national EU citizens' access to social benefits in host Member State, and did not change this in more recent cases, such as *Gusa*, *Prefeta* and *Tarola*. This restrictive trend has also extended to the social dimension of EU citizenship in the *Commission v. United Kingdom* (UK child benefit or child tax credit) case. It is suggested that this judgment probably aimed at influencing the outcome of UK Remain/Leave referendum, which failed. The consequence is understood to be that the notion of EU citizenship as a fundamental and political status with no link with the economic market is being dismantled and the free movement of citizens and workers in the EU remains incomplete.

Daniel Thym and *Mattias Wendel* discuss one of the most topic issues throughout the Brexit debate – immigration after Brexit. They are stressing the uncertainty of the moment and conclude that, while Brexit may facilitate legal control over the entry and stay of EU citizens, from a legal perspective it might, ironically, render control of immigration of non-Europeans, including asylum seekers, more difficult.

III. Apart from the internal market and its social dimension Brexit will influence other *EU Policies – Perspectives of Cooperation with the UK*, as it is discussed in Part III of the present book.

Jean-Victor Louis gives a legal standpoint of the presumed effects of Brexit on the Monetary Policy, as well as on financial regulation and supervision. After recalling some essential features of the Brexit negotiations up to the present no deal and the new delay, the author draws attention to the internal institutional consequences of Brexit in monetary and financial matters, as well as to the situation of the UK, the EU and other national authorities in the international financial institutions and the future cooperation. In spite of admitting negative consequences either for the UK or for the EU, the author concludes with a word of hope, asserting that once the UK becomes a third country after Brexit, this is perhaps an opportunity for the EU progressing towards a sui generis federation.

In his comments on Jean-Victor Louis's contribution, *Stefan Griller* states that he agrees with the identification of the most salient issues as well as the respective observation, therefore he opts to work on the hypothesis of no deal and after 31 October 2019 the UK would find itself as a third country. The author advocates that the dynamics of EMU-participation may change once the UK will have left, because the non-EMU Member States will lose a powerful ally. Secondly, after Brexit, the EMU-deepening and reform, including the building of a Banking Union, may become easier, once the UK has always been a brake to this kind of initiatives. Thirdly, the impact of a no deal Brexit on the freedom of establishment and, particularly, with regard to financial services located in the UK is considered to be huge. In spite of a rather optimistic scenario for the EU in this context, the author envisages also some negative effects.

Maria José Rangel de Mesquita, finally, analyses the possible modes of participation and cooperation of the UK in the EU external action both, CFSP and CSDP, with particular regard to the possible future status of the UK either as a mere third State or a special status as an 'ex-EU third State'. The analysis is based upon an assessment of the developments in the EU external action, particularly the 2016 Global Strategy for the European Union's Foreign and Security Policy and the adoption of 'three main categories of initiatives – political, institutional and financial – in some of which the UK may participate during and after the transition period'. In his very detailed and deep description of the EU and the UK perspectives on the recent developments as well as of the terms found in the Withdrawal Agreement and the Political Declaration the author concludes in shaping a (possible) differentiated third State status of the UK in the field of European Foreign and Security Policy, including Defence, based upon autonomy both sides but also on common values and shared interests both, known and to be identified though structured consultation and thematic dialogues. It could go as far as to agree on an observer status of the UK with some rights of participation in EU institutions, bodies and structures 'with financial EU counterparty ("value for money")'.

In the present introduction it is not possible to give a sufficiently precise idea of the richness and of all the challenging thoughts expressed during the conference, as updated and completed in the present volume by some reflections regarding the evolution of Brexit process since June 2017. Therefore, we invite the readers to go through the following chapters and develop your own views on the EU constitutional impact of Brexit.

The Lisbon ECLN-conference 2017, which was organized by the *Lisbon Center for Research in Public Law* in partnership with *Walter Hallstein Institut für Europäisches Verfassungsrecht* of Humboldt University of Berlin, would not have been possible without the generous financial support of *Fundação para a Ciência e Tecnologia* (the Portuguese Agency for Science and Technology), the *Luso-American Development Foundation*, and two law firms – *Quatre Casas* and *Linklaters*. We very warmly thank all these donors for their friendly support. We are also grateful to the *Open Access Publication Fund of Humboldt-Universität zu Berlin* for generous financial support as well as to *Dr. Johannes Rux* and *Stefan Grote* of NOMOS publishing, who made the publication of this book possible.

Ana Maria Guerra Martins/Ingolf Pernice
Lisbon / Berlin, July 2019

Inhalt

Part III EU Policies – Perspectives of Cooperation with the UK

Part I
Constitutional Issues – Basic Concepts Revisited?

Sovereignty In The European Way.
How the *Euro Summit* Came Into Being and Got Itself a Permanent President

Tom Eijsbouts, University of Amsterdam

Abstract

The Brexit decision to leave the EU is a miscarriage of democracy. It is an expression of UK sovereignty, proving not, however, that the Kingdom is retrieving its full sovereignty from the EU. Instead it proves that the UK's sovereignty has failed to evolve along with its membership of the EU and take on a European dimension.

This failure has seen UK sovereignty regress from a sophisticated parliamentary sovereignty to a regressive outburst of popular sovereignty. In other Member States, the same failure of evolution of sovereignty is latent and could lead to similar outbursts.

The first lesson for us jurists to learn from Brexit is that keeping the articulation of sovereignty to law and legal thinking, and to ourselves, is a mistake. Worse: constitutional and legal doctrine are to blame, in part, for allowing thought on sovereignty to be split up into incompatible positions and for leaving the notion defenseless against its hijack by populists.

Emmanuel Macron, first in his Humboldt plea for 'European sovereignty', provides a sound alternative. He denies the opposition between EU authority and Member State sovereignty and wants Member States to draw sovereign strength from their membership of the EU and from the latter's development. It is a new version of the pooling of sovereignties. We should give this a constitutional elaboration.[1]

1 Emmanuel Macron on Sovereignty: Berlin, 10 January 2017 (Humboldt-Universität) www.rewi.hu-berlin.de/de/lf/oe/whi/FCE/2017/rede-macron; Financial Times 24 January 2017, 'Europe holds its destiny in its own hands' https://www.ft.com/content/3d0cc856-e187–11e6–9645-c9357a75844a; Athens, 7 September 2017 https://en-marche.fr/articles/discours/

Sovereignty must be seen not as an immutable idea or notion, but as a specific form of authority, to wit that of a (or the) State. Apart from its axiomatic belonging to the State, it is not static, but has evolved for hundreds of years and will keep evolving over time, together with the State. Membership of the Union presses for further evolution of both the Member States and their sovereignties beyond the current forms, and involving the structure of authority and representation of the EU. This must be given a constitutional acknowledgment, in which constitutional doctrine can help.

This piece is meant to open up our thinking in the matter. It centers on one crucial event: the instant creation of a new institution at the heart of the Union, the Euro summit and its permanent presidency, on 25 March 2010. In an emergency situation, the EU created for itself a new authority and organized it instantly. This happened outside the law but was a clear case, both of EU constitutional evolution and of evolution in the sovereign authority of euro Member States.

Introduction. Article 50 TEU

Article 50 TEU is, among other things, an enduring expression of individual national sovereignty for the EU Member States. Article 50 TEU is also a token of the EU as a Union born from an agreement, not from violence, maintained under an enduring agreement and not by violence. This precludes an ultimate monopoly of violence as that of the US federation and it is among the things precluding the EU from itself becoming a State. What is more: the whole EU Treaty, in its evolution, is an enduring expression of the sovereignties of the Member States collectively. So, sovereignty is at the heart of the EU constitution.

This allows to look at the EU constitutional situation under Brexit with an eye to finding things to learn, first about what went wrong in the UK, then about our understanding of sovereignty in general, and finally about the evolution of State sovereignty in and through the EU.

---

discours-president-athenes; United Nations, 19 September 2017 https://en-marche.fr/articles/discours/discours-president-nations-unies; La Sorbonne, 26 September 2017 (English version) http://www.elysee.fr/assets/Initiative-for-Europe-a-sovereign-united-democratic-Europe-Emmanuel-Macron.pdf; E. Macron, R.volution: R.concilier la France (French and European Publications Inc 2017).

Brexit: a miscarriage of democracy

The Brexit decision is an acute expression of British sovereignty *singly*. It shows this up, however, not as a regain of ultimate control but as a whimsical and impulsive form of popular sovereignty, departing from the trusted *parliamentary* sovereignty and resulting in what must be called a miscarriage of democracy. A less sturdy constitution than the British would have been in acute difficulty of survival. It is an enlightening paradox how the UK, an accomplished constitutional State, has been in political shambles since its secession decision while EU, an incipient constitutional authority, is keeping its act together and in control.[2] This suggests that there is, at least in these *extremis*, in the face of threats to the public realm from inside and outside, a better claim of control, and of sovereignty, in the EU Member States together than there is in the UK singly.

Brexit shows, among other things, what the consequences can be of our not coming to grips with sovereignty in the European Union. For the EU it is fundamental to have a sound notion of sovereignty, if only because sovereignty is often invoked as an argument, or a solid fact, in the way of any real (political) EU constitution. More assertively, national sovereignty needs to be understood as an element of the EU constitution, even as a principle of it, as AG Kokott has ventured to call it.[3]

Sovereignty in general and in the context of EU

Traditionally law scholars has been the first to define and tend to the notion of State sovereignty. But this task has been relinquished at the creation of the European Union, and legal doctrine has split up into different often irreconcilable positions, notably about the relationship of European integration and national sovereignty. First, there is the doctrine holding that sovereignty gradually loses relevance in the context of European integration. Another reading of the situation is that the EU is gradually taking over sovereignty from the Member States in the form of competences and with the legal precedence of EU law. Then there is constitutional plur-

2 See the European Council position http://www.consilium.europa.eu/en/press/press-releases/2017/04/29-euco-brexit-guidelines/ the two years hence have only reinforced this evidence.

3 Opinion of 26 October 2012 in Case C-370/12 *Thomas Pringle v Government of Ireland*, par. 136

alism, in which sovereignty remains crucial, but is a mere 'claim to authority' of a polity in general, with the State losing its special status. In each of these readings, as in prevailing general views, there is at least a tense or even contradictory relationship between the EU and the sovereignty of its Member States.

In Emmanuel Macron's notion there is no such necessary contradiction; quite the contrary: there is possible synergy. His views are not alien to the ideas of multilevel or composite constitutions and to the old notion of 'shared sovereignty'. But while the latter primarily serves as doctrinal or justificatory tools in the realm of constitutional law, Macron's European sovereignty is militant, political, and defiant: 'we must reconquer our sovereignty'. First of all, he wants to keep the idea of sovereignty from being hijacked by populists.

Following Macron, we lawyers may stop our doctrinal squabbles and take the lead to find a notion of State sovereignty which not only agrees with the facts of European integration instead of opposing them, but which also allows for an original development of sovereignty in the EU, concerning both the Member States and the Union itself.[4]

The idea of EU sovereignty is not altogether strange to our thinking as EU lawyers, notably in the notion of 'pooled sovereignty'. Ingolf Pernice and others have developed ideas on 'divided sovereignty' in the context of multilevel constitutionalism. But it needs to be made concrete and related to actual fact.

The first thing to do is to demystify sovereignty. Sovereignty is not an idea, unfathomable or mysterious. It is, simply, a kind of authority, to wit the special authority of the State. It is distinct from other authorities, and stands above them. Sovereignty is, first, the ultimate authority of the State over societal movements and authorities such as markets, militias, religions: *internal sovereignty.* Second, it is the full membership of the State in the international community of States: *external sovereignty.* To further demystify it, we need to break the State's authority down into different spheres, or theatres where it is expressed and develops. Most difficult for us lawyers is to see it as something else but a matter of law and a matter of notion. Stefan Griller writes, typically: 'The concept of "sovereignty" is primarily rooted in the field of the General Theory of Law and State (which is in this part strongly linked to legal theory) and in Public International

4 See https://plone.rewi.hu-berlin.de/de/lf/oe/whi/FCE/2017/rede-macron/; Emmanuel Macron: 'Europe holds its destiny in its own hands', *Financial Times*, 24 January 2017.

Law'.[5] Sovereignty is not rooted in theory; it is rooted in historic development. All authority has solid foundations in crude, basic fact. So does sovereignty. This face of sovereignty is often hard to understand for the scholar, but its understanding is also most liberating and even illuminating.

The sovereignty of France, like that of Germany and of the US, is not primarily a concept, but a fact. Anyone wanting to deal with the State, internally and externally, will profit from knowing that its sovereignty is a fact and that it hurts to deny or ignore it. Forget about the notion. Of course the *notion* of sovereignty is important to support and organize the *facts* of sovereignty to greater coherence and function in their context. This is in the same way that the *notion of a car* supports and organizes *actual cars* to greater intelligibility and better function in traffic.

Likewise, sovereign authority is more than a matter of law or legal authority only or mostly, but also a matter of *political* authority. When the Federal Republic in the turmoil after the fall of Berlin's Wall in 1989 launched its plan to absorb the German Democratic Republic, it took the initiative in a political act of sovereignty. Legal acts of sovereignty would follow from this: first, treaties (Unification Treaty and 2+4 Treaty) then legislation. Then, again, treaties, notably that of Maastricht.

Thus, sovereign authority is developed and expressed in several theatres: in that of fact, in that of action, in that of structure and in that of doctrine. All these theatres are different, each with its own casts of characters, even if they communicate to keep coherence. In the form of *doctrine*, sovereignty is expressed and elaborated internally in constitutional law and scholarship and externally in diplomatic practice, by academics, courts and government officials. In the form of *structure,* sovereignty is expressed in the context of legal systems, in constitutions and legal instruments, by treaties and legislation. In the form of *action*, sovereignty is acted by State authorities nationally, and among States internationally. In the form of *fact,* sovereignty arises from events at the origin of States, and subsists in the form of the raw fact of the States' existence.

Having originated with the State, first as a fact, then as a notion supporting the fact (Bodin, Hobbes), the authority of sovereignty has evolved with the State over time, both in the abstract and in each State specifically.

5 Stefan Griller, 'The Impact of the Constitution for Europe on National Sovereignty', in Jiri Zemanek/Ingolf Pernice (eds) *A Constitution for Europe: the IGC, the Ratification Process and Beyond,* ECLN series vol. 5 (Nomos, Baden-Baden 2005), pp 151–182, at 151.

It has evolved from god-given internal authority to legally established internal and external authority; from absolutist to parliamentary, to popular, to national, to constitutional, to democratic. As all authority, even that of law, sovereignty in its structure, in its means and instruments, and in its appearance will vary over time and between States. The only thing immutable is its appertaining to the State (in the abstract and in the concrete).

And with the inevitable evolution of every State, sovereignty's structure of authority evolves; often towards greater democracy and rule of law. With the evolution of the international community, international sovereignty evolves toward including greater sophistication in international organization.

Does it also evolve towards greater authority or weight of international organizations? That is uncertain generally, but unmistakably it does in the EU. What is more, the evolution of the authority of the EU presses for a constitutional restructuring of the Member States' sovereignties.

Such pressure can be creative, as is most obvious in the case of the Bundesrepublik. Created as a sovereign State only in name and form, in 1949, the new German State has completed and boosted its sovereignty in the seventy years hence. Today it is among the world's top in any ranking of sovereign States, both as a vigorous democracy and as a member of the world community, both internally and externally. And all this evolution it has been both pressed and allowed to make by its membership of the EU. Its sovereignty has a clear European condition and qualification. This is what M. Macron understands by European sovereignty and what he vies to obtain for France also, and for the other Member States. Anyone interested can read it from the facts. Only the Bundesverfassungsgericht (and its epigonist colleagues Courts) is blinded by its own legalistic doctrine from seeing the facts. And it is cornering itself and legal doctrine in a false dilemma. Fortunately, German politics is not fooled.

While Germany, having come last, has been the first to develop this extra layer to its sovereignty, it is the opposite with the first sovereign State in Europe, the present United Kingdom. It has been the last and most reticent to allow its sovereignty to develop under European integration. Brexit is the result.[6]

6 The argument of Germany's strong evolution under EU membership I have put forward in a keynote speech before the Dutch circle of constitutionalist on 15 December 2017, published as 'Germany's Grand and Growing European Sovereignty' in Hardt, Sacha, Heringa, Aalt Willem, and Waltermann, Antonia: *Bevrijdende &*

How does such evolution of a national sovereignty work? It works similar to natural evolution of a species. Each older version of sovereignty is overlaid in further steps, but preserved in the full heritage. It is like we humans carry along our animal (and even bacterial) heritages. Our European State sovereignties still carry the remains of godly authority, of kingdom, of popular revolt. Even if they have now landed into constitutional and democratic authority, these older forces and sources lurk below and can be awakened, as shown in the US and the UK these days.

We are concerned not with the past, however, but with its future evolution. Sovereignty, carrying all the baggage from its past stages, will evolve further *inside* the Member States due to their membership, and *between* them. This is already going on. It is our business to stop quibbling and together turn our attention to how our States' *structures* of sovereignty have in fact been evolving under pressure from EU membership. From there, we may find doctrinal underpinning and coherence.

An unhistoric idea of sovereignty is false. This goes for the recurring idea that sovereignty is always or essentially popular sovereignty as well as for the idea that sovereignty lies with the power of exception and for any other fixed idea.

Sovereignty as a notion: more than legal

Sovereignty is not merely a legal notion concerning legal power, but it essentially, actually and notionally also involves political authority. The fact that sovereignty is historic and evolving, in the way of a living species or (better) of a form of culture or technology, means that there is no final limit to its development or sophistication, or to its pooling in the context of the EU, however frantically this limit is looked for by legal authority, judicial or academic. The search and the evolution is a matter of history, politics and law, not of legal definition. No *idea* of sovereignty should be in the way of a development of the facts and the notion. Certainly not the legalistic idea that sovereignty amounts to a State's legal powers and that it inevitably is reduced by transfers. The evolution of the German State from 1949, involving power transfers while being strengthened, contradicts this idea.

Begrenzende soevereiniteit. (Boom juridisch, Den Haag, 2018), pp 10–31. See also editorial *European Constitutional Law Review* 2018–1: 'European Sovereignty'.

The challenge is to see what facts of sovereignty present themselves and what notion of sovereignty fits the developing relationship between the EU Member States and their Union. This is a challenge both in fact and in understanding. Let us pick one instance of such evolution, not a legal one, in order to avoid the idea that sovereignty is all about notions and about law. A single but brilliant little historic fact may help us to explore lines of the possible evolution of Member State sovereignty in the EU.

Creation of the Euro-summit and its permanent chair, Brussels, 25 March 2010

In a meeting of the European Council on 25 March, 2010, at a first peak of the financial crisis and euro-crisis, the members of the Eurozone were to pledge their solidarity with Greece, in order to keep the Greeks and the euro from going under. This pledge was momentous as an act of authority in the face of power of the money markets, not to forget its possible conflict with Article 125 TFEU (no bail out). The nine non-members of the EU were asked to leave the room! UK's Gordon Brown left last, protesting loudly. Most of this is documented in the recent book by Luuk van Middelaar, who was chairman Van Rompuy's close assistant at the time.[7]

Under this immense pressure, what happened, constitutionally speaking? Exceptional authority was exercised and new authority created. A new institution was born, in the heart of the EU executive: the Euro-summit, as it is now called. It was created not by way of legal decision, but by way of convention. This happened in the heat of the moment and under protest of some concerned. Both conditions helped towards the birth of this new institution: the pressure of events created the necessity; British protest marked the moment of the event and helped to articulate it.

When Brown had left, the question arose who was to chair this meeting? The first and only meeting in this format, autumn 2008, was convened and chaired by then rotating chair France's President Sarkozy. With Spain now in the rotating presidency of the EU, no wonder José Zapatero walked to take the chair. But in the meantime, on 1 December 2009, the office of permanent chair of the European Council had been created. Herman van Rompuy was in the chair and did not budge.

---

7 Luuk van Middelaar, *Alarums and Excursions. Improvising Politics on the European Stage* (Agenda Publishing, Newcastle Upon Tyne, 2019), p 200. This is the English version of his book in Dutch of 2017. The event was reported in greater detail in my own (TE) newspaper column in *Het Financieele Dagblad* of 7 May, 2010 on the basis of my fact-finding then. The facts reported have never been disputed.

Zapatero looked left and right for support, but did not find it in sufficient measure. Then he turned and went back to his seat. The showdown was over. Thus, Van Rompuy not only won the clash, but also his position for the future, a new institution and a new office for the Union constitution. The whole thing would be legally codified in the Fiscal Treaty of 2 March 2012, Art. 12.

There is no doubt that what happened on 25 March 2010 changed the EU constitution. A new institution was created in the heart of the EU executive, with a new office of permanent president. The change not only affected Member States' core sovereignties but was an expression of new authority created for the EU, an authority of sovereign substance and status, however limited.

Conclusion: suggestions for reading sovereignty and the EU constitution

How sovereignty will implant itself constitutionally into the EU structure is not clear. It will have to be read from the facts. A close reading of the above case of constitutional innovation may help to summarize, to conclude and to make some suggestions:

1. Sovereignty is not a notion alone, nor legal. It is, first, a fact in the form of an authority, to wit the essential authority of the State. This goes for sovereignty both as fact and as notion, the two supporting each other.
2. Sovereignty is inherent in States and in their constitution. As a matter of fact and as one of notion, sovereignty has originated and evolved with the State and will continue to do so.
3. Sovereignty is not a given, neither as fact nor as a notion. There is no immutable idea behind neither the facts nor the notion of sovereignty. Nothing prevents its evolution towards the EU wielding original political authority in agreement with the sovereignties of its Member States.
4. Neither the facts nor the notion of sovereignty is exclusively legal. To consider sovereignty a matter of law and of legal doctrine alone leads to deception. On the other hand, to consider sovereignty as essentially non-legal, as Carl Schmitt held, is equally deceptive.
5. Sovereign authority in the context of the Union will come about and be exercised respectful of Member State's sovereignties while pressing these to evolve. It is not only a matter of dividing nor of sharing or pooling sovereignty, but of finding a new constitutional structure. The

UK Government and constitutional doctrine has failed to make clear to the public that the evolution of the EU is no necessary threat to UK sovereignty even if it provides evolutionary pressure to the structure of executive authority and representation, and even judicial authority which has to be acknowledged, expressed and given form, at the national level.

6. There is no identifiable limit in law to the evolution of the Member States or to that of their sovereignties in the context of the Union, their 'European sovereignty'.
7. We want to study the EU constitutional development to understand it as an evolution of the facts and notion of sovereignty of the member in conjunction with the constitution of the EU. The latter will concern:
   a) EU original executive authority, as developing e.g. in the Euro-context and exemplified by the case above-mentioned;
   b) EU original legislative and representative authority, as developing out of two sources. First, the Member States' treaty making power evolving into EU *primary* legislation, in name and in fact of authority. Second, in the original authority of EU *secondary* legislation. Most critically, this development will be led through the original representative authority of EU citizens by the European Parliament as provided in Arts. 10 and 14 of the EU Treaty since Lisbon.
   c) The Bundesverfassungsgericht's square denial, from the Maastricht Urteil through the Lissabon Urteil and upheld to today, of the European Parliament's representation of EU citizens is an unlawful denial of the possibility of German sovereignty to evolve and include representation of Europeans.[8]
   d) EU original judicial authority (autonomy, precedence), as claimed by the ECJ and in most part agreed by most who are subject to it (Member States, courts, private parties). The problem is that this authority articulates itself clearly only in legal terms, ignoring wider than legal claims *and* pretending these wider claims have also been agreed. But supremacy of EU law and the autonomy of the legal order are *not* expressions of full EU supremacy or of its autonomy, let alone its sovereignty.

8 BVerfG 30 June 2009, 2 BvE 2/08, para 284: Das Europäische Parlament bleibt vor diesem Hintergrund in der Sache wegen der mitgliedstaatlichen Kontingentierung der Sitze eine Vertretung der Völker der Mitgliedstaaten.

8. If we constitutionalists don't come to terms with Member State sovereignty as evolving in the context of EU, this will be a disservice to the field of EU constitutional law.
9. Member States that don't come to terms with their sovereignty as an essential remaining attribute yet necessarily evolving under Union membership, will remain a liability in and to the Union.
10. As to Brexit. At finalizing this paper (Thursday 20 April, 2019), the present author nor anyone else can know what the British miscarriage of democracy on 23 June 2017 will ultimately bring forth. But some decision is inevitable. As an optimist, whose understanding of developments is oriented by hope, I perceive a possibility for the crisis to lead to a redeeming change in the structure of UK politics and even a change in the constitution.

The saving change in UK politics needs to tackle, probably, as one never can be sure of the way redemption takes, two elements. First, the polarity between the two dominant parties; second, each of their crucial internal divisions over the EU.

The change in the UK constitution would have to involve an acceptance of the evolution of UK sovereignty in fact and its notion to include membership of the Union as one of its pillars. It would remain a parliamentary constitution under the sovereignty of Parliament, but has to become, in addition, *the European* sovereignty of the UK, accounting for the representative input of the European Parliament and for the executive input of EU executive bodies, notably the European Council and its progeny, such as the Euro-summit.

It is my hope as a scholar, that the present piece will be a help to understanding prospective events in the Brexit saga beyond the date of Easter 2019, when the piece was finalized. And that the events will have turned or channeled the immense political pressures into development, British and European. As is and will always remain in the powers and ingenuities of politics[9].

---

9 All this in the spirit of Bernard Crick's classic *In Defence of Politics*, London, Penguin, 1992, fourth edition (my copy); first: 1962.

Brexit from the Perspective of EU Sovereignty. Some Comments on Tom Eijsbouts' Contribution to this Book

Ana Maria Guerra Martins

Abstract

The author argues that the application of the idea of sovereignty to the EU can bring fears and suspicions that must be avoided in the current European context. Otherwise, by definition, the idea of sovereignty comprises an element of exclusivity, which is almost impossible to spread over more than one entity. Sharing sovereignty is to some extent a contradictory idea. The author also sustains that the presidency of the euro summit must be assessed in the context of EMU governance, and within this broader context, this is anything but an exercise of EU's sovereignty. In addition, Article 50 TEU does not express some kind of EU sovereignty, as the case Wightman *of the Court of Justice recently confirmed. Even if all these difficulties could be overcome, it remains the question whether the idea of EU sovereignty can be helpful after the withdrawal of the United Kingdom. In the view of the author, it cannot, and all in all, the EU does not need to be compromised with sovereignty.*

1 A Challenging and Inspiring Contribution but…

Commenting Tom Eijsbouts' contribution in this book is a rather challenging task because he introduced in the discussion of Brexit one of the most traditional notions that has ever been conceived in philosophy, political science and legal theory – the idea of sovereignty. Fascinated by the discourse of the President Macron of 26 September 2017 at Sorbonne,[1] Tom Eijsbouts seeks to give new clothes to the concept of sovereignty, rejecting the perspective of those who consider that the idea of sovereignty is nowadays outdated.

---

1 Available at http://www.elysee.fr/declarations/article/initiative-pour-l-europe-discours-d-emmanuel-macron-pour-une-europe-souveraine-unie-democratique/.

By contrast, he accepts that Brexit is an exercise of UK sovereignty, underlining, at the same time, that 'Brexit proves that the UK's sovereignty has failed to evolve with its membership to EU and take on a European dimension'.

For Tom Eijsbouts, at the end of the day, the Brexit decision may be explained by the failure of realizing the European dimension of sovereignty.

Apparently, for him, once sovereignty means authority, a multilevel constitutionalism must be based on some kind of multilevel sovereignty in progress that is located together in the individual Member State and in the Member States altogether as well as in the European Union.

According to Tom Eijsbouts, in order to prevent events, such as Brexit, Europe needs to build up its own sovereignty, which shall be added to the States' sovereignty. For him, the way how the *Euro summit* came into being and got itself a permanent president shall be faced as an exercise of European sovereignty.

This is a rather inspiring and innovative perspective. However, as fascinating as it may be, the transposition of the idea of sovereignty into the European Union will, in my opinion, face some insurmountable obstacles.

Firstly, applying the idea of sovereignty to the EU is a risky adventure, once it can bring more problems than contribute to solve whatever it is. From the outset, it can arouse fears and suspicions that must be avoided in the current European context at all costs. All in all, the EU does not need to be compromised with sovereignty.

Secondly, the definition of EU sovereignty is anything but simple, once it must integrate and respect the sovereignty of the Member States. Or, by definition, the idea of sovereignty comprises an element of exclusivity, which is almost impossible to spread over more than one entity. The idea of shared sovereignty, which has already been rather popular among the legal scholarship, is to some extent contradictory.

Thirdly, the presidency of the euro summit must be assessed in the context of EMU governance. Within this broader context, one can hardly accept that it was an exercise of EU sovereignty.

Fourthly, Article 50 TEU might comprise some elements that go beyond the classical idea of sovereignty but that does not mean that they express some kind of EU sovereignty. The recent decision of the Court of Justice,[2] accepting the reversibility of the notification of leaving the EU confirms that the UK sovereignty is much more powerful.

---

2 CJEU, C-621/18 *Wightman and Others* ECLI:EU:C:2018:999.

Fifthly, even if all these difficulties could be overcome, it remains the question whether the idea of EU sovereignty can be helpful after the withdrawal of the United Kingdom.

In the following pages I will elaborate on these topics.

2 *Sovereignty of the European Union – a Risky Adventure?*

2.1 *Inseparable link between sovereignty and State*

Starting by clarifying why the application of the concept of sovereignty to the European Union, is, in my point of view, a risky adventure, I would say that the idea of sovereignty was not conceived for a multilevel constitutional[3] and political entity,[4] such as the EU.

Conversely, it was conceived by Jean Bodin,[5] in the sixteenth century, intrinsically linked to the State as an institution that maintains a supreme governing authority over a defined territory and which is to be differentiated both from its constituent people and its office holders. The sovereignty was, in the internal perspective, the absolute and indivisible authority of the ruling power.[6] This theory was meant to serve a practical political purpose.[7] In order to survive the State needed to eliminate all other powers.

Secondly, the external dimension of the sovereignty, which implies the capacity of acting within the international community on an equal footing with other States, arose later (nineteenth century).

---

3 See: Ana Maria Guerra Martins, 'Opinion 2/13 of the Court of Justice in the Context of Multilevel Protection of Fundamental Rights and Multilevel Constitutionalism Revisited', in L Papadopoulou / I Pernice / J. H. H. Weiler (eds.), *Legitimacy Issues of the European Union in the Face of Crisis – Dimitris Tsatsos memoriam* (Baden-Baden, Hart / Nomos, 2017) 233–270, as well as the bibliography therein quoted.

4 I have always argued that the EU is a new form of aggregation of political power. See: Ana Maria Guerra Martins, *Manual de Direito da União Europeia* (Lisboa, Almedina, 2017) 229 ff.

5 J. Bodin, *De Republica* (1576).

6 Martin Loughlin, 'The erosion of sovereignty' (2016) *Netherlands Journal of Legal Philosophy* 58.

7 Tina Oršolič Dalessio, 'The issue of sovereignty in an ever closer union' (2014) *Croatian Yearbook of European Law and Policy* 69.

However, both dimensions were born and grew up with in the scope of the State,[8] whose affirmation as a political entity required a strong internal and external authority. To put it in other words, the idea of sovereignty arose in a very particular environment and enjoyed certain unrepeatable circumstances. That means the idea of sovereignty was – as many other ideas – a product of a certain time and a certain place.

As the circumstances have changed, so has the understanding of sovereignty.[9] In continental Europe it took the form of popular sovereignty, while in Great Britain it was transformed into the principle of parliamentary sovereignty.[10]

2.2 The EU's challenges to the idea of sovereignty

The project of the European integration has also created great challenges to the idea of sovereignty.[11] However, in my opinion, any attempt to transpose this idea into the European Union itself is at first starved for failure.

The European Union is a compound entity, created by the Member States, and its authority derives, firstly, from them and, secondly, from the citizens.

The European Union was made neither to – and it actually cannot – eliminate the authority of the Member States nor to replace them. By contrast, it comprises the Member States and it is founded on cooperation, mutual influence, reciprocal confidence and interdependence.

In my opinion, the inclusion of the idea of sovereignty in this context may jeopardize the relationship between the Union and the Member

---

8 On the concept of sovereignty and its evolution see Daniel Philpott, "Ideas and Evolution of Sovereignty", Sohail H. Hashmi (ed.), *State Sovereignty: Change and Persistence in International Relations* (Pennsylvania State Univ. Press, 1997) 15 ff; Bruno De Witte, 'Sovereignty and European Integration: the Weight of Legal Tradition' (1995), *MJ* 145 ff; Joseph A. Camilleri/Jim Falk, *The End of Sovereignty? The Politics of a Schrinking and Fragmenting World* (Edward Elgar Publishing,1992) 11–68; R.P. Anand, 'Sovereign Equality of States in International Law', *Recueil des Cours de l'Académie de Droit International* 197 (1986, II), 17–46.

9 Tina Oršolič Dalessio, (2014) 'The issue of sovereignty' 69.

10 This is not the adequate place to elaborate on these topics. In order to go further see Neil Walker, 'Sovereignty Frames and Sovereignty Claim', *Research Paper Series No 2013/14* of the School of Law of the University of Edinburgh, 4 ff; Pavlos Eleftheriadis, "Law and Sovereignty" *Legal Research Paper Series No 42/2009.*

11 See, above all, Neil MacCormick, 'Beyond the Sovereign State' (1993) *Modern Law Review*, 1–18.

States' institutions, as even may break the mutual confidence and cooperation between the Member States and the EU.

The assertion of sovereignty by the EU would certainly provoke an affirmation of sovereignty by the side of the Member States. Actually, throughout the history of the European integration, there are many examples of tension between the Member States and the European Union, due to disputes on sovereignty, as the case law of some Supreme[12] and Constitutional Courts[13] has ever shown. In their Lisbon Treaty judgements some Constitutional Courts[14] seemed to be more flexible as regards the understanding of sovereignty. However, all courts 'have made it clear that the process of European integration can only go on as far as it does not infringe upon the core national sovereign powers'.[15]

If one introduces the sovereignty narrative in the European Union, one can easily anticipate the raising of tensions between the Member States and the EU institutions.

The idea of sovereignty of the Union would also comprise an internal and an external authority, which could compete with the authority of the Member States. This competition would certainly provoke a permanent tension between the institutions of the European Union and the Member States that would not be beneficial for the future developments of the relationship between the EU and the Member States.

Therefore, I do not believe that the notion of sovereignty would be very helpful in the context of the European Union.

As regards the external dimension of the EU, it is even more questionable to accommodate the idea of sovereignty. Although the Union has the capacity to act at the international level, it is subjected to several restraints. The conclusion of mixed agreements,[16] the limited competence in the field of foreign security and defense policies[17]are only two examples of these restrictions. However, they illustrate rather well that the lack of EU's author-

---

12 See, for instance, the Irish Supreme Court in the judgement *Crotty v An Taoiseach* or the Danish Supreme Court Decision in the Maastricht case.

13 See the French Constitutional Council in the Maastricht case I, the German Federal Constitutional Court in the Maastricht case, the Spanish Constitutional Court in the Decision on the Treaty establishing a Constitution for Europe.

14 See the decisions of Lisbon Treaty of the German Federal Constitutional Court, the Czech Constitutional Court, the Hungarian Constitutional Court, the Latvian Constitutional Court and the Polish Constitutional Court.

15 Tina Oršolič Dalessio, 'The issue of sovereignty', 77.

16 Ana Maria Guerra Martins, *Os desafios contemporâneos à ação externa da União Europeia – Lições de direito internacional público II* (Coimbra, Almedina 2018) 211 ff.

17 Ana Maria Guerra Martins, *Os desafios contemporâneos*, 320 ff.

ity within the scope of some external fields. Dealing with the concept of sovereignty in this context is problematic.

Additionally, in several domains the core of international political authority still belongs to the Member States.

Contrary to Tom Eijsbouts, I do think that the historical background of the idea of sovereignty is so strong that it can hardly be freed from it.

2.3 The EU Sovereignty Idea May Cause More Damages than Gains

In my point of view the introduction of the idea of sovereignty in the European Union discourse may cause more damages than gains, once it may lead to some misunderstandings, turmoil and even may reactivate nonsense fears, which is the most propitious terrain for evolving Eurosceptic, nationalist and populist movements.

In my opinion, as the European Union has become a different and unique political entity in the world, the use of old notions, such as sovereignty or federalism, in legal and political theories may well result in more problems than solve whatever it is.

In its origins, the idea of sovereignty contains not only an element of authority but also a component of exclusivity. It is rather difficult for the Member States and, who knows, even for the citizens to accept some kind of multilevel sovereignty in progress that is located either in the individual Member State or in the Member States altogether or in the European Union.

I do believe that it is better to replace or even to abandon the idea of sovereignty,[18] which is too connected to the State, than seeking to adapt it to political entities that have nothing to do with the State and I am not alone in this belief.[19]

In my view, the introduction of the idea of sovereignty into the narrative of the European Union can only contribute to exacerbate the current internal tension between the Member States and the EU institutions. And Brexit is a good example of how the introduction of the idea of sovereignty in the European Union discourse may well lead to negative Member States' reactions.

---

18 Against: Bruno De Witte, 'Sovereignty and European Integration' 172–173.

19 See: Pavlos Eleftheriadis, 'Law and Sovereignty', *maxime* 37–39. Michael Newman, *Democracy, Sovereignty and the European Union* (London, St. Martin's Press, 1996), 12; Michel Leroy, 'Requiem pour la souveraineté, anacronisme pernicieux', in *Mélanges offerts à Jean Vélu*, tome I, (Brussels, Bruylant, 1992), 91 f.

It is never too much to remember that Brexit relied on the rhetoric of State sovereignty before and after the referendum of 23 June 2016.

'Taking back control' over laws, borders, democracy, and money means nothing but 'taking back control' over the most significant issues of the State sovereignty and its constitutional system.

Notwithstanding, the rhetoric of sovereignty does not take many factors into account. Firstly, the effects of the withdrawal of a Member State are not restricted to the Member State that leaves the EU, but they are also felt in the other Member States. That means the sovereignty of the remaining Member States is also threatened. Secondly, it is true that the referendum is one means to express the will of the people, but it is not the sole legitimate tool in the context of the exercise of democracy. To put it bluntly, sometimes it is not the most accurate one, especially when nobody seriously considered the consequences of a negative result. Many scholars, including in the UK, criticized the political decision of launching a referendum on the exit of the EU. For instance, Jo Shaw drew attention to the particularities of the UK as a Union State and to the fact that some voices were not heard in the referendum vote and that those voices were also neglected during the debate that preceded the referendum.[20]

In the perspective of the remaining Member States, the withdrawal may be conceived as an "authoritarian" decision, since their citizens will lose certain rights – for instance, the ones inherent to EU citizenship – without having been consulted.

Accepting that Brexit is an expression of the UK sovereignty– which is rather consensual and recently confirmed by the Court of Justice of the EU[21] – implies at the same time the rejection of EU sovereignty.

Therefore, if one does not want to introduce more sand into the gear, it is better to leave some words, such as sovereignty or federalism, where they are – within the State. That means aside the EU.

2.4 *Other difficulties Raised by the Extension of the Concept of Sovereignty*

Extending the concept of sovereignty beyond the State raises other questions, such as the one of its scope of application. Is it reduced to the EU or

20 V. Jo Shaw, "The quintessentially democratic act? Democracy, political community and citizenship in and after the UK's referendum of June 2016" (2017) *Journal of European Integration*, 12.

21 CJEU, C-621/18 *Wightman and Others* ECLI:EU:C:2018:999.

is the idea of sovereignty potentially applicable to every political entity? Is it applicable to the international community in general, namely, to international organizations? Is it applicable to global governance, which comprises all sorts of actors (either public authorities or private)?

I am not saying that Tom Eijsbouts suggested going that far. Actually, I do not think so. However, if one opens the Pandora's box of the sovereignty beyond the State, one must be ready to extend it, at least, to some international organizations, such as United Nations or the Council of Europe.

In my view, if the application of the idea of sovereignty to the EU raises enormous problems, extending the said application to international organizations, which are dominated by the Member States, will face even greater obstacles. And the sovereignty of the global governance is even more unconceivable. This is true that global governance includes informal entities that exercise authority without clear legal and political limits and sometimes against the decisions of the States and of other legitimated international actors, such as the international organizations. However, that does not mean they are exercising sovereignty. By contrast, such situations only highlight the difficulties of drawing a clear boundary between the exercise of sovereignty and a pure exercise of power (force). Not all acts originating from a political authority should be regarded as sovereign acts.

In the event that the idea of sovereignty only applies outside the State within the European Union, as it seems to be the reasoning of Tom Eijsbouts, I do not see what is the difference of some well-known concepts, such as 'pooled sovereignty', 'shared sovereignty',[22] or 'divided sovereignty', which have been theorized by the EU law scholarship since the very beginning of the European integration.

22 Stefan Oeter, 'Souveränität und Legitimation staatlicher Herrschaft im europäischen Mehrebenesystem', in Astrid Epiney et al, *Direkte Demokratie und Europäische Union. Démocratie directe et Union européenne* (Freiburg 1998), 29 ff; idem, 'Souveränität und Demokratie als Probleme in der "Verfassungsentwicklung" der Europäischen Union' (1995) *ZaöRV*, 666 ff.

3 *Denial of EU Sovereignty*

3.1 *The evolution of EMU Governance denies the EU Sovereignty*

Contrary to Tom Eijsbouts, I do not assess the way how the *Euro summit* of 25 March 2010 in Brussels came into being and got a permanent president as an exercise of European sovereignty.

In my viewpoint, this isolated act should be evaluated in the wider context of the response of the EU and the Member States to the sovereign debt and euro crises. When one puts this act in context, one can hardly accept that the way how the EMU governance evolved during the crisis represents any kind of exercise of EU sovereignty. By contrast, as it is well known, in order to challenge the crisis not only a panoply of legislative measures through the procedures established by the Lisbon Treaty were approved, but also some inter-governmental treaties (the European Stability Mechanism, the Treaty on Stability, Coordination and Governance in the Economic and Monetary Union, the so-called Fiscal Compact, and the Single Resolution Fund in the context of the banking union[23]) and the executive agreements (EFSF2 and the Euro Plus Pact). These treaties were approved by the EU Member States outside the Lisbon Treaty and bound only the signatory Member States. As Bruno De Witte put it, 'a group of EU Member States 'stepped outside' the EU legal order and the Union's institutional framework, and instead resorted to instruments of public international law for organizing their cooperation'.[24]

The Euro summit and its presidency are currently enshrined in Article 12 of the Treaty on Stability, Coordination and Governance in the Economic and Monetary Union, the so-called Fiscal Compact, of 2 March 2012, which entered into force on 1 January 2013. The president of the Euro summit is not anymore the President of the European Council, but an elected President. That means the so-called expression of EU sovereignty has suddenly turned into the most evident expression of Member States' sovereignty, since the Fiscal Compact is an international treaty approved and signed by the Member States and not by the EU.

---

23 On the inter-governmental agreement on the Single Resolution Fund see Federico Fabbrini, 'On Banks, Courts and International Law – the Intergovernmental Agreement on the Single Resolution Fund in Context' (2014) 21 *MJ* 3, 444 ff.

24 Bruno De Witte, 'Using International Law in the Euro Crisis – Causes and Consequences', Working Paper, *ARENA Working Paper* No. 4, June 2013.

In the short term the TSCG may be fully integrated into the EU legal framework, following the recommendation of the Five Presidents' report[25] and a proposal of the Commission of December 2017.[26] However, up to now the Fiscal Compact remains an exercise of Member States' sovereignty. The EU sovereignty has not been exercised yet.

We will probably need to revisit this topic, if the above mentioned recommendation and proposal become hard law in the future, but with the currently available data, the way how the Euro summit got the permanent presidency was the result of a constellation of factors that cannot be assessed as an exercise of sovereignty.

Anyway, this was not the first time that law was overcome by facts in European integration. The crisis of the *chaise vide*, the Schengen Agreements, the Social Agreement, the successive opting outs of some Member States are good examples that can be invoked in this context.

To sum up, the way how the Euro summit got the permanent presidency was only a drop in a bucket that does not allow any definitive conclusion. After that episode there were so many manifestations in the opposite direction, which do neither permit to consider that the EU sovereignty has already emerged nor that it is in progress.

3.2 *The reversibility of the UK decision of leaving the EU*

Another example that denies the EU sovereignty concerns the reversibility of the UK decision of leaving the EU. This question has been discussed in the academy[27] since the UK referendum of 23 June 2016.

---

25 Available at https://ec.europa.eu/commission/sites/beta-political/files/5-presidents-report_en.pdf.

26 Proposal of the Commission of 6 December 2017 for a Council Directive laying down provisions for strengthening fiscal responsibility and the medium-term budgetary orientation in the Member States (COM(2017) 824 final 2017/0335 (CNS)). Available at http://eur-lex.europa.eu/legal-content/EN/TXT/PDF/?uri=CELEX:52017PC0824&from=EN.

27 See 'Editorial Comments' (2016), *Common Market Law Review*, 1491 ff; Christophe Hillion, 'Le retrait de l'Union européenne – une analyse juridique' (2016), *Revue trimestrielle de droit européen* 719 ff; Paul Craig, 'The Process: Brexit and the Anatomy of Article 50', in Federico Fabbrini (ed.), *The Law & Politics of Brexit* (Oxford Univ. Press, 2017) 49 ff; Catherine Barnard, 'Law and Brexit' (2017) *Oxford Review of Economic Policy*, 4 ff; Dora Kostakopoulou, 'Brexit, Voice and Loyalty: Reflections on Article 50 TEU' (2016), *European Law Review*, 484 ff;

Many scholars have suggested[28] that the UK decision was not irreversible. According to them, the UK might well change its mind and nothing in Article 50 prohibits the revocation of the notification, as long as it respects the constitutional requirements of the State. As Piet Eeckhout and Eleni Frantziou put it 'if a Member State could not remove its notification after changing its mind, and was thus forced to leave upon the conclusion of a two-year period under Article 50(3), that would effectively amount to an expulsion from the Union – a possibility that was considered and rejected during the *travaux*. It would also be contrary to the principles of good faith, loyal cooperation, the Union's values, and its commitment to respect the Member States' constitutional identities'.[29]

On 10 December 2018, the Court of Justice of the European Union puts an end to any doubt on this issue. Within the scope of a preliminary ruling request made by decision of the Court of Session, Inner House, First Division (Scotland, United Kingdom), the Court of Justice of the EU ruled that 'Article 50 TEU pursues two objectives, namely, first, enshrining the sovereign right of a Member State to withdraw from the European Union and, secondly, establishing a procedure to enable such a withdrawal to take place in an orderly fashion.'[30]

Agreeing with its Advocate General, based on 'the sovereign nature of the right of withdrawal', the Court admitted that 'Article 50(1) TEU supports the conclusion that the Member State concerned has a right to revoke the notification of its intention to withdraw from the European Union, for as long as a withdrawal agreement concluded between the European Union and that Member State has not entered into force or, if no such agreement has been concluded, for as long as the two-year period laid down in Article 50(3) TEU, possibly extended in accordance with that provision, has not expired'.[31]

According to the Court, the reversibility of the notification 'reflects a sovereign decision by that State to retain its status as a Member State of the

---

Tamara Capeta, 'Brexit and the EU Constitutional Order: A three Act Tragedy' (2016), *Croatian Yearbook of European Law and Policy,* 1 ff.

28 See Paul Craig, 'Brexit: A Drama in Six Acts' (2016), *European Law Review*, 464–465; Piet Eeckhout / Eleni Frantziou, 'Brexit and Article 50 TEU: A Constitutionalist Reading' (December 2016), *UCL European Institute Working Paper*' 37 ff.

29 Piet Eeckhout / Eleni Frantziou, 'Brexit and Article 50 TEU' 41.

30 CJEU, judgment of 10 December 2018, *Wightman and Others*, C-621/18, ECLI:EU:C:2018:999, para. 56 and 57.

31 Ibidem, para. 57.

European Union, a status which is not suspended or altered by that notification[32] (…), subject only to the provisions of Article 50(4) TEU'.[33]

And the Court stressed that 'given that a State cannot be forced to accede to the European Union against its will, neither can it be forced to withdraw from the European Union against its will'.[34]

The emphasis put on the sovereignty of the Member State by the Court contrasts with the lack of reference to the EU sovereignty. Actually, the EU sovereignty is rather irrelevant in this context.

Having said that, one has to underline that the Court also set up limits to State sovereignty. According to the Court, 'the purpose of that revocation is to confirm the EU membership of the Member State concerned under terms that are unchanged as regards its status as a Member State, and that revocation brings the withdrawal procedure to an end.'[35] That means the revocation of the withdrawal's decision shall not be transformed into a renegotiation of the remaining terms of the Member State in the EU.[36]

In conclusion, the decision of not leaving should be taken, at first instance, by the UK, in accordance with its sovereignty. The EU is, to a certain extent, subjected to that decision, unless it constitutes an abuse of law.[37]

32 See judgment of 19 September 2018, *RO*, C-327/18 PPU, EU:C:2018:733, paragraph 45.

33 CJEU, judgment of 10 December 2018, *Wightman and Others*, C-621/18, ECLI:EU:C:2018:999. para. 59.

34 Ibidem, para. 65.

35 Ibidem, para. 75.

36 For a comment on this decision see Oliver Garner, 'Case C-621/18, Wightman v Secretary of State for Exiting the European Union: the European Court of Justice Confirms that Article 50 Notification can be Unilaterally Revoked' (11 December 2018) *European Law Blog available at* https://europeanlawblog.eu/2018/12/11/case-c-621-18-wightman-v-secretary-of-state-for-exiting-the-european-union-the-european-court-of-justice-confirms-that-article-50-notification-can-be-unilaterally-revoked/; Dagmar Schiek, "The ECJ's Wightman Ruling, the "Brexit" Process and the EU as a Constitutional Entity" (7.1.2019) *Frankfurter Newsletter zum Recht der Europäischen Union,* available at https://www.europa-uni.de/de/forschung/institut/institut_fireu/newsletter/fireu-Newsletter-34.pdf.

37 Piet Eeckhout / Eleni Frantziou, 'Brexit and Article 50 TEU', 40.

4 *The Role of Sovereignty within the Negotiations of Brexit*

In spite of the current uncertainty of the Brexit's process, I would shortly like to elaborate on the role played by the idea of sovereignty in the negotiations of Brexit.

Regardless the final result of the Brexit process that nobody can predict by now, the negotiations of Brexit also revealed to some extent a common exercise of Member States' sovereignties.

Firstly, at the very beginning, the rejection of the negotiation strategy of Theresa May, who demanded parallel discussions regarding the withdrawal and trade, illustrates very well the leadership of the Union in the Brexit's process and the common exercise of Member States' sovereignties. According to the President of the European Council, the negotiations should be informed by the following principles: minimization of disruption caused by UK withdrawal; securing agreement on the rights of EU citizens living in the UK; ensuring that the UK honors its financial commitments; and avoiding a hard border between Northern Ireland and Ireland. "These four issues are all part of the first phase of the negotiations. Once, and only once, we have achieved sufficient progress on the withdrawal, can we discuss the framework for our future relationship. Starting parallel talks on all issues at the same time, as suggested by some in the UK, will not happen."[38]

The EU's 27 leaders unanimously adopted the phased strategy at the European Council meeting on 29 April 2017. Instead of contributing to divide Member States, Brexit aggregated them around a negotiating strategy that was proposed and supported by the European institutions.

From my point of view, although this decision has a constitutional component and may well be regarded as a constitutional moment, it can hardly be assessed as an exercise of EU sovereignty.

Secondly, the procedure of adoption of the future withdrawal agreement shall also be assessed as a common exercise of the Member States' sovereignties. This agreement shall be concluded on behalf of the Union by the Council, acting by a qualified majority that represents at least 72 % of the members of the Council representing the participating Member States, comprising at least 65 % of the population of these States, after ob-

38 Remarks by President Donald Tusk on the next steps following the UK notification, available at https://www.consilium.europa.eu/en/press/press-releases/2017/03/31/tusk-remarks-meeting-muscat-malta/.

taining the consent of the European Parliament (Articles 50 (2) TEU, 218 (3) and 238 (3) (b) TFEU).

The adoption of the withdrawal agreement by the Council, acting by a qualified majority, could even be seen as a first signal of the exercise of EU external sovereignty. Actually, the withdrawal agreement is concluded between the EU (not by the Member States) and the exiting Member State. However, in my opinion, this is not enough to characterize the treaty-making power of the Union as a pure exercise of sovereignty, due to the composition of the Council. It never acts independently of the Member States collectively. Furthermore, the future withdrawal agreement – if it exists – must follow the constitutional requirements of the leaving Member State. Therefore, the successive rejection of the draft agreement by the UK Parliament shows once again the Member State (rectius: the UK) sovereignty prevails.

Thirdly, the recent extension of the 29 March deadline to 31 October 2019, according to Article 50 (3)TEU, may also be assessed as an expression of the common exercise of the 27 Member States sovereignties and the UK sovereignty, once it is taken by a unanimous decision of the European Council and the agreement of the withdrawal Member State.

5 May EU Sovereignty emerge after Brexit?

Finally, although it is nowadays impossible to predict whether the exit of the United Kingdom from the Union will contribute to deepen the European integration or will constitute a fertile ground for disintegration, question whether the Brexit can have the effect of launching the EU sovereignty is always possible.

Despite the circulation of some proposals before Brexit, such as the Global Strategy for the European's Union Foreign and Security Policy presented by the High Representative of June 2016,[39] the Brexit led to the increasing of the discussion of the future of Europe. In March 2017 the Commission launched the White Paper on the Future of Europe,[40] which did not enclose any concrete proposal but scenarios for discussion. Since then,

39 Available at https://europa.eu/globalstrategy/sites/globalstrategy/files/regions/files/eugs_review_web_0.pdf.

40 Available at https://ec.europa.eu/commission/sites/beta-political/files/white_paper_on_the_future_of_europe_en.pdf.

the debate of the future of Europe has intensively increased both at political and at the academic level.

With or without an agreement concerning the future relationship between the United Kingdom and the EU, the Brexit will without doubt impact in several fields of the Union. For instance, without the UK the institutional framework will not be the same, as it loses one of the biggest Member States. Similar reasoning applies to the financial framework of the Union, once the United Kingdom is a liquid contributor to the EU budget. The impact of Brexit in the EU's Common Foreign and Security Policy (CFSP) and Common Security and Defense Policy (CSDP) will also be remarkable, since the UK is not only the Member State that spends more on security and defense but it is also a Permanent Member of the UN Security Council.[41] According to Whitman, '...for the EU the loss of UK's diplomatic and military resources will diminish the collective capabilities at the disposal of EU foreign and defence policies'.[42]

Depending on the future relationship between the UK and the EU agreement, the impact of UK's exit may still be minimized either for the UK or for the EU.

Let me concentrate on the topic of the rights of EU citizenship and fundamental rights in general. The withdrawal of a Member State – whatever it may be – from the Union will have an impact on EU citizens' rights either they are UK citizens or not. That means the impact of Brexit overcomes the boundaries of the UK. Agreeing with Piet Eeckhout and Eleni Frantziou, 'the withdrawal of a Member State from the European Union creates significant possibilities of regression in terms of fundamental rights, and of panoply of other rights of persons and companies'.[43]

---

41 On the impact of Brexit into the CFSP see Ramses A. Wessel / Adam Łazowski, 'Legal Consequences of 'Brexit' for the Role of the EU and the UK in Global Affairs', Paper presented at the EUSA Conference, Panel 7 A The Consequences of Brexit on Europe's role: Reinvigoration or Atrophy, Miami, 4–6 May 2017, available at file:///C:/Users/Ana%20Martins/Downloads/Wessel%20and%20Lazowski%20-%20Legal%20Consequences%20of%20Brexit%20-%20EUSA%20Miami%202017%20-%20Panel%207A%20(1).pdf; James Black et al, *Defence and Security after Brexit – Understanding the possible implications of the UK's decision to leave the EU – Compendium Report* (Cambridge, Rand Corporation, 2017), 25 ff.

42 Richard G. Whitman, "The UK and EU Foreign, Security and Defence Policy After Brexit: Integrated, Associated or Detached?" (2016) *National Institute Economic Review*, 238–44.

43 Piet Eeckhout / Eleni Frantziou, 'Brexit and Article 50 TEU', 19.

It is still possible to prevent some consequences of the losing of rights of EU citizenship,[44] through the conclusion of an international agreement between the UK and the EU, but it is impossible to prevent the losing of rights. This loss does not depend on the exercise of EU sovereignty, rather on the exercise of UK sovereignty, on the one hand, and on the common exercise of Member States' sovereignties within the Union, on the other hand. That means the EU sovereignty does not play any significant role in the future relationship between the UK and the EU.

In addition, there are some fundamental rights that are very difficult to maintain, such as the right to access to the Court of Justice of the European Union either directly or through national courts by means of a reference in the context of a preliminary ruling and the fundamental rights acknowledged by the Charter, which are not part of the ECHR.

Another remark should be made about the EU competences after Brexit.

In my viewpoint, the EU competences will not change as a direct consequence of Brexit. However, after the leave of the UK, it might be easier to exercise some of them[45] as well as to modify the Treaty, in conformity with Article 48 EU Treaty.

Provided it actually happens, one has to underline that this will not be an exercise of EU sovereignty but an exercise of sovereignty of the Member States, acting collectively.

To conclude, constitutionally speaking, we firmly believe that the EU sovereignty will be a so useless idea after Brexit, as it has been before.

---

44 See: Guayasén Marrero González, "BREXIT' – Consequences for Citizenship of the Union and Residence Rights', (2016) 23 *MJ* 5, 796–811; Oliver Garner, 'After Brexit: Protecting European Citizens and Citizenship From 'BREXIT' – Consequences for Citizenship of the Union and Residence Rights', (2016) 23 *MJ* 5 (2016) 796–811; Oliver Garner, 'After Brexit: Protecting European Citizens and Citizenship From Fragmentation', *EUI Working Paper LAW* 2016/22.

45 The authors of the Clingendael Report argue that EU defence might well be one of the fields where the exit of the UK may be beneficial. See Anne Bakker / Margriet Drent / Dick Zandee, 'European Defence: how to engage the UK after Brexit?' (The Hague 2017), 8.

Differentiated Integration in Europe After Brexit: An Institutional Analysis

Giacinto della Cananea

Abstract

It is self-evident that the European Union has evolved over time and so has the relationship between unity and differentiation. Understanding the nature of this evolution is more difficult. This essay seeks to explicate this development, not by a temporal analysis, but by delineating two opposite political visions of the European construction. The first is the vision that is centred on the idea, or ideal, of an "ever closer union among the peoples of Europe". The other vision of Europe postulates a wide and loose union, a sort of 'club' where the members do not necessarily wish to change the current state of things. The differing solutions provided by these visions are examined with regard, first, to some mechanisms of differentiated integration, which are considered against the twin criteria of clarity and coherence and, second, with regard to other legal mechanisms, which imply an interaction between EU members and third countries. This can be useful for a better understanding of the institutional and legal options that are available for the relations between the UK and the EU in the post-Brexit period.

I. Introduction

The outcome of the referendum that has been held in the United Kingdom about leaving the European Union (*Brexit*) has fuelled the debate, in political and academic circles, about the future of the EU, in particular from the perspective of differentiated integration.[1] This essay seeks to contribute to the debate, by arguing that it should be made clear that the differing solutions that are proposed for the challenges with which the Union

---

1 For a discussion of the theories of European integration, see FG Snyder, *European Integration*, Encyclopedia of Law and Society (Sage, 2004); A. Stone Sweet, Integration and the Europeanization of the Law, in P Craig & R Rawlings (eds), *Law and Administration: Essays in Honour of Carol Harlow* (Oxford University Press, 2003), 197.

is confronted are based not only on different legal foundations, but also on distinct visions of the European construction. For analytical purposes, two opposite political visions can be delineated. At this stage, it suffices to characterize each of them in the briefest terms. There is, first, the vision that is centred on the idea, or ideal, of an 'ever closer union among the peoples of Europe', as provided by the Treaty of Rome's preamble. The other vision of Europe postulates a wide and loose union, a sort of 'club' where the members agree only on a few fundamental principles and do not necessarily wish to change the current state of things.

It is precisely because these are political visions that they provoke passionate debates. But, for all their importance in social and political life,[2] passions do not help analytical clarity and coherence.[3] My intent is, first, to show the distinctive traits of each vision and to argue that the differences between them are so profound that the significance of some central elements of European integration will differ depending upon the framework within which they are considered. This applies, in particular, to the various mechanisms of differentiated integration. The ensuing analysis will make this patently clear, but the idea can be briefly exemplified here. The vision of unified Europe that is based on the idea of the 'ever closer union', whilst recognizing the diversity of European peoples not only, descriptively, as an element of the real, but also, prescriptively, as an element that must be preserved, aims at strengthening the ties between them. The other vision, which aims at achieving a wider and looser union, pays less attention to those ties and favours greater flexibility. Secondly, after showing the different background of these political visions, we shall see that both pose particular problems, legally and institutionally.

The essay is divided into four parts. The first two parts will illustrate the vision of the European construction that purports the achievement of the 'ever closer union' and that of a wide union, with less intense ties and obligations for its members, respectively. Next, some mechanisms of differentiated integration will be considered against the twin criteria of clarity and coherence. Finally, there will be a discussion of other legal mechanisms, which imply an interaction between EU members and third countries. This might be helpful for a better understanding of how the issues arising from Brexit can be dealt with.

---

2 See AO Hirschman, The Passions and the Interests: Political Arguments for Capitalism before Its Triumph (Princeton, Princeton University Press, 1977).

3 P Craig, Constitutions, Constitutionalism and the European Union, 7 Eur. L. J. (2001) 125.

II. Two Visions of Europe (I): An "Ever Closer Union"

With regard to the first political vision of Europe, three are the main themes underlying it: first, the meaning and relevance of the "ever closer union"; second, the emergence of a 'community of destiny'; third, a set of institutional and legal mechanisms, with specific regard to the principle of loyal cooperation – governing the action (and inaction) of both common institutions and national authorities. Adequate attention must be paid to some elements of flexibility too.

A. A Union of Peoples

The first vision is well grounded in the genetic act of modern European integration, the Declaration of 9 May 1950 as well as by the founding treaties. The Declaration was premised on the necessity to eliminate the 'age-old opposition of France and Germany'. However, its drafters were fully aware of the importance, for a polity, of the cultural and social construction of the sense of belonging. They thus proposed the creation of a community, viewed as a 'first step in the federation of Europe', through the achievement of a '*de facto* solidarity' between the Member States. The Treaty of Paris establishing the European Coal and Steel Community was based on the same strategy, but with an important linguistic shift. It did no longer refer only to the States, but aimed at laying the foundations of a community of peoples (a '*communauté plus large et plus profonde entre des peuples longtemps opposés*'). The Treaty of Rome sought to achieve the same goal. According to its preamble, this Community was created '*among peoples* long divided by bloody conflicts'. An adequate awareness of such conflicts was not, however, an obstacle to the choice of those peoples to give, through the institutions thus created, 'direction to *their future common destiny*'. The Community was thus the first step towards 'an ever closer union among the peoples of Europe'. This formulation was explicitly teleological, in the sense that it sets out the *telos* of European integration.[4].

The thesis that not only the founding States, but also their peoples, are constitutionally relevant is of remarkable importance in helping us to understand the nature of the legal order of the Community. The ECJ, for ex-

4 For this terminology, see JHH Weiler, *The Constitution of Europe* (Cambridge University Press, 1999) and id, Europe in Crisis – On 'PoliticalMessianism', 'Legitimacy' and the 'Rule of Law', 53 Singapore J. Leg. St. 248 (2012).

ample, referred to it in its famous ruling in *Van Gend en Loos*, when it argued that the EEC constituted a 'new legal order of international law' and established the direct applicability of the Treaty of Rome.[5] This is not to say, however, that the Treaty was based on strong democratic mechanisms in the sense that all public power was channelled through Parliaments.[6] Quite the contrary, it simply set up a Common Assembly, certainly not an all-powerful body, though its institutional connection with national Parliaments could be viewed in a different light today, in a period in which new attempts are being made to strengthen the ties between representative institutions.

That said, the shift from States to peoples has had a number of important repercussions, the first of which is the pluralist conception of the social element. The Community was not simply premised on the recognition of the existence of a plurality of peoples but, precisely because its *telos* was to give rise to an 'ever closer union' between those peoples, on the common understanding that no step would be taken to forge a single people or *demos*. Put differently, the ties existing between the peoples of Europe that accepted to forge a 'future common destiny' were to be progressively intensified and strengthened, but without eliminating their distinctiveness.[7] Similarly, the preamble of the Charter of Fundamental Rights, which under Article 6 TEU has the same legal value of the treaties, provides that 'The *peoples of Europe*, in creating an ever closer union among them, are resolved to share a peaceful future based on common values'. The underlying philosophy thus differs from that which underlies the US Constitution, which begins with the identification of its unitary author, 'We the People of the US'.[8] This conclusion, which attenuates the possible tension between the recognition of a pluralistic Europe and the aspiration to

5 ECJ, Case 26/62, *Van Genden Loos v. NederlandeseAdministratie der Belastingen*, holding that the 'Treaty is more than an agreement which merely creates mutual obligations between the contracting states. This view is confirmed by the preamble to the Treaty which refers not only to governments but to peoples'.

6 See P Craig, The Community Political Order, 10 Indiana J. Global L. Studies (2003), 79, 84.

7 For further analysis, see R. Dehousse (ed), *Europe after Maastricht: an Ever Closer Union?* (Springer, 1994); J.L. Quermonne, Trois lectures du Traité de Maastricht: essai d'une analyse comparative, 42 Revue fr. sc. pol. (1992) 802, 813 (arguing that a federal vision was not incompatible with the Treaty of Maastricht, though with important adjustments).

8 See B Ackerman, *We the People: Foundations* (Harvard University Press, 1991), for an analysis of the foundations of the US Constitution; C Nicolaidis, We, the Peoples of Europe, 83 Foreign Affairs (2004) 97, and M Zuleeg, What Holds a Nation

strengthen the ties between its various parts,[9] is coherent with the emphasis that the TEU's preamble has placed more recently on the ambition to 'reinforce' the 'European identity'. From the wording of the Treaty this is clearly something that pre-existed in the Union.

B. A Community of Destiny

There is another fundamental consequence of the shift from States to peoples, which concerns the social element. The founding Treaties clearly rejected the idea of a community of origin and embraced that of a community of destiny (*'a destin partagé'*). There is a striking difference between this conception of the social element and that of the German *Volk*, with its strong sense of identity and belonging.[10]

Precisely because the goal to achieve an 'ever closer union' is connected with the creation of a community of destiny, it implies a dynamic conception of integration, as opposed to a static conception.[11] This means that the Member States have not simply joined a club and agreed on a set of obligations. Rather, they have created a community aiming at strengthening the ties among their peoples.[12] More recent political and legal documents have confirmed this, including the Solemn Declaration of 1983[13] and the TEU, according to whose first provision 'this Treaty marks a *new stage in the process of creating an ever closer union among the peoples of Europe*, in which decisions are taken as closely as possible to the citizen'. European integration is

---

Together? Cohesion and Democracy in the United States and in the European Union, 45 Am. J. Comp. L. (1997), 505, 506, pointing out the difference between the philosophies underlying the US Constitution and the EC Treaty.

9 See, however, the report published by the LSE, *Ever Closer Union. Report of the Hearing of 15th April 2015* (2016), 6, holding that a tension does exist.

10 See JHH Weiler, *The Constitution of Europe*, cit., 295, tracing the roots of the overemphasis on the organic understanding of peoplehood to Carl Schmitt.

11 See LJ Constantinesco, La nature juridique des Communautés européennes, in Ann. Fac. dr. Liège (1979), 179-180, emphasizing the dynamic character of European integration.

12 See W Hallstein, *The European Economic Community*, 78 Pol. Sc. Quart. (1963) 161, holding that the Community was 'not 'static..., it is a process of continuous creation'.

13 The Solemn Declaration on European Union of June 1983 reiterated the 'awareness of a common destiny' and their 'commitment to progress towards an ever closer union among the peoples' of the EC and their Member States, thus introducing a new element.

thus viewed as a process. As a result of this, we may wonder whether the refusal of either one partner or a group of partners to proceed in the path of the 'closer union' is in irreducible contrast with this dynamic conception, with the further consequence that it could be regarded as an infringement of the *foedus*.

This is not without practical consequences. Consider, for example, the deal that the UK and the other members of the EU concluded a few months before the referendum of June 2016, a deal that would exempt the UK from being involved in the achievement of the "ever closer union".[14] Politically, while David Cameron's intent was not to have his "country bound up in an ever closer political union in Europe",[15] his predecessor John Major accepted to keep the reference to the 'ever closer union', in order to avoid any reference to a federal Europe. Whatever the intrinsic soundness of the deal for the rest of the EU, all its members accepted it. On constitutional grounds, however, the remarks just made suggest that the deal was in contrast with the Treaties.

The ideal of the 'ever closer union' is important also for understanding the criteria for membership. Since its early decades, the Community has been much more than a free market area. Without question, if we look back to the Treaty of Paris, it provided no less than making the key industries (coal and steel), that are indispensable to make war, subject to a common supranational control, in the logic of a federation of States, which would have been completed by a common defence.[16] Without question, too, the Treaty of Rome was regarded by its founders as being much more than a common market. They saw it as a community of liberal democracies. This was clear in the 1950's and was equally clear in the following decades. An illuminating example is the denial to include Spain in the 1960's, when it broadly accepted market economy but was still governed by Franco's authoritarian regime. Such denial was based on a doctrine of

---

14 The deal provided that: 'It is recognised that the United Kingdom, in the light of the specific situation it has under the Treaties, is not committed to further political integration into the European Union. The substance of this will be incorporated into the Treaties at the time of their next revision in accordance with the relevant provisions of the Treaties and the respective constitutional requirements of the Member States, so as to make it clear that the references to ever closer union do not apply to the United Kingdom'.

15 See David Cameron's statement to the House of Commons on 3 February 2016.

16 A treaty establishing the EuropeanDefence Community was signed in 1952, but it was not ratified by the French Parliament.

membership that underlined the importance of the political values that are common to liberal democracies.

More recently, the members of the EU have clarified the type of societies in which the peoples that wish to forge a 'common destiny' must live. The European Council in Copenhagen, in 1993, took the first step, when it sets out some criteria. Such criteria included: i) stable institutions guaranteeing democracy, the rule of law, human rights and respect for and protection of minorities; ii) a functioning market economy and the capacity to cope with competition and market forces in the EU; iii) the ability to take on and implement effectively the obligations of membership, including adherence to the aims of political, economic and monetary union. These criteria have been enshrined into the treaties. Their repercussions can be appreciated from a twofold point of view. On the one hand, only a State that respects those principles and is committed to promoting them may thus apply for membership. On the other hand, the States that have obtained membership are no longer free. They have renounced to their freedom to adopt an authoritarian regime. In this sense, the reference to the Rule of Law and to fundamental rights, as well as to liberty and democracy has effects similar to those of national constitutions that prevent any departure from a set of principles concerning the form of government.[17] Unless a State chooses to leave the Union, it must respect those principles, even though there is a variety of opinion about their meaning and significance.

C. *A Unitary Institutional Framework*

Under the present political vision of Europe, there is a necessity to ensure that the action of the members is coherent with their determination to achieve an 'ever closer union' and this has two principal implications for the constitutional framework. First, it requires an institutional framework that permits them to elaborate and manage common policies. Second, it postulates the adoption of legal mechanisms that serve to ensure the unity of the legal order and the equality of the Member States therein. These mechanisms, including the infringement procedure and the preliminary reference procedure, will be considered later. Meanwhile, it is helpful to consider the implications of the model of the 'ever closer union' from the

17 JL Quermonne, Trois lectures du Traité de Maastricht: essai d'une analyse comparative, cit., 814.

first point of view, which concerns the organization and functioning of common institutions.

As far as the institutional framework is concerned, despite the initial distinction between the three communities created between 1952 and 1957 (the ECSC, the EEC, and the Euratom), the Brussels Treaty of 1965 ensured the unity of the institutional framework, by 'fusing' their executives. There were thus a single Commission and a Council of Ministers, together with the Court of Justice and the European Parliament. Almost thirty years later, the Treaty of Maastricht (1992) distinguished between the EC and the two areas of cooperation between the Member States (external security and justice and home affairs). The risk of fragmentation thus emerged.[18] Given that the Union's actions and policies were increasingly differentiated, institutions were the unifying element. The Treaty thus stressed the existence of a '*single* institutional framework', having the goal of enhancing the 'efficient functioning of the institutions'[19] or, in a slightly different terminology, of ensuring the 'consistency, effectiveness and continuity' of such policies and actions.[20] The Lisbon Treaty eventually abolished the distinction between those forms of integration and cooperation. It established that 'the Union shall replace and succeed to the' EC,[21] thus confirming the continuity between the Community and the Union. All public power was thus channelled through the EU.[22]

Another implication of the vision of the 'ever closer union' concerns decision-making processes. The precise implications are, however, disputed, because of a tension between the provisions of the Treaties and their implementation. On the one hand, it has been pointed that, unlike most international organizations, in many cases the EC was enabled to reach its decisions by way of majority voting. This strengthened the Commission's agenda-setting power and, more importantly, the conception of the 'common' interest as something distinct from the interests of the members. On the other hand, there is a more cautionary note in the literature that em-

---

18 D Curtin, The Constitutional Structure of the Union: A Europe of Bits and Pieces, 30 Common Mkt L. Rev (1993), 19.

19 Preamble of the TEU, emphasis added.

20 Article 13 (1) TEU. For further analysis, see R. Dehousse, *From Community to Union*, in R. Dehousse (ed.), *Europe After Maastricht* (Beck, 1994).

21 Article 1 (3) TEU.

22 A von Bogdandy & M Nettesheim, Ex Pluribus Unum: Fusion of the European Communities into the European Union, 2 Eur. L. J. (1996), 267. See also HP Ipsen, *Europaisches Gemeinschaftsrecht* (Mohr Siebeck, 1972), 1050, for the thesis that the unity of the legal structure of the EC derived from the rationale of itsconstruction and its tasks.

phasizes the reluctance, if not the refusal, by national governments to use majority voting. This becomes clear when considering not only the long period during which the so-called 'Luxembourg compromise' produced its effects, weakening 'normative supranationalism',[23] but also the persistence of the requirement of unanimity for decisions affecting certain areas, such as taxation.

There is still another salient implication of the present model. It is the principle of loyal cooperation between supranational and national institutions. This principle has been laid down by Article 5 TEC with a broad scope of application and the ECJ has clarified its contents.[24] On the one hand, the Court has applied it to the relationship between common institutions, and in this guise it has been used, in particular, to strengthen the role of the European Parliament. On the other hand, it has been applied to the relationship between EC and national institutions. The Court has used it not only as a negative norm, that is to say a prohibition to perform policies and issue acts or measures in contrast with the obligation to cooperate, but also as a positive norm, thus condemning the inaction of national authorities. This is just an example of the power of judicial review that the ECJ has exercised. In exercising this power, the Court has had to decide what the language of the constitution means and it has decided that the principle of loyal cooperation precludes States from operating against the common interest of the Community and now of the Union.[25]

Once the action of common institutions is justified, the question that arises is how its results can be achieved if a State is unwilling to respect it or is unable to do so, for example due to its internal organization. In the language used by the ECJ this necessity has been conceptualized in terms of 'coherence' of the legal order. Practically, it has been ensured by several mechanisms, including the higher legal status of the norms laid down by the treaties, the system of centralized enforcement centred on the Commis-

---

23 JHH Weiler, The Community System: The Dual Character of Supranationalism, 1 Ybk Eur. L. (1981), 267.

24 See, for example, the ECJ's ruling in Case C-246/07, *Commission v. Sweden* and, for further analysis, J Temple Lang, Article 5 of the EEC Treaty: the Emergence of Constitutional Principles in the Case Law of the Court of Justice, 10 Fordham Int'l. L. J. (1986), 503, showing that, though this general principle had largely been underestimated, it was very important.

25 What is considered in the text is the internal action of common institutions. As far as their external action is concerned, loyal cooperation must be kept distinct from pre-emption, as observed by M Cremona, Defending the Community Interest: the Duties of Cooperation and Compliance, in M Cremona & B De Witte (eds.), *EU Foreign Relations Law. Constitutional Fundamentals* (Hart 2008), 168.

sion, and the jurisdiction of the ECJ. The first element was implicit in the Court's mandate to ensure that the law was observed in the interpretation and application of the Treaty of Rome, and more particularly in the provision concerning the infringement of any provision of the Treaty itself.[26] But it owed much to the jurisprudence of the Court on the primacy and direct effect of the Treaty, which were eventually accepted by the higher courts of the Member States. EC law was to be either valid or invalid for all the Member States, as well as to business and citizens within their borders.

Another salient element is the system of centralized enforcement centered on the Commission, as provided by Article 169 TEC, according to which the Commission could bring 'disobedient' States before the ECJ.[27] This marked a profound difference with other mechanisms that are still used today by international organizations such as the WTO. However, since this mechanism places the entire burden of supervising national compliance on the shoulders of the Commission, it does not only entail a considerable administrative workload, but also a huge amount of discretion. The Commission may not know that a breach of the Treaty or implementing legislation has occurred or it may prefer to postpone its intervention. This could give rise to a prejudice for citizens and business whose rights are affected by delayed or partial compliance.

For this reason, the Court's doctrine of direct effect has had fundamental importance. It was by giving weight to their rights that the ECJ established the fundamental principle of direct effect, thus empowering individuals to enforce EC norms before national courts.[28] This was a salient step not only in the transformation of the Community from a compact between States to a legal order of a new kind, but also in the achievement of the 'closer union among the peoples of Europe'.[29] At the same time, this doctrine had a practical advantage, because EC norms could be enforced without any need for the Commission to sue the States by way of the infringement procedure. Action brought by interested individuals before national courts would suffice, if necessary by giving the Court of Justice the possibility to interpret EC law in the context of the preliminary reference

---

26 See Articles 164 and 173 EC Treaty.

27 This is the 'standard' procedure: A Gil Ibanez, *The 'Standard' Administrative Procedure for Supervising and Enforcing EC Law: EC Treaty Article 226 and 228*, 68, Law & Cont. Probl. 135 (2004). Other mechanisms concern, for example, the surveillance on excessive government deficits, under Article 126 TFEU.

28 ECJ, Case 26/62, Van Genden Loos v. NederlandeseAdministratie der Belastingen.

29 P Craig, *Administrative Law* (Sweet & Maxwell, 2003), 311.

procedure. The margin of discretion left to national authorities was even more limited by the Court's rulings that awarded damages in case of non-compliance with directives.[30]

D. *Flexibility Within Unity*

For all its concern for ensuring coherence, this vision of Europe does not neglect the necessity of flexibility and of the differentiation that it can allow. Since the beginning, the legal order of the EC has been characterized by the existence of legal mechanisms allowing some form of flexibility. They can be justified in a simple manner: without some degree of flexibility the execution of legislation in very different areas of the same legal system can be very hard, if not impossible.

The Treaty of Rome provided for both, a transitional period and for special arrangements. The transitional period was provided in order to give all the Member States enough time to adjust their internal institutional and legal arrangements to cope with the obligations stemming from their membership. Special legal arrangements were laid down either for some policies, by way of specific derogations, or for some parts of the territory of the Member States that were outside Europe. Interestingly, the Treaty of Rome expressed the partners' will to 'to associate with the Community, the non-European countries and territories which have special relations with Belgium, France, Italy, and the Netherlands'.[31] It also specified that nothing precluded the existence of a regional union between Belgium, Luxembourg and the Netherlands, which stipulated an agreement in 1958. After the accession of Denmark, Ireland and the UK, other norms gave the latter some opt-out clauses and specified that the EC Treaty applied only partially to the Isle of Man and did not apply as such to the Faroe Islands, though it could have been extended to them subsequently. However, these were very limited and specific areas, which could justify limited exceptions without undermining the postulates of the other conception of the constitutional framework of the Community.

An important element of differentiation also emerged from the famous ruling of the ECJ in *Cassis de Dijon*. Confronted with a measure having

30 ECJ, Joined Cases 6 & 9/90, Francovich, Bonifaci et al. v. Italy.

31 Article 131 (1), TEC. For further analysis, see D Hanf, *Flexibility Clauses in the Founding Treaties: From Rome to Nice*, in B De Witte, D Hanf & E Vos (eds.), *The Many Faces of Differentiation in EU Law* (Antwerpen, Intersentia, 2001), 4.

equivalent effect to a quantitative restriction, the Court found that a product lawfully marketable in a Member State could be freely marketable in another.[32] It established, therefore, a sort of functional equivalence of national standards. The Commission endorsed this functional equivalence, or mutual recognition as many began to call it and it became part of the *acquis*. It provided EC institutions with a viable alternative to the harmonization of national legislative, regulatory and administrative rules. It should not be forgotten, however, that the Court recognized several exceptions, in the guise of 'overriding reasons of public interest', including public health and the protection of consumers, thus legitimizing national political preferences.

E. The Difficulties of this Vision of Europe

As observed earlier, this vision of Europe shaped the pace and form of integration for decades. However, it was not unchallenged. First of all, it was based upon a mistrust of the Nation-State, which was not unjustified after World War II (WW2). However, retrospectively, some observers argued that, far from ceding the centre stage to the institutions, the Member States were rescued by European integration.[33]

Secondly, some lawyers criticized the exercise of the Union's power to harmonize national legislative and administrative rules, on grounds that it would unnecessarily reduce the autonomy of national legal orders.[34] Similarly, some commentators observed that the Court did not show its willingness to defer to such national preferences.[35] There are certainly some elements of truth in these remarks. The overall force of this critique is, however, attenuated by a fact that is not disputed and which has an undeniable importance, politically and legally; that is, not only national governments accepted harmonization within the Union's decision-making processes,

32 ECJ, Joined Cases 6 & 9/90, Francovich, Bonifaci et al. v. Italy.

33 A. Milward, The European Rescue of the Nation-State (Routledge 1992).

34 On such autonomy, there is a wide literature: see, in particular, DU Galetta, Procedural Autonomy of EU MemberStates: Paradise Lost? A Study on the "Functionalized Procedural Competence" of EU Member States (Springer, 2010).

35 See AW Green, Political Integration by Jurisprudence (Sijthoff, 1969) and H Rasmussen, On Law and Policy in the European Court of Justice. A Comparative Study in Judicial Policy-making (Nijhoff, 1986). But see also the opposite views of M Cappelletti, Is the European Court of Justice 'Running Wild'?,12 Eur. L. Rev. (1987), 3, and JHH Weiler, The Court of Justice on Trial, 24 Common Mkt. L. Rev. (1987), 555.

but also their Parliaments constantly ratified all treaties providing it, including the Lisbon Treaty. Moreover, every enlargement was decided under the condition that the union between European peoples should be deepened. The initial constitutional clause was confirmed by all the treaties that amended the Treaty of Rome, as well as by all accession treaties, including that concerning the UK.[36]

Thirdly, since the end of the 1980's there was a growing awareness that, though the Member States could and did keep a key role, European integration did not leave their structures and processes unchanged, in terms of both centralization and perceived disempowerment of citizens. This provoked a cultural and political reaction. It was no longer taken for granted that European integration was a good thing in itself, because it undermined the sense of belonging and identity, which was allegedly rooted in national constituencies. This explains, in part, the emergence of a different vision of Europe, which is based on the idea of a wider and less demanding or looser union which will be examined in the next section.

There is a final element of the picture, which should not be neglected; that is, the perceived failure of the neo-functional approach that was associated with the idea of an ever closer union. Some of those who advocate greater flexibility do so because they think that European integration has simply gone too far and must, therefore, be reconsidered.[37] Others point out that what is increasingly controversial is precisely the dream of a better future, based on peace and prosperity.[38]

III. Two Visions of Europe (II): A Wider and Looser Union

A. A Broad Community of Nation-States

It is important to say at the outset that the other vision of Europe, going ideally from the Atlantic Ocean to the Urals is not new, though it has gained consent in the last two decades.

Some elements of this vision can be traced in the Treaty of Paris. Its Preamble emphasized the intent to create a 'broad' community. Accord-

---

36 I am grateful to Ingolf Pernice for drawing my attention of this important issue.

37 See, for example, G Majone, Rethinking the Union of Europe Post-Crisis: Has Integration Gone Too Far? (Cambridge University Press, 2014).

38 JHH Weiler, Europe in Crisis – On 'Political Messianism', 'Legitimacy' and the 'Rule of Law', cit, 258.

ingly, the Treaty established that '[a]ny European State may request to accede to the present Treaty'.[39] However, as observed earlier, it should not be forgotten that membership would inevitably be common supranational control of the key industries for both peace and war, coherently with a federalist approach.

The Treaty of Rome used slightly different words. It established that 'any European State may apply to become a member of the Community'.[40] It added a new element; that is, the Community's capacity not only to conclude treaties with third countries and international organizations, but also to 'establish an association' involving reciprocal rights and obligations.[41] It was precisely when dealing with the failure of the first series of negotiations for the UK entry into the Common Market (as it was then called) and with the Uruguay round of GATT that Walter Hallstein reiterated that the Community was, and had to be, an 'open Community'.[42]

This political vision of the Community was converted into reality during the following decades. While membership has remained unchanged until 1973 and has changed by way of limited accessions during the following three decades,[43] it has changed more radically after 2000, when ten new members have acceded the EU, followed by another three in the following years. An important step has thus been made towards the 'broad' union envisaged fifty years earlier and a new policy has replaced that of gradual and limited extension of membership, with the consequence that the number of Member States was almost doubled[44].

This was not without institutional consequences. If the 1990's had seen the rise of subsidiarity, which appeared both as a rationale and an operating tool for resolving the practical problems raised by the widening scope of Community policies, the following decade has been characterized by discourses about flexibility and differentiation. Many have argued that new and more flexible policy methods were necessary,[45] including various forms of differentiated integration. Others have underlined the necessity to

---

39 Article 98 (1), Treaty of Paris.
40 Article 237 (1), TEC.
41 Article 238 (1), TEC.
42 W Hallstein, The European Economic Community, cit, 174.
43 Denmark, Ireland and the UK in 1973; Greece in 1980; Portugal and Spain in 1985; Austria, Finland and Sweden in 1995.
44 See C Lequesne, Les perspectives institutionnellesd'une union élargie, 69 Pouvoirs (2004), 129.
45 See H Wallace, *Flexibility: A Tool of Integration or a Restraint on Disintegration?* (Oxford, Oxford University Press, 2000).

respect of national constitutional identities. Both arguments can be better understood in the context of an analysis of the values upon which the Union is founded.

B. A 'Community of Interests'

Like other legal orders that of the EC/EU has laid down certain gateways, methods for allowing interests to be recognized and weighed within the system. Initially, these gateways were centred on individual interests, as opposed from collective interests, which are promoted by social groups, such as trade unions and environmental associations.

Only at a later stage, have such collective interests gained recognition and protection, for example, through the 'dialogue with civil society'.[46]

There is another sense in which interests are of central importance for understanding the role of the EU; that is, the problematic relationship between the 'common' interest and national interests. This relationship can be considered both conceptually and institutionally. Conceptually, as observed earlier, at the heart of the first vision of unified Europe there is a conception of the 'common' interest, which is truly distinct from the interests of the individual States and which, within certain limits, must prevail on them. Within the other vision of unified Europe, that of a broad and loose union, there is a very different conception of the common interest. If the EC/EU is a community of Nation-States, so the reasoning goes, it is also a community of interests, where the common interest is nothing more than the aggregation of national interests.[47] It is perhaps no exaggeration to say that, if the main function of the EU is to ensure that the market is not distorted, the political arena functions similarly to the market.

This conception of the common interest has three principal implications. First, the role of the Union within this vision of a broad community is not regarded as a challenge to the Nation-State, but as a mechanism for

46 See Articles 10 (1) and 11 (2), TEU.

47 See C Harlow, A Community of Interests? Making the Most of European Law, 55 Modern L. Rev. (1992), 331. But see also D Mueller, Federalism and the European Union: A Constitutional Perspective, 90 Public Choice (1997), 255, 267 (qualifying the UK Government's threat to veto the accession of new members in 1994 as an "illustration ... of an essentially constitutional choice only in terms of its impact on the narrow geographic interests ... represented").

preserving it.[48] EU institutions are considered instrumentally, as means for achieving policy goals, what no Member State could obtain alone. Second, EU legislation must be narrowly confined for two related reasons. On the one hand, there is the objective of limiting the Union's legislative action.[49] There has been concern for 'creeping competence',[50] as it was often said before the Treaty of Lisbon confirmed that the Union is founded on the principle of conferred powers. On the other hand, even when common action is in principle legitimate, it is argued that in many instances the States are in a much better position for understanding and maximizing their interests than is the EU. The principles of subsidiarity and proportionality impose a rigorous scrutiny of any intervention by the EU.

Third, because every government operates so as to maximize its own individual interest within the decision-making processes of the EU, the central institutions are those that are composed by national representatives. Legislation is seen as a product that will be 'produced' by the legislature, in particular by the Council of Ministers, in response to the demand from the members of the club, that is to say the States. Accordingly, the role of the Commission is that of implementing the balance of interests determined by the Council. Even within the European Parliament, which is no longer an assembly composed of delegates of national Parliaments, the choices to be made are sometimes regarded in a national perspective.[51] However, on one hand, the internal organization of the EP does not reflect national boundaries. On the other hand, there are several examples of parliamentary debates that do not reflect national boundaries, for example, when MPs discuss about the rules concerning the reduction of the tariffs paid by consumers for roaming services. Nor is it the case when parliamentary groups are called to discuss about agreements with third countries. The preceding description is even less suitable to explain the choices that are made by other institutions, in particular by the European Central Bank.

---

48 For a historic approach, see A. Milward, *The European Rescue of the Nation-State* (University of California Press, 1992).

49 J. Temple Lang, EC Constitutional Law: the Division of Powers between the Community and the Member States, 39 N. Ireland Legal Q (1988), 209.

50 This expression became popular after the 1980s: see M. Pollack, *Creeping Competence and the Agenda of the European Community*, 14 J. Public Policy, (1994), 95.

51 S. Mazey & J. Richardson, Interest Groups and EU Policy Making: Organizational Logic and Venue Shopping, in J. Richardson (ed.), European Union: Power and Policy Making (Routledge, 2001), 217.

C. The Shift from Principles to 'Values'

For an adequate understanding of the importance of national constituencies within this vision of unified Europe, it would be wrong to consider only the 'prosaic' interplay of interests. At least two other elements ought to be taken into account: the weight accorded to national constitutional identity and the shift from common principles to 'values'.

The term 'national constitutional identity' has been introduced by the Maastricht treaty. This is not at all a very clear legal concept. Perhaps the underlying idea can be understood as a temperament of the emphasis that the other vision of Europe has placed initially on the general principles of law common to the legal systems of the Member States and subsequently on 'common constitutional traditions'. At the heart of this idea there is a concern for the preservation of the sense of identity and belonging that in the last centuries has been forged within the Nation-States. Coherently with this concern, whilst confirming the importance of 'common constitutional traditions' under Article 6 TEU, the drafters of the recent Treaties, from Maastricht to Lisbon, have referred to national traditions. National traditions, in a generic sense, are mentioned by the TEU's preamble, together with history and culture, though in an indent which begins with the desire to deepen the solidarity between European peoples. Interestingly, the TFEU recognizes national 'legal traditions' in a particular, but fundamental area, that of freedom, security and justice. It does so with the intent of balancing the 'respect for fundamental rights' with the guarantee of the 'different legal systems and traditions of the Member States'.[52]

This shows a difficulty concerning fundamental rights, which becomes more evident when considering an ambiguity of the Lisbon Treaty that has been seldom noticed and that is under-theorized. Since the early 1950's it has been settled case-law of the ECJ that not only the institutions and bodies created by the treaties, but also national authorities must respect the general principles of law common to the legal orders of the Member States, including legal certainty, proportionality and due process of law[53]. Since the late 1960's the Court has also ensured the respect of fundamental rights, as they are listed by the European Convention of Human Rights. The Preamble of the Maastricht Treaty confirmed the Member States 'at-

52 Article 67 (1), TFEU.

53 See JA Usher, *General Principles of EC Law* (Longman, 1998) and T Tridimas, *The General Principles of EU Law* (Oxford, Oxford University Press, 2015, 2nd ed.), both highlighting the role of the ECJ.

tachment to the principles of liberty, democracy and respect for the fundamental freedoms and the rule of law'. This choice was confirmed by Article F TEU, according to which the Union had to respect the national identities of the Member States 'whose systems of government are founded on the principles of democracy"', as well as fundamental rights. The language used by the Treaty thus was the same of the Court and was the language of 'principles'. There was only one provision which used a different concept, that of 'values', but it was a sector-specific provision, that did so with regard to the common foreign and security policy and significantly, referred to the necessity to safeguard "the common values" and fundamental interests of the EU.

The Lisbon Treaty has reiterated the 'attachment to the principles of liberty, democracy and respect for the fundamental freedoms and the rule of law'. But, after so doing, it has shifted from the concept of 'principles' to the concept of 'values'. According to Article 3 TUE, the Union's aim is 'to promote peace, its values and the wellbeing of its peoples'. The question that thus arises is which are the Union's values. The answer is provided by Article 2, which lists such 'values', including 'respect for human dignity, freedom, democracy, equality, the rule of law and respect for human rights'. There is not only, therefore, a longer list, but also a shift of concepts, although there is a certain overlapping between them, for example, with regard to fundamental rights and the rule of law, even though Article 7 TEU sets out a political mechanism for their enforcement. More recently, the Rome Declaration of 25 March 2017 has reiterated the emphasis on 'common' and strong values.[54]

Three comments can be made on the preceding textual analysis. The first is conceptual. Some legal theorists have stressed the distinction between general principles and values,[55] in the sense that the latter is susceptible of emphasizing divisions within the social body.[56] The second is institutional and concerns judicial bodies. Viewed in conjunction with the emphasis placed on national identities, the reference to values may lead national constitutional courts or other judicial institutions to affirm their

54 See *infra*, Part 5.

55 For further discussion, see G dellaCananea, *Due Process of Law Beyond the State. Requirements of Administrative Procedure* (Oxford, Oxford University Press, 2016), arguing that general principles have a foundational value.

56 See C Schmitt, Die Tyrannie der Werte (1964)..

role as defenders of such identities.[57] The third concerns the role of the Union's political institutions. Under Article 7 TUE, there are two mechanisms: there is the action by the Council, acting by a qualified majority, when it is requested to determine whether there is a serious breach of those values by a Member State; there is the action by the European Council, acting by unanimity when it is called to determine the existence of a serious and persistent breach by a Member State. Clearly, the objective is to protect common values and there is an obligation, for common institutions, to attempt to reach this goal. However, there may be no certainty that this objective will always be attained in fact, because the various peoples may well disagree as to the content of those values, as well as to the best way to reach the goal of protecting them. National rulers may not only disagree on both aspects, but also use their voting powers instrumentally or tactically, in order to prevent a negative assessment of their conduct.

D. From Transitional to Permanent Differences

As observed earlier, some elements of flexibility have been laid down since the early period of European integration and are perfectly compatible with the first vision of Europe, that centred on the idea of an 'ever closer union'. What characterizes the other vision of Europe, therefore, is not the recognition that some form of flexibility and differentiation is simply necessary. It is rather the use of normative and functional arguments in favour of institutional mechanisms that allow the Member States to follow different rules and paths, not just for a limited period of time, but for a longer period or forever.

Normatively, two main arguments might be used to support an increased differentiation of EU institutional and legal mechanisms. Firstly, it is coherent with the increasing internal differentiation of the EU. Secondly, it accords a prominent role to pluralism.[58]The consequences of this change in attitude are important. There is the provision according to

57 See E Cloots, National Identity, Constitutional Identity, and Sovereignty in the EU, 45 Netherlands J. Leg. Phil. 82 (2016) and B Guastaferro, Beyond the Exceptionalism of Constitutional Conflicts: The Ordinary Functions of the Identity Clause, 32 Ybk. Eur. L. (2012), 263.

58 For this perspective, see C Harlow, Voices of Difference in a Plural Community, 50 Am. J. Int'l. L. (2002), 339. See also P Manin – JV Louis (eds.) *Vers une Europe différenciée? Possibilité et limites* (Paris, A Pedone, 1996).

which the Union 'respects the national identities' of its Member States.[59] Other provisions aim at protecting cultural diversity. Interestingly, there is a shift between the Charter of Fundamental Rights and the Lisbon Treaty. While the former imposed on the Union the obligation to respect 'cultural, religious, and linguistic diversity',[60] the latter provides that the EU shall respect its '*rich* cultural and linguistic diversity'.[61]

Functionally, it might be argued that a Union of almost thirty members, with very different political cultures and policy processes, requires a much greater degree of flexibility and differentiation. This is not necessarily an obstacle to the traditional functional or neo-functional strategy of creating *de facto* solidarity between the peoples of Europe on concrete issues. Rather, an approach that leaves much room for different national choices may preserve the dynamic of integration. In this sense, some observers have pointed out that without the distinction between the various phases of the Economic and Monetary Union and the opt-out clauses for Denmark and the UK, it would not have been possible for the other Member States to proceed in this path. This is an important point to which we shall return in the next section. Meanwhile, it is important to observe that, for all its appeal, the increasing recourse to differentiation is not without difficulties. In particular, it raises serious issues from the point of view of accountability, which is always more difficult in non-unitary frameworks than in unitary ones.[62]

E. *The Difficulties of this Vision of Europe*

Certain of the problems raised by the second political vision of Europe have been touched on in the preceding discussion. A more structured survey of these and other difficulties is however warranted.

First and foremost, for all the appeal of a broad and loose union, every enlargement of the Community was decided under the condition that the union between European peoples should be deepened. The initial constitu-

---

59 Article 4 (2) TEU, according to which national identities are 'inherent in the fundamental structures, political and constitutional, inclusive of regional and local self-government' of each country.

60 Article 22, Charter of Fundamental Rights.

61 Article 2 TEU (emphasis added).

62 For this remark, see P Craig, European Governance: Executive and administrative powers under the new constitutional settlement, 3 J. Int'l. Const. L. (2005), 407, 436.

tional clause was confirmed by all the treaties that amended the Treaty of Rome, as well as by all accession treaties, including those concerning the UK and more recently various countries from Central and Eastern Europe.[63] It can be understood that politicians and electors in some of these countries are reluctant to accept what has been described as 'integration by stealth'.[64] However, constitutionally, their accession has been premised, among other things, on the acceptance of the initial clause, even though there was not full awareness of the ramifications of this.

Secondly, functionally, there are clearly more problems in managing a Union with 28 or 27 Member States than there would be if membership were still limited to six or twelve countries.[65] This puts a burden of proof on the shoulders of those who argue for a more flexible and differentiated Europe.

For all its importance, decision making is not the only element that really matters. A constitutional framework that recognizes and protects rights provides expectations and determines constraints that it is unwise for politicians to ignore. Within liberal democracies an assertion that a certain course of action is contrary to constitutional requirements or to some goals set out by the constitution or to a procedure that it sets, is a potent argument for invoking some kind of correction either by the courts[66] or by other public agencies. We may surely ask ourselves whether the mechanism set out by Article 7 TEU is the right solution for the problem of noncompliance with the values upon which the EU is founded. However, one thing should be clear; that is, treating such values as generic ideas, from which no meaningful answer can be deduced for the problems that emerge and, *a fortiori*, an instrumental use of voting mechanisms under Article 7 would seriously undermine mutual trust between partners and, in the end, the Union itself.

This debate about fundamental rights is very significant also historically and comparatively. In the US, in the ratification debate the Anti-Federalists opposed to the Constitution on grounds that the new system would lead to excessive centralization and would thus fail to protect individual

63 I am grateful to Ingolf Pernice for drawing my attention of this important issue.

64 G Majone, Dilemmas of European Integration. The Ambiguities and Pitfalls of Integration by Stealth (Oxford, Oxford University Press, 2009).

65 As observed almost thirty years ago by L Dubouis, *Peut-on gouverner à Douze?*, 48 *Pouvoirs* 105 (1989).

66 For a pioneer comparison between judicial institutions, see H Kelsen, *Judicial review of Legislation. A Comparative Study of the Austrian and the American Constitution*, 4 Journ. of Politics (1942), 183.

rights, while Madison and others argued that only a wide republic could limit factions, though Madison himself later presented the Bill of Rights to Congress. In today's Europe, instead, those who oppose to a new centralized government that would allegedly have the characteristics of despotism do not use the argument of rights. Quite the contrary, they do not seem to be concerned with the dangers or unrestrained national government. The arguments of rights is, instead, used by those who fear that, if the EU is weakened and the ties between European peoples are loosened it is only a matter of time before several fundamental rights are jeopardised and this explains why the debate about judicial independence is so important.

IV. The Institutional Mechanisms of Differentiated Integration within the EU

A. Clarity and Coherence

Thus far, we have seen that there is a tension inherent between two visions of Europe, with important consequences about the goals of the Union, the conception of its peoplehood and the legal tools for ensuring coherence and unity. We cannot, however, content ourselves with delineating this distinction. We must subject existing or proposed institutional mechanisms to careful scrutiny under the twin criteria of clarity and coherence. Intellectual clarity is traditionally regarded as a requisite for academic works, in the sense that any thought or statement must be sufficiently clear and must avoid contradictions. There can perhaps be a policy without intellectual clarity, but not a scientific argumentation. Even for a policy, however, coherence matters, at least in the sense of coherence between ends and means. From this point of view, if we value something intrinsically, in our case either an ever closer union between the peoples of Europe or a union with less intense ties between them, an increase of it, all else being equal (there might be side effects), can be assessed favourably, while what reduces it or is incompatible with it should be considered unfavourably. An attempt will thus be made to understand whether a certain existing or proposed institutional mechanism that can be said to be coherent with one vision of Europe is hardly compatible with the other, or not at all.

It can be helpful to begin by observing that the idea of differentiated integration is expressed by way of several terms, including enhanced cooperation, two-speed Europe, variable geometry, Europe *à la carte* and concentric circles. Even a quick look at official discourses and academic works show that these terms are increasingly important, both descriptively and prescriptively. Descriptively, the various terms just mentioned are used to designate situations in which the members of the EU make policy choices with different effects for the different partners. The prescriptive side seeks to build an increasing legitimacy for these types of decision making processes.

As observed earlier, there is nothing wrong in this. However, legally, some distinctions are necessary, because there are various forms of differentiation.[67] Only some of those terms designate mechanisms that are provided by the treaties, such as enhanced cooperation. Moreover, and more importantly from the institutional perspective that is followed in this essay, the mechanisms that involve, at least potentially, only the Member States of the EU must be kept distinct from those that are susceptible of involving third countries. Last but not least, the terms just mentioned are not simply different, but mean different things, in the sense that a closer look reveals that they support contrasting strategies of integration.[68] There is thus the need to ensure coherence between ends and means. Keeping this in mind, our discussion will continue with an analysis of what has been probably the single most important achievement after Maastricht; that is, EMU. As a second step, enhanced cooperation procedures will be considered. Next, we will look at a recent and controversial treaty between most EU members, but not all; that is, the Fiscal Compact.

B. *No 'Ever Closer' Monetary Integration within the EMU*

Given the object and purposes of this essay, no attempt will be made here to synthetize the complex legal and institutional arrangements on which the EMU is based.[69] Suffice it to mention few legal norms and facts that

---

67 See B De Witte, D Hanf & E Vos (eds.), *The Many Faces of Differentiation in EU Law* (Intersentia, 2001).

68 See, however, JA Usher, *Variable Geometry of Concentric Circles: Patterns for the European Union*, 46, 243 at 253 (1997), putting on an equal basis 'variable geometry' and 'two speeds'.

69 On the road to the EMU, see N Thygesen, The Delors Report and European Economic and Monetary Union, in 65 International Affairs 637 (1989). For an outline of the main issues, see JV Louis, The Economic and Monetary Union: Law and Institutions, 41 Common Mkt. L. Rev. (2004), 575, and FG Snyder, *EMU – integration and differentiation: metaphor for European Union*, in P Craig & G de Búrca (eds), *The Evolution of EU Law* (Oxford, Oxford University Press, 2011), 687. But see also G Majone, *Rethinking the Union of Europe Post-Crisis: Has Integration Gone Too Far?* (Cambridge, Cambridge University Press, 2014), 20, referring to the EMU as an example of the more general crisis of the EU.

are substantially undisputed. First of all, the EMU is the main innovation from the viewpoint of the transfer of sovereign powers from the Member States to the EU, which is particularly visible in the adoption of a single currency. Secondly, and as a specification of this, institutionally the EMU consists of three distinct though related parts. There is the economic part, which rests in the hands of national government, though under a set of common rules, while national budgetary policies are constrained by common targets, standards and checks, within the procedure of multilateral surveillance. There is, finally, monetary policy making, which is conferred to the ECB. Thirdly, institutional differentiation has been increased by the different choices made by the Member States. Three phases or stages were envisaged and while all the States that were members of the EU were included in the first one and could move to the next, the norms governing the EMU did not impose on them to ask to be included in the third stage, as it will soon be explained. A differentiated membership has thus emerged. Last but not least, unlike traditional common policies, EMU is characterized by a complex variety of rules, including guidelines and technical opinions, and by the exemption from the ordinary mechanisms for ensuring compliance. All the rest is controversial, to say the least. In particular, it is disputed whether the policies followed by the ECB have saved the euro, and with it the EU itself, or has just dissipated resources that should have been used otherwise.

The main question that arises is, however, another; that is, how the first and the third aspects mentioned earlier – that is, the fundamental importance of the EMU and its differentiated membership – can be reconciled. Jean-Victor Louis has suggested a twofold explanation, pragmatic and normative. Pragmatically, granting to Denmark and the UK an 'opt-out' clause was the only way to obtain their consent to the revision of the treaties, in view of the unanimity that was required. Normatively, he acknowledged that the special status granted to these members was 'singular'. But he argued that, although such status appeared to be of indefinite duration, it was '*de facto* only temporarily if the objective of an ever closer union is to be safeguarded'. He added that it was with this idea in mind that such status was conceded.[70] This is a very helpful contribution to the understanding of the complex decisions taken by the European Council. The normative argument that he has advanced is however problematic in some respects, in particular with regard to the potential dismissal of the

70 J.V. Louis, *Differentiation and the EMU*, cit. at 45, 43-44.

goal of the 'ever closer union'. A distinct but related question is whether the course of events made such goal unattainable.

Let us begin by clarifying a preliminary issue. It is often asserted that Denmark and the UK were granted an opt-out clause from EMU, but this is not wholly correct. In fact, they were included in EMU, but were not required to participate in its third stage, with the further caveat that Denmark obtained the acknowledgement of its right to take part in the third phase, after a positive assessment by the Council.[71] As regards to the UK, all EU countries 'recognized' that it 'shall not be obliged or committed to move to the third stage' of EMU without a decision of its representative institutions,[72] which according to the standard account means that it was granted an opt-in clause.

That said, normatively, the fact that the concession of a specific status to the UK and Denmark was '*de facto* only temporary' because of the necessity to safeguard the goal of the 'ever closer union' is a weak counter to the literal argument that such status was conceded without any explicit deadline. There is a strong argument that runs in the contrary direction. As the Protocol on EMU specified unequivocally, the UK 'shall retain its powers in the field of monetary policy according to national law'.[73] As a consequence of this, a different law was to be, and was, applied.

Moreover, and as a variant of the preceding argument, the Maastricht Treaty was an agreement between sovereign States and conventional international law is based, though not exclusively, on their explicit consent. As a result, it is hard to see how the fact that the specific status was conceded to the UK with the idea in mind that this situation would not last for a long time could influence the exercise of rights and duties under the Treaty. Even if it could be said that all partners agreed on this, this would not be conclusive against the ordinary criteria of interpretation.

Finally, the argument advanced by Louis with regard to the necessity to safeguard the goal of the 'ever closer union' is ambiguous, in the sense that it can be read in two distinct ways. It is one thing to say that the treaties and the other parts of the constitutional framework of the EU must be interpreted systematically, with the consequence that the specific status conceded to Denmark and the UK had to be used in the light of their commitment to contribute to the achievement of the 'ever closer union'. It is an-

71 Protocol on certain provisions relating to Denmark, Article 1 (1).

72 Protocol on certain provisions relating to the United Kingdom, Articles 1 and 9, last indent.

73 Protocol on certain provisions relating to the United Kingdom, Article 4.

other thing to say that, in the light of this commitment, their specific status *de facto* has a limited duration. We must be very careful when deducing particular consequences from a very general clause of the Treaty's preamble. It is hard to see how it would be possible to convert a permanent clause into a temporary one.

These findings support the conclusion that the solution envisaged by the drafters of the provisions governing the EMU, whilst allowing Denmark and the UK to join the Euro when they meet the requisite prescribed by the Treaties, at least potentially, deviated from the goal of the 'ever closer union'. It remains to be seen how this potentiality was converted into reality and in this respect that the explanation provided by Louis is particularly helpful. Even a quick look at the course of the events shows, on the one hand, that both British and Danish officers participated in a variety of decision-making processes concerning the EMU and on the other hand soon after 1992 several measures were taken by national policy makers in particular within the UK in order to make full membership possible.[74] For example, between 1993 and 1999, the Bank of England constantly monitored the preparation for the adoption of the single currency. Some years later, Gordon Brown, then Chancellor of the Exchequer, set out the economic conditions that had to be fulfilled so that this could occur.[75] This was not the case, however, though the adoption of the single currency was still supported by some economists when the crisis begun.[76] A different choice has been made and its consequences are so well known that few hints will suffice for our purposes here. The UK has kept its money and has remained relatively insulated from the effects of the policies carried out by the European Central Bank. Institutionally, this implies that the Governor of the Bank of England takes part only in the meeting of the General Council, a body with limited powers, but is not involved in decisions concerning the fixing of rates or to refer to the most salient decision taken by the ECB in the last year, in the purchase of national bonds. More concretely, the consequence of all this for citizens is that, unlike in other EU coun-

74 See, however, T Prosser, *The Economic Constitution* (OUP, 2014), 142, noting the 'partial acceptance by the UK' of the objectives set out by the ECB.

75 See the statement by Gordon Brown on *UK Membership of the Single Currency*, HM Treasury (2003).

76 See W Buiter, Why the United Kingdom Should Join the Eurozone, 11 International Finance 269 (2008). For a survey of the literature, see T Sadeh & A Verdun, Explaining Europe's Monetary Union, 11 International Studies Rev. 277 (2009).

tries, in the UK a visitor needs to change currency.[77] In sum, the provisions of the Treaty determined a potential breach with the ideal of the 'ever closer union', though they left the door open.

Looking at the course of the events has a further advantage. It reveals that there is not simply a two-tier legal regime, whereby all EU countries are within the third stage except those who either cannot join it or do not wish to do so. Indeed, there is a more complex situation, with: a) nineteen countries within the Eurozone; b) other EU countries that are obliged to meet convergence criteria and do so with some difficulties (with the exception of Sweden); c) Denmark and the UK (until the end of negotiations for its exit from the EU) that have a specific status; d) some smaller European States (Andorra, Monaco, San Marino and Vatican City) that are using the euro on the basis of a specific agreement; e) two Balkan countries that are unilaterally using the Euro (Kosovo and Montenegro). This last element shows the existence of asymmetric relationships between legal orders, which is not unknown to legal theorists[78] and that raises interesting issues from the viewpoint of both effectiveness and accountability.

C. *Enhanced Cooperation: Nature, Rationale and Impact*

As a second step, it is interesting to examine enhanced cooperation. There is a brief overview of the provisions on enhanced cooperation that have been laid down since the Treaty of Amsterdam (1997). On this basis, the rational for enhanced cooperation is examined. Finally, we must consider some difficulties that have emerged in institutional practice.

Although some consider the provisions enacted by the Treaty of Amsterdam as a generalization of previous experiments in flexibility that had been agreed within the Treaty of Maastricht, institutional mechanisms differed, particularly with regard to the role of EU institutions.[79] Moreover, those provisions initially excluded common foreign and security policies. A

77 G Dinan, Ever Closer Union. An Introduction to European Integration (Palgrave McMillan, 2005, 3rd ed.), 1.

78 From the viewpoint of general theory of law, see S Romano, *L'ordinamento giuridico* (Sansoni, 1946, 2nd ed.), Engl. transl. *The Legal Order* (Routledge, 2017).

79 See JHH Weiler, *Editorial:* Amsterdam, Amsterdam, 3 Eur. L. J. (1997), 309, for the claim that the Treaty was important not only for its existence, but also for its institutional contents; for further details on enhanced cooperation, H Kortenberg, Closer Cooperation in the Treaty of Amsterdam, 35 Common Mkt. L. rev. (1998), 833.

change occurred with the Treaty of Nice, though it still excluded all 'matters having military or defence implications'. It has been the Treaty of Lisbon, therefore, that has generalized enhanced cooperation, though within the substantive limits and procedural constraints that will now be clarified.

The essence of enhanced cooperation is that some Member States, not all, 'may make use' of the Union's institutions. It is, therefore, a mechanism that is 'constituted' and regulated by the Treaty and which takes place within the institutional framework of the EU, unlike those of purely intergovernmental nature that will be examined earlier. The justification for the use of EU institutions is that the goal of enhanced cooperation is to 'further the objectives of the Union, protect its interests and reinforce its integration process'.[80] However, its scope is limited to the areas for which the Union has non-exclusive legislative competence. Moreover, it is only if the Council has 'established that the objectives of such cooperation cannot be attained within a reasonable period by the Union as a whole' that an enhanced cooperation may take place. The Treaty also sets out a requisite concerning the minimum number of EU members (nine) that must be involved[81] and specifies that the procedure laid down in Article 329 TFEU shall be used. This requires the authorization issued by the Council, acting on a proposal made by the Commission and with the assent of the European Parliament. Participation in an enhanced cooperation has relevant legal consequences, in the sense that, though all members of the Council are enabled to participate in its deliberations, only those that represent the Member States participating in it 'shall take part in the vote'.[82] On the other hand, their decisions will neither be binding on the other members of the EU nor will be regarded as part of the *acquis communautaire*.

Three comments can be made on the preceding textual analysis. They concern the nature, the rationale and the impact of enhanced cooperation. Functionally, there is an analogy between enhanced cooperation and treaty revisions, because they both seek to adjust the process of European integration to the varying necessities and to the difficulties that inevitably arise in a Union of twenty-seven (or twenty-eight) Member States.[83] However, there is also a fundamental difference. Unlike treaty revision, enhanced cooperation leaves the existing constitutional framework unaltered and is,

80 Article 20 (1) TEU.
81 Article 20 (2) TEU.
82 Article 20 (1) TEU.
83 On this linkage, see P Craig, *The Lisbon Treaty* (Oxford, OUP, 2013, 3rd ed.).

therefore, not subject to ratification processes within national legal systems.

The rationale of enhanced cooperation becomes clear when considering that, according to the Treaty, enhanced cooperation is viewed as a 'last resort', when it has become undisputed that the members of the EU either cannot or do not wish to proceed in the same direction and with the same pace, though all members can join at a later stage, if they wish to do so. It is, therefore, an institutionalized differentiated integration, in the sense that it differs from the closer integration that can be achieved by the members that choose to sign an agreement outside EU treaties, as it happened with the Schengen Agreement (1985) and more recently with the Prüm Convention (2005). To the extent to which enhanced cooperation can work as an instrument of the 'ever closer union', without obliging all the Member States to accept the same ties simultaneously, it can be said to be a flexible tool, which is compatible with both visions of the Union. Precisely for this reason, however, it has a certain ambiguity.[84]

Moreover, despite its flexibility, enhanced cooperation has been less relevant and significant than expected by its proponents. Soon after the entry into force of the Treaty of Amsterdam, EU institutions expressed concern about the development of enhanced cooperation outside the treaties, as a consequence of enlargement[85]. After the big enlargement, few steps have been taken by national governments to use enhanced cooperation, even when they intended to 'reinforce the process of integration' in the area of the EMU. They have preferred to stipulate international treaties, as they did in 2012 for the 'Fiscal Compact'. It is interesting, therefore, to take it into consideration.

84 For this remark, see H Bribosia, Les coopérationsrenforcées, in G Amato, H Bribosia & B De Witte (eds), Commentaire du traité établissant une Constitution pour l'Europe à la lumière des travaux préparatoires et perspectives d'avenir (Bruxelles, Bruylant, 2007). See also D Thym, The Political Character of Supranational Differentiation, 31 Eur. L. Rev. (2006), 781, seeing in this the emergence of an 'asymmetric constitutionalism'.

85 See B De Witte, Chameleonic Member States: Differentiation by Means of Partial and Parallel Agreements, in D Hanf & E Vos (eds), The Many Faces of Differentiation in EU Law (Intersentia, 2001), 236, 239, noting that the Amsterdam rules were too rigid.

D. *'Internal' International Agreements: the Fiscal Compact*

In addition to enhanced cooperation, there is another instrument that can be regarded as an alternative to the revision of the treaties; that is, the conclusion of international agreements between either all Member States or only some of them. These are international treaties. They are, therefore, subject to the principles and rules of public international law, including the Vienna Convention on the Law of Treaties, in addition to the limits stemming from EU law,[86] for example with regard to the relations with third countries, under the doctrine of pre-emption. However, this 'parallel track' has always existed, as was observed earlier with regard to the Treaty establishing the Benelux. It had become increasingly important during the economic and financial crisis. An interesting example is the Treaty on Stability, Coordination and Governance in the Economic and Monetary Union (TSCG), which is better known as the 'Fiscal Compact'. An analysis of its process, rationale and relationship with EU law can help us to understand the distinctive features of this form of differentiated integration.

When the crisis burst out, most political leaders affirmed that the existing legal framework needed to be adjusted. On the one hand, it was adjusted for all the Member States, through a further change of the Stability and Growth Pact, enacted in 1996 and already modified in 2005. On the other hand, it was adjusted by way of an international agreement negotiated by most members, but not by all. Initially, there was a Franco-German proposal to amend the treaties in order to tighten the framework of budgetary rules for the Member States. That proposal was vetoed by the UK, on the grounds that its representatives had not managed to obtain adequate safeguard against the undesired impact of those tightened rules on the UK's financial services industry, an aspect that certainly has not lost its relevance in the context of Brexit. The negotiation process that followed was not easy for some members, who were afraid of meeting strong opposition during their ratification processes. In particular, the Czech Republic, decided that it was not in a position to sign the treaty. Quite the contrary, Italy used that process instrumentally, in order to secure an amendment of the national constitution. Eventually, on 30 January 2012, twenty-five Member States agreed to the TSCG or 'Fiscal Compact'.

---

86 See B De Witte, *Chameleonic Member States: Differentiation by Means of Partial and Parallel Agreements*, cit., 232, distinguishing partial agreements, concluded between some Member States within the institutional framework of the EU, from parallel agreements, involving all of them, and placing less emphasis on the involvement of third countries.

At its roots there is not only the fact that, even when action by a group of Member States is regarded as justified from the viewpoint of the Union's goals and processes, national politicians often show a strong preference for cooperating outside the treaties. There are also two important factors, greater flexibility and time. If the decisions to be taken are left to be determined through unconstrained political processes, then an even greater flexibility can be attained. Accordingly, decisions will be reached on shorter time horizons than for comparable behavior regulated by EU rules. But there can be another justification for doing so: the opposition by one or more members to the proposed innovation, as it happened with the Fiscal Compact.

It is precisely because the TSCG is not an EU treaty that it has a complex relationship with EU law. The preamble clearly reveals that the intent of the contracting parties is to proceed on the path of integration. They regard their economic policies 'as a matter of common concern' and express their desire to 'develop ever closer coordination of economic policies within the euro area'.[87] This intent is confirmed by Article 2, which refers to the parties' will to 'foster budgetary discipline through a fiscal compact'. However, the Fiscal Compact has but a limited impact on existing EU rules for two reasons that are related but distinct. Firstly, the general basis of the rules set out by EU treaties is the prior consent of the States. It is this consensus that performs the basic legitimizing function. Without their consent, the two EU members that have not signed the TSCG, are not bound to respect the canons of conduct that it lays down, in particular the 'rule' that 'the budgetary position of the general government ... shall be balanced on in surplus'.[88] Secondly, and consequently, several provisions of the Fiscal Compact clarify that the new treaty entails no change of the obligations stemming from existing EU treaties. While Article 2 does so in a general way, by ensuring that the Fiscal Compact will be interpreted and applied consistently ('in conformity') with EU treaties,[89] Article 3 does so with regard to the more innovative and controversial rule about budget

87 See the first two indents of the TSCG's Preamble.

88 TSCG, Article 3 (1) b).

89 TSCG, Article 2 (1), which refers to both 'the Treaties on which the European Union is founded' and to 'European Union law, including procedural law'. The following indent puts even more emphasis on the necessity of consistency, by affirming that compatibility is requisite for applying the TSCG. See, however, P Craig, The Stability, Coordination and Governance Treaty: Principle, Politics and Pragmatism, 37 Eur. L. Rev. 231 (2012), arguing that the TSCG raises the question concerning the extent to which a treaty outside the confines of the Lis-

deficits, which will be applied by the contracting parties 'in addition and without prejudice to their obligations under' EU law. In addition to these limits, the new rules have a differentiated application. While they 'apply in full' to the Member States whose currency is the euro,[90] they apply to the other parties under the conditions set out in Article 14. Leaving aside the conditions that referred to the entry into force of the TSCG, it can be observed that it will apply to the States with a derogation or with an exemption, as in the case of Denmark, as from the date when the decision abrogating that derogation or exemption takes effect.[91] This, incidentally, confirms that the position of Denmark (and the UK) differs from that of the other members of the EU. There is, finally, a provision that is increasingly important in the political debates about the EMU; that is, Article 16 of the TSCG, which regulates the process of 'incorporation'. It establishes that 'within five years ..., the necessary steps will be taken ... with the aim of incorporating the substance of this Treaty' into the legal framework of the Union. But precisely with regard to the substantial part of the Fiscal Compact in some Member States there is much less consensus than there was five years ago concerning the soundness of the tighter rules on public debt and deficit. Tighter budgetary standards have been criticized on grounds that they codify debt-reduction policies with a huge and negative impact on social programs. What is controversial is moreover their imposition by a treaty, as opposed to a national constitution.[92]

In the light of these findings, the distinctive features of this form of differentiated integration, from an institutional point of view, can be viewed more clearly than hitherto. First, State consensus performs the usual basic normative function, in the sense that it is of central importance in shaping the interaction between the Member States. However, while in the case of

---

bon framework can confer new powers on EU institutions; for further remarks, K Tuori, *The European Financial Crisis –Constitutional Aspects and Implications*, EUI Working Paper LAW 2012/28.

90 TSCG, Article 1 (2).

91 TSCG, Article 14 (5).

92 For critical remarks, see M Everson & C Joerges, Between Constitutiona lCommand and Technocratic Rule: Post Crisis Governance and the Treaty on Stability, Coordination and Governance ('The Fiscal Compact'), in C Harlow, P Leino & G della Cananea (eds), *Research Handbook on EU Administrative Law* (Elgar, 2017), 351, but see also P Craig, *The Stability, Coordination and Governance Treaty: Principle, Politics and Pragmatism*, cit. at 87, 235, arguing that the TSCG 'does not advance matters much' with respect to existing EU rules. New changes have been envisaged by the 'five presidents' report': *Towards a Genuine Economic and Monetary Union* (Brussels, 2012).

the Maastricht clauses their consensus was expressed by all members and within the provisions of the treaties, in this case it concerns most members, but not all. As a further consequence, while the Maastricht Treaty distinguished between members with or without specific clauses, the TSCG makes EU membership more differentiated than before, with two categories of contracting parties, those within and outside the Eurozone, and the remaining two members of the EU that did not sign the new treaty. The question that thus arises is whether this type of agreement reinforces the perspective of a sort of Europe 'à la carte'. This question will now be addressed.

E. *Two-speed Europe: Concept and Issues*

As observed initially, few topics have aroused as much controversy in the literature about the EU as differentiated integration. Opinions differ markedly both as to the justification for the existence of such form of integration and as to the shape that it should assume. It is, therefore, not surprising that different concepts are used in differing ways. However, if we move beyond nominalism, in an attempt to understand the nature of the interactions between the Union's partners, it becomes evident that a juxtaposition of some forms of differentiated integration is unjustified. This is the case of two-speed Europe and Europe *à la carte*. While some observers, including Usher, put them on an equal basis,[93] they differ. The term 'two-speed Europe' designates processes that are used to reach more expedite decisions for some members of the EU, who sooner or later are joined by the others.[94] Quite the contrary, the term 'Europe *à la carte*'[95] designates a scenario in which certain countries would join some policies while others would join other policies, with the consequence that there can only be a very low common denominator. For this reason, unlike the idea of two-speed, the idea of a Europe *à la carte* is hardly coherent with the first vision of a unified Europe, that which seeks to achieve an 'ever closer union' between the peoples of Europe.

This does not mean, however, that the other idea, that of a two-speed Europe, is without difficulties. These become evident when considering

93 JA Usher, Variable Geometry of Concentric Circles: Patterns for the European Union (1997) 46, 243 at 253.

94 For further analysis, see JC Piris, *The Future of Europe: Towards a Two-Speed EU?* (Cambridge, Cambridge University Press, 1997).

95 See R Dahrendorf, *A Third Europe* (Florence, EUI, 1979).

the joint Declaration of 25 March 2017, in the sixtieth anniversary of the Treaty of Rome.[96] The Declaration has both a retrospective and a prospective, which deserve a detailed analysis.

The retrospective is a bit rhetoric, as it often happens in these types of documents. There is a strong emphasis on the decision 'to bond together and rebuild our continent from its ashes' and on the construction of a 'community of peace, ... with unparalleled levels of social protection and welfare'. For sure, that of the EC/EU can rightfully be seen as a success story from the point of view of the achievement of the initial goals of peace and prosperity. The Declaration proudly states 'we have built a unique Union with common institutions and strong values, a community of peace, freedom, democracy, human rights and the rule of law'. This statement is not unreasonable if we compare Europe and more particularly the EU with other regions of the world. However, as we shall argue later, there are some difficulties with it.

The prospective part of the Declaration seeks to combine unity and diversity. Its *incipit* underlines the importance of the 'construction of European unity'. The importance of unity is reiterated by the second paragraph, according to which 'today we are united and stronger'. There is still another paragraph (the fourth) that begins by affirming the ambitious goal of 'even greater unity' and continues with this challenging statement:

> 'we will act together, at different paces and intensity where necessary, while moving in the same direction, as we have done in the past, in line with the Treaties and keeping the door open to those who want to join later'.

There is, again, a similarity with enhanced cooperation; that is, flexible integration. But there is also a distinctive trait, in the sense that a two-speed Europe can be achieved in more than one way. Its essence is that integration requires some 'pioneers'; that is, some members of the club choose to be more closely integrated in a new policy field, on the assumption that, if it works, the others will join them. This idea can be appealing for several reasons. It appears to be susceptible to revitalize the functional method, by encouraging sector or issue-specific coalitions of partners willing to proceed with the same pace. From the viewpoint of economic theory, it can

96 Declaration of the leaders of 27 Member States and of the European Council, the European Parliament and the European Commission, available at http://www.consilium.europa.eu/en/press/press-releases/2017/03/25-rome-declaration/.

make sense to say that, unlike other 'clubs' or organizations, the EU provides several 'goods', which may have different relevance or significance for its members.[97] This may foster competition between different policy approaches.[98]

There are, however, some difficulties with the strategy delineated by the Declaration. First, it rests on an unclear assumption. It is questionable whether in the past what was really allowed was the acceptance of 'different paces and intensity where necessary'. Arguably, the mechanisms concerning EMU did much more than allowing different paces. They allowed some members of the club not to proceed on the path of monetary integration. This is of significance when thinking about a strategy aiming at achieving unity, whatever the veracity of the intent of the Declaration's authors.

Secondly, the idea to 'act together, at different paces and intensity where necessary' may take different forms. Some are based on the treaties, such as enhanced cooperation. Other forms of cooperation between the Member States lie outside the treaties, as the 'Fiscal Compact', because not all EU countries agreed about it and its inclusion within the architecture of the EU requires a series of steps and of course the consensus of all partners. Those who think that it suffices to say that the EU will proceed 'at different paces and intensity where necessary' are therefore mistaken. To borrow a term used in one of the first studies on differentiated integration, this was but a 'misleading simple idea'.[99]

Thirdly, it is not clear how the partners would move in the same direction. There is an inner tension between the desire to get all members of the EU involved and the role of the promoters or pioneers. For example, some political leaders who did not wish to join the Eurozone feared to be left behind. Their fear becomes more evident when, instead of multi-speed Europe, other terms are used, such multi-tier Europe, which has a hierarchical and pejorative connotation.

97 See J Pisani-Ferry, Intégration monétaire et géométrie variable, 48 Revue économique 495 (1996), for the thesis, that preserving the single market and enhancing convergence are distinct objectives.

98 G Majone, *Europe as the Would-Be World Power: the EU at Fifty* (Cambridge University Press, 2009). On 'pioneer groups', see B de Witte, Future Paths of Flexibility: Enhanced Cooperation, Partial Agreements and Pioneer Groups, in in JW de Zwaan et al., *The European Union: An Ongoing Process of Integration – Liber Amicorum Alfred E Kellermann* (The Hague, T.M.C. Asser Instituut, 2004), 140.

99 F De La Serre & H. Wallace, *Flexibility and Enhanced Cooperation in the European Union: Placebo rather than Panacea*, Notre Europe, research and policy paper n. 2, (1997), 5.

F. A Synthesis

An analysis of differentiated integration within the EU confirms the claim made initially about the implications of the two contrasting visions of the European construction. Differentiated integration is often considered in a functional fashion; that is, with a focus on the opportunity to allow some members to proceed faster on the path of integration, without precluding the other members from joining them at a later stage. This type of explanation is helpful but incomplete.

There are four reasons why an exclusive concern with functional aspects fails to provide an adequate understanding of differentiated integration. First, even supposing that the arguments supporting differentiated integration are of functional nature, the question that arises is why there is a variety of forms, some within and some outside the provisions of the treaties. This explanation is therefore not sufficient.

More importantly, there is another side of the coin. The various forms of differentiated integration are susceptible of promoting different visions of the European construction. For example, whatever the original intent of the drafters of the EMU, it has allowed some members not to proceed towards the goal of the 'ever closer union between the peoples of Europe', though the rules they agreed are very different from those that would govern a more or less free trade area, that some British (but also Polish) politicians seem to wish.

Thirdly, an explanation that focuses only on functional or pragmatic considerations fails to devote adequate attention to the dynamics of power. It is not fortuitous, for example, that the UK has contrasted the idea that an enhanced cooperation could be launched without a unanimous decision. Nor is it fortuitous that some of the new members that are reluctant to engage in enhanced cooperation are afraid that, if they remain outside of it, they will be indirectly subject to the new rules without being able to influence their content, an aspect to which we shall return when considering the post-Brexit scenario.

Finally, paying attention to the functional features of differentiated integration can be helpful to understand whether integration may proceed, in a perspective that focuses on the conduct of the States. It will in no sense be sufficient from a perspective that instead focuses on individual and collective (as distinct from national) interests. Although the shift from general principles to values does not necessarily undermine the importance of the respect for the rule of law and fundamental rights, it can be observed that, by placing the focus on national traditions, some institutional safeguards have been weakened. This is the case, for example, of the independence of the judiciary in Poland.

V. Legal Mechanisms of Integration Beyond the EU

With these *caveats* in mind, let us consider the forms of differentiated integration that involve other European countries. They include the treaties that are agreed by all the members of the EU with other groups of countries, such as the Treaty of Oporto establishing the EEA, or by some members with third countries, as it happens with the rules established under the Schengen Agreement. Space limits preclude an examination of other legal mechanisms, including those with the European countries that wish to become members of the EU, such as Serbia and Montenegro, and those with non-European countries that wish to establish a closer partnership with the EU, particularly in the Mediterranean area.[100]

A. A Single Market Beyond the Union: the European Economic Area

What has been said earlier with regard to monetary policy raises the further question whether a similar asymmetry occurs with regard to the other main instrument of the EU, the single market. This question is interesting in itself, for an understanding of the legal mechanisms of integration beyond the EU and for its practical implications, because some observers suggest that the UK might be a member of the European Economic Area (EEA).

The standard account about the EEA highlights three main features: first, that the EEA is an area where persons, goods, services and capitals can circulate freely, which exists since 1 January 1994, upon entry into force of the Treaty of Oporto; second, that membership of EEA is open to EU countries as well as to the members of European Free Trade Area Association (Iceland, Liechtenstein and Norway); third, that EFTA members must adopt most EU legislation concerning the single market and, correspond-

100 See, for further analysis, R Wessel, Fragmentation in the Governance of EU External Relations: Legal Institutional Dilemmas and the New Constitution for Europe, in J.W. de Zwaan*et al*, *The European Union: An Ongoing Process of Integration – Liber Amicorum Alfred E Kellermann* (The Hague, T.M.C. Asser Instituut, 2004), 123.

ingly, are able to influence the content of such legislation by way of 'decision-shaping' processes at an early stage of EU legislation.

There is nothing basically wrong with this standard account. However, for an adequate understanding of the available options, at least two other aspects must be taken into consideration. On the one hand, while the forms of differentiation that were examined previously imply an institutional differentiation within the Union, the EEA is a regulatory regime for applying the rules governing the single market beyond its borders. Consequently, some non-EU countries have simply accepted large amounts of substantive EC/EU law. There is, therefore, an asymmetric relationship between their legal orders and that of the EU. On the other hand, within the other members of EEA, there is a difference between the paths followed by Norway and Switzerland. While Norway has negotiated through the EEA, Switzerland has not joined the EEA, but has entered into a series of bilateral agreements with the EU.

These findings support the following four conclusions: First, the EEA does not constitute a form of differentiated integration between the Member States of the EU. It is, rather, a form of cooperation between the EU and other European countries. Secondly and consequently, although it could be said that such cooperation might be beneficial to a further integration of non-EU members, this is just a potentiality. Meanwhile, it is a cooperation that is limited to the rules governing the Single Market and is, therefore, coherent also with the vision of a wide and loose union. Thirdly, such cooperation is based on a variety of legal sources, as it can be established either by accessing EFTA or by negotiating several bilateral agreements. Accordingly, referring to the EEA only provides a generic solution; that is, the devil is in the details. Finally, the asymmetry that has been noticed is relevant from a twofold viewpoint: theoretically, it confirms that relations between legal orders can be either symmetric or asymmetric; institutionally, it is problematic with regard to democratic standards.

B. *Schengen's Mixed Membership*

As observed initially, there are two distinct frames in the present analysis: one concerns the institutional mechanisms of differentiated integration within the EU and the other the legal mechanism of integration outside the Union. It might, therefore, come as a surprise that the rules of the Schenghen agreement are examined here, but this is not unjustified.

It can be helpful to begin by saying that, while the Maastricht Treaty allowed differentiated integration within a partially new area, that of monetary policy, the Schengen Agreement of 1985 was more problematic, because its object was the regulation of free movement of persons, as distinct from citizens or workers. This was one of the pillars of the European Community, as it was envisaged by the Treaty of Rome in 1957; that is, a Community where the citizens of the Member States could freely travel. However, almost thirty years later, systematic controls of identity documents were still in place at the borders between most Member States, with the notable exception of the Benelux countries. It was precisely these countries, together with France and (West) Germany, which in 1985 signed the agreement aiming at progressively dismantling common border controls. The contracting parties agreed on the harmonization of their visa and asylum policies, allowing their nationals and other residents to cross borders without police controls.

This legal framework has been subsequently modified in three ways. First, in 1990 the Agreement was supplemented by the Schengen Convention, which established an area without border controls.

Secondly and more importantly, during the Intergovernmental Conference that drafted the Amsterdam Treaty (1997) all the Member States, except the UK and Ireland, agreed to incorporate the Schengen rules within the Union's legal framework. The Protocol annexed to the Treaty clarified that such incorporation was achieved with a view to developing more rapidly 'an area of freedom, security and justice'. It also noticed that Ireland and the UK had not signed the Schengen Agreement, though they could accept some of its provisions and could at any time request to take part in the entirety of the *acquis.*[101] Conversely, the Protocol mentioned the intent of Iceland and Norway to become bound by the Schengen rules. The form of 'cooperation'[102] that thus emerged was based on a 'mixed' membership. This feature has been confirmed by later agreements, for example with Switzerland. In brief, the enhanced cooperation that initially was promoted only by some members of the EU has been opened to other European countries.

Thirdly, the incorporation of the Schengen *acquis* allowed EU institutions to step in. In particular, the Council replaced the Executive Committee and the Court of Justice was enabled to exercise judicial review within

---

101 Protocol integrating the Schengen *acquis* into the framework of the European Union, Article 4.

102 Protocol integrating the Schengen *acquis* into the framework of the European Union, Article 1.

certain limits,[103] which have mainly been eliminated by the Lisbon Treaty, together with the 'three-pillars' structure of the EU.[104] For example, the ECJ has found that the application of a rule set out by the Schengen Convention is incompatible with the right of free movement that stem from Community law for third country nationals who are family members of EU citizens.[105]

Once again, when considering differentiated integration, it is clear that the voluntary consensus of the State, of each State, is of central importance. Two elements are crucial in determining the nature of the voluntary consensus. First, the voluntary nature of the agreement is not vitiated by inequality in the bargaining power of the parties, because the rules that are incorporated have been set out only by some of them. On the one hand, as noticed by the Protocol's Preamble, those rules 'aimed at enhancing European integration'. Their goal was thus a deeper integration. On the other hand, though the *acquis* must be preserved, EU institutions can develop it. For example, they have established a European Border Surveillance System.[106] Second, with the Treaty of Amsterdam it has become clear that even with regard to one of the central elements of the EC, the free movement of persons, where Union's action would have been justified, a deepened integration remains subject to the voluntary consensus of each State. It is in this sense and within these limits that the Schengen agreement has been considered as a sort of *interim* arrangement, in view of a communautarization of its rules.[107]

---

103 Protocol integrating the Schengen *acquis* into the framework of the European Union, Article 2. For further analysis, see H Wallace, *Flexibility:* A Tool for Integration or a Restraint on Disintegration?, in K Neunreither & A Wiener (eds), *European Integration after Amsterdam: Institutional Dynamics and Prospects for Democracy* (Oxford, OUP, 2000) 175.

104 Article 276 TFEU keeps some limits, on which see P Craig, The Treaty of Lisbon: Process, architecture and substance, 33 Eur. L. Rev. (2008), 137, at 144.

105 ECJ, Case C-503/03, *Commission v Spain*, §§ 33-35. On the issues concerning non-EU nationals, see C Harlow & E Guild (eds), *Implementing Amsterdam: Immigration and Asylum* (Oxford, Hart, 2001) and GI Wolf, Efforts toward 'An Ever Closer' European Union Confront Immigration Barriers, 4 Indiana J. Global Leg. Stud. 223, 228 (1996), noting the increased perception of a 'fortress Europe'.

106 See Regulation No 1052/2013 and the ruling of the ECJ in Case C-44/14, *Spain v. European Parliament and Council* (rejecting the action brought by Spain against the possibility that the UK is involved in the new regime).

107 See B De Witte, Chameleonic Member States: Differentiation by Means of Partial and Parallel Agreements, cit., 241.

C. *A Europe of Concentric Circles: a 'Misleading Simple Idea'*

In the light of the remarks that have made thus far, another interesting and important question arises; that is, whether the various forms of interaction within and beyond the EU can be summarized by the referring to the idea of a 'Europe of concentric circles'.

As it has been observed for other terms, this metaphor has both a descriptive and a prescriptive side. Descriptively, it is noticed that some non-EU countries have accepted to apply the principles and rules of the single market, an aspect to which we will return later. Likewise, Turkey has accepted certain parts of EU law in the framework of the custom union that it agreed with the EU. Other Balkan countries have accepted part of the *acquis communautaire* and in particular the general principles of law developed by the ECJ, as is normally requested to the States that wish to become members of the EU. Conversely, the UK is not involved in the border-free Schengen area, which is so strategic for the freedoms of EU citizens to travel without visas or passports, and other five members of the EU followed it, including Ireland, which does not wish to take part in common actions in the field of defence. The general conclusion that is drawn from all this is that there is a greater differentiation of EU law than there was in the past. The description turns into a prescription, when it is observed that this is the inevitable price to pay for the construction of a larger area of peaceful cooperation in Europe.

There are, however, some difficulties with this irenic view of a Europe of concentric circles. First of all, the outer circle, that of non-EU countries, is far from being homogeneous, because some of them joined the EEA, while another have only agreed on a custom union.

Secondly, the inner circle – the EU – is itself differentiated not only with regard to monetary and fiscal issues. On the one hand, within the EU there are different views about the construction of the area of freedom, security and justice, as we have seen with regard to the Schengen *acquis*. Moreover, only fourteen Members have ratified the Convention of Prüm, which aims at strengthening police cooperation through exchange of information and, thus, security. On the other hand, there are very different views with regard to one of the main values upon which the EU is founded; that is, the respect for fundamental rights. When the last IGC discussed about the incorporation of the Charter of Fundamental Rights, some Member States dissented. A protocol added to the Lisbon Treaty now affirms that the Charter does not extend to Poland and the UK the 'ability' of the ECJ to 'find' that their 'laws, regulations or administrative provisions, practice or actions' are inconsistent with the Charter.[108] Legal scholarship has expressed strong reservations concerning the legal value and effects of this Protocol, which on other hand reaffirms the obligations stemming from EU law, including its general principles and thus fundamental rights as they stem from the ECHR and common constitutional traditions.[109] A more critical remark might be that any attempt to limit the scope and effectiveness of individual rights, even indirectly, for example through a limitation of judicial independence,might lead to the destruction of the moral foundations on which the 'legal order of a new kind' has been built. Interestingly, this was precisely the point of attack of the Commission in respect of Polish legislation and the Court of Justice endorsed its argument. The Venice Commission, too, criticized certain measures taken by Polish policy-makers from the viewpoint of the Council of Europe's standards concerning the Rule of Law.[110]

For the sake of clarity, I am at present making no claim about the nature of this controversy and the measures that could be adopted in order to solve it. This is a complex question that must be considered on its own, not tangentially. The present aim is more limited. It is to enquire whether one can coherently construct a theory of differentiated integration that rests on the assumption that there is an inner and more integrated circle – the EU – and a an outer and less integrated circle. The conclusion that suggested here is that this is not plausible. Whatever its apparent appeal, the idea of a Europe of concentric circles is but another 'misleading simple idea'.[111]

---

108 Protocol n. 30, Article 1 (1). See also Polish Declaration n. 61 on the Charter, affirming that the Charter does not affect in any way the Member States' capacity to legislate in the sphere of family law and public morality.

109 See J Ziller, *Les nouveaux traités européens: Lisbon et après* (La Découverte, 2005), 105; I Pernice, The Treaty of Lisbon and Fundamental Rights, in S Griller & J Ziller (eds), *The Lisbon Treaty. EU Constitutionalism without a Constitutional Treaty?* (Springer, 2008). See also P Craig, *The Treaty of Lisbon: Process, architecture and substance*, cit, 163 (observing the UK's insistence on the Protocol is 'problematic').

110 The Opinion was adopted by the Commission at its 113th session, on 8-9 December 2017.

111 F. De La Serre & H. Wallace, Flexibility and Enhanced Cooperation in the European Union: Placebo rather than Panacea, cit., 5.

E. *Implications for the post-Brexit Scenario*

It is in the light of the various legal mechanisms just examined that the post-Brexit scenario will be considered. The Bill approved by the English Parliament to authorize the referendum (the European Union Referendum Act 2015), the referendum's outcome and the decision to trigger Article 50 TEU brought about major changes for the UK, 'a fundamental reorientation in ... law and policy',[112] as well as for the EU as a whole. Taken together with the magnitude of such changes, the evident lack of adequate awareness of the available institutional and legal options before the referendum took place, explain the difficulties with which policy makers are confronted.

Limits of space preclude treatment of several important issues concerning public policies in range of sectors including work and environment, security and trade with the rest of the world. The following discussion will focus on some issues concerning institutions and rights and will rest on an assumption, that is, it can rightfully be said that is 'axiomatic' that the future relations between the UK and the EU will be deeply affected by the content of the withdrawal agreement,[113] but at the same time the content of the agreement will be influenced by the nature of the relationship that can be envisaged. This applies even to the scenario characterized by the absence of an agreement (the 'no-deal'). That being the case, the UK would not leave just a wide range of policies, but also the Single Market, under which most of its trade in goods and services has taken place for almost fifty years. Absence of an agreement, at least about a transitional period, this would happen very quickly and would force the UK to use World Trade Organization rules. Whether such rules are more or less favourable to the UK is a question that requires specific treatment,[114] which is precluded by space limits. Suffice it to mention that WTO rules are by all means a vehicle of legal globalization, more than those of the EU.

The question that is more related with our previous analysis is another; that is, whether the UK may remain aligned with the EU, either within the Single Market or within the Custom Union (this scenario is often called

112 M Dougan, Introduction, in Id (ed), *The UK after Brexit. Legal and Policy Challenges* (Intersentia, 2017), 1. For an account of the institutional consequences of *Brexit*, see P Craig, Brexit: A Drama in Six Acts, 41 Eur. Law Rev (2016), 447.

113 P Craig, Brexit and Relations Between the EU and the UK, in M. Dougan (ed.), *The UK after Brexit. Legal and Policy Challenges*, cit, 302.

114 See M Cremona, UK Trade Policy, in M Dougan (ed.), *The UK after Brexit. Legal and Policy Challenges*, cit, 247.

'soft Brexit', whatever the adequacy of this term). Some observers suggested that the UK might be involved in the single market as a member of the EEA.[115] There is no doubt that such a scenario could be economically beneficial for all, though in a different degree. It would also be beneficial to all individuals who have benefited of free movement and right of establishment.

However, it is not immune from difficulties. There is, first, the difficulty concerning the choice of legal instruments. As observed earlier, while Norway signed a single treaty with the EU, Switzerland chose to sign a set of agreements. Whatever the choice, the process of negotiation will tend to be long and cumbersome, as the experience of the last two years shows.

There is a further difficulty with this solution; that is, the close connection between the four freedoms of circulation of persons, goods, services and capitals. Of course, the UK may ask, as it did, to exclude the former, but the common position of the EU has been that those freedoms cannot be separated. For this reason, a scenario of a Europe '*à la carte*' in this respect seems very unlikely. This might induce negotiators to consider a custom union. But this would severely limit the capacity of the UK to enter into relations with other countries. In other words, if this was the model to be followed, instead of bringing sovereignty home, as many supporters or the '*Leave*' front argued during the political campaign, Britons would be subject to the rules established elsewhere, with a very limited influence on their contents.[116]

A further difficulty concerns enforcement mechanisms. Those who govern the UK constantly expressed their intent to be no longer subject to the jurisdiction of the Court of Justice. While this may be a politically legitimate purpose, institutionally it is not easy to understand how it could be achieved in the short run, because the EU Council's negotiating policy is that the Court must have jurisdiction concerning the term of the agreement. Nor, in the medium term, is it easy to understand how a solution different from the one that exists in the context of the EEA could be meaningfully envisaged. It is true that the Council has not excluded an alternative mechanism of adjudication, provided that it offers equivalent guarantees of independence and impartiality. However, an elementary necessity of coherence within the EEA would run against anything – for example,

115 This is a contentious political issue, as it is demonstrated by the fact that some shadow ministers of the Labour Party resigned after they joined the MPs who supported a rebel amendment to the Queen's Speech calling for Britain to stay in the single market and customs union (*The Independent*, June 30, 2017).

116 P Craig, Brexit and Relations Between the EU and the UK, cit, 320-1.

arbitral procedures – that differs from the existing judicial mechanism, in its essence the Court of Justice integrated by judges coming from the other partners. Similarly, the interpretation given by the Court to the *acquis communautaire* would continue to have weight as a persuasive authority for national courts, when they elaborate their own interpretation of the nationalized *acquis*, in terms indicated by the Repeal Bill.

VI. Conclusion

This essay has two major themes. The first is that there is a tension inherent between two political visions of Europe, one centred on the 'ever closer union' and the other on the achievement of a wide and loose union. Precisely because these are not simply different, but conflicting political visions of what the EU is and should be, it is necessary to be fully aware of their consequences, which is not always the case. A clear example is provided by the illusion, which emerges from the recent Declaration of Rome, that it is possible to live together harmoniously for a prolonged amount of time despite conflicting ideas about the ultimate ends of the European construction and, to some extent, about what its common values concretely mean. The second theme concerns differentiated integration. Although there is a variety of opinion about the desirability of those political visions of Europe, the institutional and legal mechanisms of integration that exist within and outside the EU must be considered in the light of the twin criteria of clarity and coherence. Such criteria are necessary requisites for a rigorous scientific analysis. They are also helpful for a better understanding of the institutional and legal options that are available for the relations between the UK and the EU in the post-Brexit period. Clarity and coherence, of course, do not replace passions and interests, which shape political preferences. They are nonetheless important.

The Future of the Protection of Fundamental Rights after Brexit

Jiří Zemánek

Abstract

The Union fundamental rights can become a medium of a real – two direction – dialog between European and national judicial authorities. The judicial reasoning by the British courts, reflecting the long tradition of the British system of conversations between the courts, will be missing after Brexit.

To meet the legitimate aspirations of the Union citizens means to leave the strict application of the CFR by the CJEU that should have to be more open to a discourse with national courts, which might be as well positioned to assess conflicts of constitutional values even beyond the standard instrumentalities of preliminary ruling. A more courageous use of the CFR means for judicial authorities at both levels to take their commitments in this area more seriously. The British judiciaries had been responsive in this respect. Their leaving the Union means slowing down the process of assertion of the CFR as the authoritative document on human rights protection in Europe.

I. Introduction

A process of rapprochement of three autonomous, but functionally interrelated, levels of protection of fundamental rights – national constitutions, European Convention of Human Rights and Fundamental Freedoms (the ECHR) and, for the Member States of the European Union, the Charter of Fundamental Rights (the CFR) – is running in Europe, initiated by the free movement of EU citizens within the internal market and the shared space of security and justice. The Britain's departure from this 'community of destiny', where the United Kingdom holds in certain respects a reserved position, will entail more than a mere withdrawal from its rights and obligations.

The enforcement of Union law at national level, whether it is applied directly or through implementation acts of Member States, relies on the effectiveness of national sanctions and other coercive measures for keeping under control the margin of appreciation or limits of exception conferred on national authorities by Union law. The judicial review of their acts by ordinary and constitutional courts refers – besides the principle of rule of law – to the principle of protection of fundamental rights. The direct normative reception of the CFR is taking place on an alternative basis, where the higher level of protection is replacing the lower ones (Article 53), not – as in cases without the Union law dimension – on a cumulative basis, where the national constitution is in a subsidiarity position towards the ECHR or other human rights treaties. 'A total convergence'[1] of all standards of protection has been made difficult due to warries of some constitutional courts about the extensive interpretation of the CFR by the Court of Justice of the European Union (the CJEU), which could allegedly override the identity-building core elements of their national constitutions. The British reservation followed by a Polish one against the CFR at the intergovernmental conference in Lisbon 2007 has evidenced this approach.[2]

A convergence-supporting potential of references to the CJEU as well as by national judicial authorities to general principles of law with binding force, stemming both from the ECHR and from common constitutional traditions of the Member States, is evident and functionally complementing the CFR. This process results in merger of concepts originating in different legal orders by mutual communication of their interpreters, forming an autonomous frame of protection, which is not identical with the original sources. The real permeability of shared national and supranational values, which are nominally listed in Article 2 TEU, can be verified in the judicial dialog.[3]

Distinct positions towards direct application of the CFR appeared in the case-law of the constitutional courts in some Central and East European countries. The Czech Constitutional Court (the Court) admitted earlier an indirect influence of the CFR through its 'irradiation' in the national catalogue.[4] By this reserved position to the CFR the Court displayed an asym-

1 R Arnold, 'Introduction' in R Arnold (ed), *The Convergence of Fundamental Rights Protection in Europe* (Springer, 2016), 2.

2 Protocol no. 30 on the application of the Charter of Fundamental Rights of the European Union.

3 M Wendel, Permeabilität im europäischen Verfassungsrecht. Verfassungsrechtliche Integrationsnormen auf Staats – und Unionsebene im Vergleich (Mohr Siebeck, 2011), Teil 3 (Einheitsbildende/Vielfaltswahrende Formen primärrechtlicher Permeabilität).

4 Judgment of the Czech Constitutional Court in the case *Sugar quotas III*, Pl. ÚS 3/14 (N 50/40 SbNU 443 = no. 154/2006 Coll.).

metric approach, since – after the adoption of the monistic concept in the Constitution[5]– international treaties on human rights and fundamental freedoms have been expressly declared as having the same legal status as the norms of the constitutional order[6], forming a reference point for the constitutional review of domestic law,[7] whereas – after the accession of the Czech Republic to the European Union – the same status has not been expressly granted to the CFR (yet). However, an equivalent standing is recognized to the CFR de facto by the case law of the Court on constitutional complaints.

The CFR has been referred to with certain reservation in Slovakia, what was a matter of a sharp criticism. The absence of reasoning with reference to the CFR at the level of ordinary courts 'deprives the Constitutional Court of the opportunity to establish the basics of its doctrine in relation to the Charter'.[8] Otherwise it 'infringes the principle of the prohibition of *denegatio iustitiae*', its approach to the Charter was found to be 'unreasonably dismissive, particularly in comparison with its attitude to other international documents on human rights and fundamental freedoms'.[9] A deeper analysis of the relevant case law to date leads to the conclusion that this gap has been progressively narrowed.

After 2015 a disobedience – 'a clear risk of a serious breach of the values referred to in Article 2 TEU'– in Poland has been determined by the European Commission.[10] It could result in violation of principles of rule of law as well as protection of fundamental rights.[11]

If Brexit would mean also cutting the communication between the British courts and the jurisprudence of the CJEU, it could amount to narrowing the plurality of national experiences of protection, impeding the Europe-wide convergence in the field of fundamental rights. A couple of

5 International treaties binding the Czech Republic form a part of the legal order with priority over status in case of a conflict, Article 10 Const. as amended by Act no. 395/2001 Coll.

6 It is determined by Article 112 Const.

7 The case *Bancrupcy Trustee*,Pl. ÚS 36/01 (N 80/26 SbNU 317; no. 403/2002 Coll.).

8 J Mazák and M Jánošíková (eds), The Charter of Fundamental Rights of the European Union in proceedings before courts of the Slovak Republic (Košice, 2016), 179.

9 *Ibid*, 180.

10 See meanwhile the judgment of the ECJ, Case 619/18, *Commission v. Republic of Poland*, ECLI:EU:C:2019:531.

11 Opening remarks of the First Vice-President Frans Timmermans, *Readout of the European Commission discussion on the rule of law in Poland*, Brussels, 20 December 2017.

law students from the Central and Eastern Europe, forming the new generation of judges and practicing lawyers now, made use after 1990 of the unique opportunity to study at universities in the United Kingdom under the EU programs Socrates/Erasmus and learned the fundamental rights-based approach to law there. The treaty arrangement of the leaving of the United Kingdom the European Union should have to take the need for preservation of the link between judges at ′both sides′ into account. The access of UK′s persons to the EU internal market as well as the access of Member States′ persons to the UK′s market should have to remain supported by the shared constitutional values and fundamental rights, the execution of which, indispensable for the effective functioning of the whole system of the post-Brexit cooperation between the EU and the UK, is to be guaranteed by judicial authorities at the both sides. The mutual communication and exchange of opinions between them, enjoying also future developments of the jurisprudential standards of protection, needs an anticipating open-ended treaty frame without any isolated self-assertion in this field.

II. The position of the EU charter in United Kingdom

There has been a dispute about the application of the CFR in the United Kingdom. The Protocol no. 30 to the Treaty of Lisbon states that the ability of the Union or British courts will not be extended to 'find that the laws, regulations or administrative provisions, practices or action of the United Kingdom are inconsistent with the fundamental rights, freedoms and principles' of the CFR. As the CFR reaffirms the general principles of Union law having been developed by jurisprudence, they have binding effect on British courts, when they interpret the CFR and form part of criteria of review of British laws on their compliance with them [Article 52(4) CFR]. For instance, under Article 4 CFR the British courts 'may not transfer an asylum seeker to the "Member State responsible" ...where they cannot be unaware that systemic deficiencies in the asylum procedure and in the reception conditions of asylum seekers ... amount to substantial grounds for believing that the asylum seeker would face a real risk of being subjected to inhuman and degrading treatment' [the judgment of the CJEU in the joint cases *N. S.* (C-411/10) and *M. E.* (C-493/10)]. Whether Article 1(2) of the Protocol no. 30 exempts the United Kingdom from applying social rights as justiciable under Title IV has not been cleared yet.

The CFR has been given normative effect within the United Kingdom by Section 2 of the 'European Communities Act 1972'. This basic concept differs from continental systems of Union law reception and is in contrast with the principle of its direct validity and enforceability as developed by the CJEU case law and has not been modified by 'European Union Acts 2008 and 2011'.

The United Kingdom's 'Human Rights Act 1998' has established a system, which combines judicial and political intervention, guaranteeing compliance of national laws with the ECHR. The declaration of incompatibility by higher courts challenges the legislative bodies to make laws compatible. The most fundamental principle of the British constitutional order – sovereignty of the Parliament – seems to remain only formally respected by this system. It is the Government (the Minister responsible for the legislation in question), which takes a measure reflecting the respective decision of the European Court of Human Rights (the ECtHR), whereas the Parliament is expected to give its consent, in urgent cases ex post.

According to the Conservatives' proposals for changing Britain's human rights laws of May 2015, both the recent practice of the ECtHR, using the ECHR under a 'living instrument doctrine' leading to a 'mission creep', and the domestic legislation passed in this respect and overruling decisions of the democratically elected Parliament, 'damaged the credibility of human rights at home'. They undermined the role of British courts, that 'have to take into account' ECtHR rulings, when they are interpreting ECHR's rights, as well as the sovereignty of the Parliament, when the 'Human Rights Act 1998'goes far beyond the United Kingdom's obligations under the ECHR.

The Conservatives, therefore, earlier proposed fundamental changes by repealing (Labour's) 'Human Rights Act 1998' and restoring common sense ('put Britain first') through a new 'Bill of Rights and Responsibilities', which should have to 'prevent British laws from being effectively rewritten through interpretation'. As even after Brexit the experience of the British judicial authorities in human rights protection would continue (at least for some time), their performance would have to be counted for by the Union and Member States' judiciaries and political bodies, even when looking for a new arrangement of the Union's accession to the ECHR.

However, the British Government has given priority to negotiating and concluding a post-Brexit treaty. The long anticipated British Bill has been further delayed because of the Brexit judgment of the Supreme Court *R (on the application of Miller and another) v Secretary of State for exiting the European Union* given on 24 January 2017 as well as by the outcome of parliamentary election in June 2017 and later, due to turbulences in decision making process of Brexit policy, left open for post-Brexit times.

III. The relevance of the CFR for the areas of EU policies

The intensity of application of the CFR relies on the area *of Union law* considered. Where a stronger Union interest exists (e.g. internal market, competition), the CFR is more likely to be a frame of references for constitutional review of national measures. When the application of the CFR could lower the effective enforcement of Union law (like in asylum or European Arrest Warrant matters), the uniform compliance with a minimum standard of protection by Member States is presumed and precedes over the potential breach of fundamental rights in a given case.[12] When, on the other hand, the objectives of European integration can be realized only by coordinating the exercise of Member States competencies (e.g. family law, social policy), the obligation of national authorities to refer to the CFR by taking it into consideration is limited solely for the specific purposes of interpreting a piece of Union law without an assessment of national law as such.[13] In all other cases the CFR will most likely not be applied. Substantive (higher level of protection) as well as procedural (supremacy) advantages for individuals could have been always favoring the Union rather than national fundamental rights.

The relevance of the CFR in areas reserved to Member States, where the Union has not been authorized to full harmonization, is constitutionally questionable as it might result in a latent extension of competences, even when the CJEU constructed – through an extensive interpretation of the scope of application of Union law – a remote link to it, sufficient enough to refer to the CFR.[14] However, the CJEU rather attempts to ensure that the CFR should not become a vehicle for broadening the impact of Union law on national law through further limitation of the field, in which national courts must apply the CFR directly. When assessing the scope of discretion in the execution of an asylum claim, the Member State is implementing Union law; however, to ensure the full effectiveness of the Dublin II Regulation, the CFR would be as relevant as in an 'exceptional' situation.[15] The CJEU is somehow reducing the impact of the CFR even when national courts are enforcing Union law. The CJEU renounced to a broad application of fundamental rights also to avoid an intervention in the sovereignty of the Member States, in particular, in cases of migration of

12 Judgment of the CJEU in the case no. C-399/11 *Melloni*.
13 Judgment of the CJEU in the case no. C-400/10 PPU *McB*.
14 Judgment of the CJEU in the case no. C-617/10 *Akerberg Fransson*.
15 Judgment of the CJEU in the case no. C-411/10 and C-483/10 *N. S. and others*.

third country nationals within the Union. However, the CJEU did not identify such an intervention in national sovereignty in pleas of Hungary and Republic of Poland Decision (EU) 2015/1601 on provisional measures in the area of international protection in an emergency situation characterized by a sudden inflow of nationals of third countries into certain Member States.[16]

The above-mentioned findings have been in the United Kingdom, the most exposed Member State to (im)migration with its social impacts, a stock of displeasure leading to Brexit.

IV. Recent developments

The integration in sensitive matters is imaginable, when mutual trust between the Member States in adequate fundamental rights protection across the Union is underlying the legal instruments of cooperation. National authorities should not be exposed to the need to scrutinize the 'adequacy' of fundamental rights compliance in cooperating States, otherwise the effectiveness of the pieces of Union law in question would be impaired. However, national constitutional courts could be unwilling to rely only on Union guarantees, as the German Federal Constitutional Court recently demonstrated in a ruling which claimed its jurisdiction on the review whether the principle of mutual trust does not violate the constitutional guarantees of fair trial as a part of national identity.[17]

The quick answer from Luxembourg was unusual – in contrast to its earlier decisions,[18] the CJEU adjudicated, that the full effect of Union law is not the only objective to be aimed at. It is rather the elimination of any inhuman treatment in the country the court of which has been asking the extradition. The obligation of mutual recognition of standards of protection of an individual in criminal proceedings under the framework decision on the European Arrest Warrant must be supported by an impartial information about non-existence of degrading treatment of prisoners, based on a direct communication between the respective national criminal

---

16 Judgment of the CJEU of 6 September 2017 in joint cases no. C-643/15 and C-647/15.

17 Judgment of the German Federal Constitutional Court 2 BvR in the case no. 2535, 14 concerning European Arrest Warrant (called *Solange III*, too).

18 Case *Melloni* (supra n 11).

courts. Otherwise the process of surrender can be – rather is to be – brought to an end.[19]

This indicates that the Union fundamental rights can become a medium of a real – two direction – dialog between European and national judicial authorities. The judicial reasoning by the British courts, reflecting the long tradition of the British system of conversations between the courts, will be missing after Brexit.

V. Conclusions

It is open to debate, whether the approach of the CJEU to the application of the CFR in the Member States is not arbitrarily restrained, weakening the protection and frustrating the expectations of Union citizens. As an effective Union procedural mechanism for the enforcement of fundamental rights obligations in the Member States (regardless of the infringement procedure under Article 258 TFEU and the 'nuclear bomb' of Article 7 TEU) has been still under construction, the space for presumption of a minimum compliance within the Union would be narrowed. It can be considered whether or in which way the next draft Treaty on the accession of the Union to the European Convention of Human Rights, the first draft having been rejected by the CJEU,[20] could be supportive in this respect. The hypothetical question about the prospects of supporting the accession by United Kingdom need not to be raised now any more.

Both the CJEU case law on coordinating legislation and on Article 51 CFR seem to suggest an inferiority of Union fundamental rights in the interest of European integration (a. o., rejection to reflect the constitutional reservations of Spanish courts against the execution of European Arrest Warrant in *Melloni* case,[21] calling into doubt Article 53 CFR). National guarantees are the main source of protection for Union citizens against acts of the Member States when exercising discretion in a field occupied by Union law, whereas the CFR is a medium guaranteeing the conformity of national authorities′ obligations in the area of fundamental rights and freedoms. A generous application of the CFR might limit national autonomy and entail the loss of constitutional diversity, forming part of national

---

19 Judgment of the CJEU in the joint cases no. C-404/15 and C-659/15 *Aranyosi and Caldararu*, initiated by preliminary questions of German courts.

20 Opinion of the CJEU no. 2/13.

21 Supra, n 12.

identity, which is to be observed by the Union (Article 4 para 2 TEU) in a way that could be difficult to justify with regard to the principle of conferral of powers.

To meet the legitimate aspirations of the Union citizens means to leave the strict application of the CFR by the CJEU that should have to be more open to a discourse with national courts, which might be as well positioned to assess conflicts of constitutional values even beyond the standard instrumentalities of the preliminary ruling. A more courageous use of the CFR means for judicial authorities at both levels to take their commitments in this area more seriously. The British judiciaries had been responsive in this respect. Their leaving the Union means slowing down the process of assertion of the CFR as the authoritative document on human rights protection in Europe.

The question, whether the European Union does possess remedies adequate to the task of protecting its values, has been recently a matter of assessment of the CJEU, initiated by the reference for preliminary ruling concerning conditions for execution of the European arrest warrant. On the basis of the European Commission's reasoned opinion of 20 December 2017[22] submitted in accordance with Article 7 (1) TEU and the findings of the Venice Commission for Democracy through law of the Council of Europe regarding the rule of law in Poland the CJEU has deepened its conclusions in the judgment of 5 April 2016 *Aranyiosi and Caldararu*[23] by the ruling that 'where the executing judicial authority ... has material ... indicating that there is a real risk of breach of the fundamental right to a fair trial ... on account of systemic or generalized deficiencies so far as concerns of the independence of the issuing Member State's judiciary, that authority must determine, specifically and precisely, whether ... there are substantial grounds for believing that that person will run such a risk if he is surrendered to that State'.[24]

The further course of human rights in the Union thus faces an uneasy dilemma: is it better for the Member States, who control the Treaties and therefore the rules of the game, to give up the national autonomy they have anxiously guarded, so that the Union may react decisively to restrictions on fundamental rights? Or should they rather accept the Union,

22 Supra, n 11.
23 Supra n 19.
24 Judgment of 25 July 2018 in the case C-216/18 *PPU*, para 80.

which does not intervene in fundamental rights' issues at the expense of tolerating new authoritarians emerging in some other Member States?[25]

25 'The interpretation of Article 51 of the EU Charter of Fundamental Rights: the dilemma of stricter or broader application of the Charter to national measures. Study for the PetiCommitee of the European Parliament, 2016'.

Brexit – Exercise of Democracy or a Challenge to Democracy?

Ingolf Pernice, Berlin

Abstract

The Brexit process is no doubt a challenge to the EU. Is it also a challenge to democracy? Or is it just an exercise of democracy? Looking closer at both, the provisions for the withdrawal from the EU and their application by the UK and the EU no serious violation of democratic principles can be determined. Some doubts, however, arise with regard to certain aspects of the process in practice, starting from the conditions and preparation of the referendum up to the effect given by a broad majority to its result, notwithstanding the advisory nature only. The present contribution discusses questions of appropriate democratic participation to a referendum of the given kind, of dealing with systemic lying and manipulation in political processes, binding effects of a referendum in a parliamentary democracy and the role of courts in relation to the parliament and the government when it comes to decide upon far-reaching constitutional issues. Some lessons are drawn from the experience of Brexit so far, not least for the rising awareness of citizens of the Union for political developments across borders and of challenges to democracy the abuse of new information technologies can bring about at all political levels. Whatever the outcome of the process with all its threats to democracy it brings about, it will trigger a transformation both of the UK and the EU. Should Brexit really happen, the door so remains open for an enlightened return as an expression of democracy.

Introduction

The Brexit story so far is full of surprises, unexpected turns and disappointments. Nobody really expected that the referendum of 23 June 2016 would result in a success for the Brexiteers, and that the government would strive to execute it with such decisiveness and rigor. Many argued that the government simply had to follow what 'the people' had decided and forgot about the consultative nature of the referendum as well as the constitutional principle of the supremacy of Parliament. Surprisingly for them, the High Court and the Supreme Court has very clearly confirmed the constitutional need for the government to obtain parliamentary authorisation in order to trigger Article 50 TEU and also surprisingly clear was the Parliament's final vote on this authorisation, in spite of the fact that before the referendum a majority of the Parliament had defended exactly the opposite point of view: Remain.

That Theresa May, having an absolute majority in Parliament for her party, would decide to call new elections in order to gain support for her strategy of a hard Brexit, was unexpected as well, and so was the clear refusal of the British people to follow her. Nothing suggests that Theresa May will politically survive the process or even remain in office for the full period of the process. Given her failure in the 2017 general elections, it came as a surprise that the negotiations on a withdrawal agreement started at all: 19 June 2017.

The only obvious certainty was at this time that the remaining part of the two years period provided under the Treaty for coming to an arrangement on the conditions of Britain's withdrawal would be over by 29 March 2019. Given the complexity of the subject there was little hope that this deadline would be met. Surprisingly, the negotiators did emerge with an agreement in time. And this "Draft Agreement on the withdrawal of the United Kingdom of Great Britain and Northern Ireland from the European Union and the European Atomic Energy Community", as agreed at negotiators' level on 14 November 2018,[1] was even accepted by the Council of 27, as required by Article 50 TEU. It was also expected to receive the consent of the European Parliament. As it was rejected by the UK Parliament, however, it was difficult to see how a timely ratification could be reached to avoid a hard Brexit, as it was the wish of the majority voting in the UK Parliament on 14 March 2019. Would a second referendum be needed, or new elections, before such a step is taken? An extension of the Article 50 TEU deadline with the agreement of the 27 was necessary in any event. This agreement even seemed to be questioned for a while, since Italy was thought possibly to veto the extension.[2] The only way to avoid a hard

1 Draft Agreement, TF50 (2018) 55–Commission to EU27, full text available at: https://ec.europa.eu/commission/sites/beta-political/files/draft_withdrawal_agreement_0.pdf (accessed 19 March 2019).

2 For an attempt of blocking: see Georgi Gotev, 'Farage to lobby EU countries in search of Brexit extension veto', at: https://www.euractiv.com/section/eu-elections-2019/news/farage-to-lobby-eu-countries-in-search-of-brexit-extension-veto/ (accessed 19 March 2019); see also: Focus online of March 19, 2019: 'Geheim-PaktmitSalvini? Wie Brexit-Vater Farage die EU austricksen will', at https://eulawanalysis.blogspot.

Brexit in this case would have been the revocation of the Article 50 notice.[3] Yet, at the EU summit of 22 March 2019, an extension was granted until 31 October 2019, though nothing indicates that an agreement will be found and finally be ratified by all parties until then. – Following the 2019 European elections and after Theresa May stepping down, the new Prime Minister Boris Johnson even more strongly envisages a no-deal Brexit. This is as suprising as audacious, given the clear majority in the Parliament is against this solution. Probably the Parliament will not allow it to happen, though time is too short for new elections or for organising the second referendum. The next surprise, thus, is to come. The second extension of the Article 50 deadline may be unavoidable.

The 2019 local elections in the UK had shown a manifest move away from the Tories and the Labour Party, and commentators saw this as an expression of disappointment of people with the way the Brexit process was handled by the Government and in the Parliament so far. Since no solution could be found, the UK had decided to participate in the European elections of 26 May 2019. This was a new challenge since the question may be asked: What was the point of participating in the elections for a Member State that is about to leave the Union. Or is it not?

A second referendum or new elections in the UK may lead to no-Brexit at all. Millions of petitioners asked for revoking the Article 50 notice,[4] and again, hundreds of thousands anti-Brexit campaigners were marching in London demanding a second referendum at the 'Put it to the People march' of 23 March 2019. Given the increasing weight of young British voters compared to that of the elderly, whose votes were decisive in the June 2016 referendum, and with a view to the fact that Brexit is decisive for the young generations' future above all, the last word is not spoken yet.[5]

---

com/2019/03/extension-and-elections-we-need-to-talk.html?fbclid=IwAR3sRomrzRbRRAVnh7ProT9M7VPdrRO2TXxTayljNu1h3pbQM8AMku88BfA&m=1 (accessed 19 March 2019).

3 For the possibilities of this option from a legal point of view see the judgment of 10 December 2018 of the ECJ in case C-621/18 – *Wightman*, ECLI:EU:C:2018:999.

4 See Petition: Revoke Article 50 and remain in the EU, with 4,366,791 signatures by March 23, 2019, 16:32, at: https://petition.parliament.uk/petitions/241584 (accessed 23 March 2019).

5 For the legal aspects of the remaining outcomes a fortnight before the 29 th of March 2019 see the blog of Catherine Barnard & Steve Wheatherill, 'Extension and elections: We need to talk about Article 50', at: https://eulawanalysis.blogspot.com/2019/03/extension-and-elections-we-need-to-talk.html?fbclid=IwAR3sRomrzRbRRAVnh7ProT9M7VPdrRO2TXxTayljNu1h3pbQM8AMku88BfA&m=1.

What we are experiencing these days in the UK and the EU with regard to the Brexit process is closely related to the meaning of democracy. If my task at this Lisbon conference, as the title of the present paper suggests, was to develop some thoughts about the choice between characterising Brexit as an exercise of, or a challenge to democracy, perhaps the only certainty is, wherever the process may finally lead the Union to, that the outcome *must* be democratic. Let me develop my thoughts on the basis of these three:

1. The Brexit process is no doubt an exercise of democracy in some respect;
2. It must be understood as a challenge to democracy in some other respect;
3. And it is a process from which some lessons can be drawn for the future.

Some questions cannot be examined in depth at this place: 'What actually is democracy?', or whether 'democracy' is a term that can be easily applied in EU contexts at all. Reference may be made insofar to the proceedings of the last ECLN Conference in Thessaloniki in May 2015, published under the title 'Legitimacy Issues of the European Union in the Face of Crisis'.[6]

The present paper rather focuses, first, on the provisions of the EU-Treaty regarding the withdrawal of a Member State: They seem, indeed, to provide for an exercise of democracy (infra I.). Second, the process leading to the UK Government's notice of withdrawal under Article 50 TEU: With a view, in particular, to the democratic rights of the citizens directly affected by a Brexit and how EU citizens are represented, it rather looks like a challenge to democracy (infra II.).This leads to the question what lessons can be learned from this process: What does it tell us about democracy in the EU (infra III.)?

I. The Brexit Process as an Exercise of Democracy

Paul Craig has described the first phases of the process in a brilliant essay titled: 'Brexit: a drama in six acts'.[7] After a long public debate, David

6 Lina Papadopoulou/Ingolf Pernice/Joseph H.H. Weiler (eds), *Legitimacy Issues of the European Union in the Face of Crisis. Dimitris Tsatsos in Memoriam* (Nomos, Baden-Baden 2017).

7 Paul Craig, 'Brexit: a drama in six acts', *European Law Review* (2016), 447.

Cameron was given a clear mandate in the parliamentary elections of 2014 to carry out his strategy in the form he had proposed in the famous Bloomberg Speech of 23 January 2013.[8] As promised, he led negotiations with the EU on an arrangement satisfying the demands of the UK and after these negotiations had been concluded, he submitted the question to the British people so that they could decide whether to remain in the EU under these new conditions or to withdraw from it. The answer was Brexit. But even more than 3 years after the referendum of June 2016 the UK is still a Member State of the EU, it participated in the European elections of May 2019, and its future role in – or relation to – the EU remains undefined.

The conclusion that this process was an exercise of democracy can, at least, be based on four aspects of it: David Cameron's strategy was democratic (infra A.); putting the question of Brexit to an advisory referendum is an exercise of democracy (infra B.); the conditions and the procedure that Article 50 TEU provides for a withdrawal from the EU are democratic (infra C.), and the result of the Brexit process so far has been a surprising increase in democratic awareness among people throughout the EU (infra D.).

A. *The Cameron Strategy was democratic*

David Cameron understood that strong feelings existed in Britain against the EU and that people had problems with (a) the increasing flow of immigrants into the country, with (b) the financial burden of EU membership and with (c) the constraints that EU legislation and policies seemed to place on sovereign UK policies, primarily in the social sector and health care. The EU seemed to have competences that were too far-reaching. Contrary to his expectations, however, the 'balance of competences review' David Cameron had initiated in 2012 revealed that there was no unjustified EU competence.[9] With a view to finding an appropriate arrangement with the EU, Cameron puts emphasis rather on a stronger subsidiarity control over the exercise of EU competences, an enhanced role of the national

---

8 David Cameron, 'EU speech at Bloomberg', 23 January 2013, at: https://www.gov.uk/government/speeches/eu-speech-at-bloomberg (accessed 18 August 2017).

9 See GOV.UK, 'Guidance. Review of the balance of competences', at: https://www.gov.uk/guidance/review-of-the-balance-of-competences (accessed 19 March 2019). An official conclusion upon all the documents and work published has not been published yet.

Parliaments over EU policies and the deletion of the 'ever closer Union'-clause in the Treaties. If his strategy was to negotiate these issues with his colleagues in the EU and to submit the resulting arrangement to the scrutiny of the British people as a basis for the 'remain' option, it is difficult to contest the democratic character of this process.

The problem was that the outcome of these negotiations was neither strong nor convincing in substance, nor clear regarding the legal implications.[10] It was not the 'far-reaching fundamental change', nor the 'updated European Union' he had called for in the Bloomberg speech, nor the return to the 'common market'.[11] Nonetheless, to put the question of 'Brexit or remain' to the British people was a great risk, to say the least, and his campaign for 'remain' on this basis was more than difficult. This does not mean, however, that the strategy was undemocratic. On the contrary, in the 2014 elections it received full backing, and the Brexit referendum was expressly authorised by the Parliament in 2016.

B. *Advisory Referendum and Democracy*

Is an advisory referendum, as it was authorised by the Parliament, democratic? Difficult to deny! A referendum is an expression of direct democracy. Even in a representative democracy that is based upon the principle of parliamentary sovereignty, like Britain, there cannot be doubts about this, at least in a case where the Parliament in the exercise of its prerogatives expressly authorises a referendum that is not legally binding. In the present case the referendum was advisory, so the Parliament allowed the government to ask for the opinion of the people without implying that the outcome would determine the policies of the government or the Parliament. While the principle of parliamentary sovereignty may well exclude an act of Parliament – or a popular vote, authorised by the Parliament – from being binding for the Parliament in future and so restricting the Parliaments' own freedom to decide at any time whatever it considers necessary, no such restriction follows from an advisory referendum.

10 See the critique by Sylvie Goulard, *'Goodby Europe'* (Flammarion, Roubaix 2016).

11 David Cameron, Bloomberg speech (n 8), summarising his view of what the British peoples' 'disillusionment with the EU is': 'People feel that the EU is heading in a direction that they never signed up to. They resent the interference in our national life by what they see as unnecessary rules and regulation. And they wonder what the point of it all is. Put simply, many ask "why can't we just have what we voted to join – a common market?"'.

Meanwhile, the Divisional Court of England and Wales and, on appeal, the UK Supreme Court were asked to decide upon the question 'whether a formal notice of withdrawal can lawfully be given by ministers without prior legislation passed in both Houses of Parliament and assented to by HM The Queen'.[12] With Judgment of 20 January 2017 the UK Supreme Court has confirmed the view taken by the High Court[13] that an express authorisation by the Parliament is required for the government to file the notice under Article 50 TEU. The Supreme Court stressed, in particular, that 'Parliamentary sovereignty is a fundamental principle of the UK constitution'. Quoting from Dicey's *Introduction to the Study of the Law of the Constitution* the Court emphasises that the 'Parliament, or more precisely the Crown in Parliament, lays down the law through statutes – or primary legislation as it is also known – and not in any other way'. And as the withdrawal from the EU would necessarily change the law applicable within the UK and the rights of her citizens, Brexit would not be possible without an act of Parliament.[14] In rejecting the government's argument that filing the notice under Article 50 TEU would not be an exercise of the Royal prerogative the Supreme Court so protected the constitutional rights of the Parliament and democracy in Britain.

It was for the Parliament, thus, to give or not to give the green light for the notice. And voting upon the authorisation of the government to give notice of withdrawal to the President of the Council as specified by Article 50 TEU, each individual Member of Parliament was called to make his or her own personal judgment of conscience whether or not to follow the people's vote. If they felt bound, politically, to follow it, this was no doubt an expression of democracy.

C. *The Terms of Article 50 TEU as an Expression of Democracy*

Democracy means free self-determination of people, citizens of a political community. According to the concepts of post-national democracy and

---

12 See (2017) UKSC 5 Judgment of 24 January 2017 – *Miller*, para. 2, at: https://www.google.com/search?q=uk+supreme+court+brexit+judgment&oq=uk+supreme+court+brexit&aqs=chrome.2.69i57j0l3.20422j1j7&sourceid=chrome&ie=UTF-8# (accessed 21 March 2019).

13 Divisional Court of England and Wales, Judgment given on 3 November 2016 – *R (Miller) v The Secretary of State for Exiting the European Union* [2016] EWHC 2768.

14 UKSC (n 12), paras 43, 100, 101.

multilevel constitutionalism, democracy is not limited to States only.[15] People can organise self-determination at diverse levels, and this is what the citizens of the Member States did when they accepted, according to their respective constitutional requirements, the European Treaties and their amendments as negotiated, on their behalf, by their governments. With the constitution of the EU people, citizens of the Member States, have not only created this particular supranational setting for pursuing their common political objectives, and defined themselves as citizens of the Union; they have also set up the procedure allowing EU membership to remain voluntary. Thus, like the Constitution of the EU as a whole, the right of withdrawal reflecting the 'principle of voluntariness' laid down in Article 50 TEU,[16] is also an expression of the citizens' democratic self-determination in the profoundest sense of the term. The citizens of the Member States exercised their sovereign right to establish the EU, the membership to which similarly remains the sovereign choice of each of the participating peoples.

There is an important difference to the constitution of a State, even of a federal State: Article 50 confirms the voluntary character of the membership to this particular joint venture, with all the consequences it may imply. Though originally not thought to be of practical relevance, the exit option is part of the deal and an expression of a constitutional principle, which is formative of the EU. It underlines the openness, which the principle of democracy requires as a matter of self-determination, for peoples at any time to revise previous decisions whenever deemed necessary.

But democratic self-determination is not without limits. It is based upon the recognition and respect of human dignity and the fundamental rights of others. This is the reason why the withdrawal from the EU is subject to a specific procedure. The terms of Article 50 TEU can, thus, be understood as an expression of these limits. They reflect the fundamental requirements of solidarity, the principle of loyal and sincere cooperation and respect for the rights of EU citizens under the Treaties, in particular the rights of free

---

15 Ingolf Pernice, 'Multilevel Constitutionalism and the Crisis of Democracy in Europe', 11 *EuConst* (2015), pp 541–62, available also as: WHI-Paper 02/2015.

16 On this principle as a particular characteristic of the EU see Ingolf Pernice, 'The EU – A Citizens' Joint Venture. Multilevel Constitutionalism and Open Democracy in Europe', in: José M Magone (ed), *Routledge Handbook of European Politics* (Routledge, Abingdon, 2015), pp 184–201. See also: Kalypso Nicolaidis, Exodus Reconing Sacrifice. Three Meanings of Brexit (Unbound, London 2019), p 188: Brexit as a demonstration of "how the freedom to leave defines the very essence of the EU".

movement and non-discrimination or, technically speaking 'national treatment' of foreign EU citizens. Therefore, though established by a democratic process, the question of whether or not the procedure and conditions set out in this provision are sufficient to ensure the effective protection of these rights and principles needs further consideration.[17]

D. *Stimulating democratic Processes in the EU*

As part of the Brexit story, not only the developments in the UK, but also the reactions they provoked in other Member States are of interest. It was a shock for many people, an alarm bell warning of the decline not only of the EU but also of national democracies. People feared that the British referendum would have a negative impact on national political developments in Austria, the Netherlands, France and others, including Germany, due to populist, xenophobic and nationalist movements gaining ground at the same time as the European idea was coming under increasing pressure. As a result, new citizens' initiatives and movements arose spontaneously in reaction to these threats to integration and peace in Europe.

One of them, Pulse of Europe, begun in January 2017 and has since brought tens of thousands of Europeans onto the streets in up to 130 European cities, to demonstrate each Sunday at 2 p.m. for a United Europe of the citizens.[18] The general fear that the Brexit process could stimulate disintegration and push Europe back into a situation that we thought we had overcome over the past 70 years thus had the positive effect of mobilising citizens who had hitherto been silent to engage and take ownership of the EU. After some silence in 2018 this movement has taken up speed in the run-up to the European elections in May 2019 and must continue to counter those who see their future in political structures devised in the 19th century with consequences nobody would wish to see again.

It may be going too far to construct some kind of causality, but the victory of *Van der Bellen* in Austria, the defeat of *Wilders* in the Dutch elections, and the victory of *Macron* 2017 with his clear commitment to the European Union in France seemed to signal an awakening of people all over Europe, people who have realised that the current period of crisis and

---

17 See infra II.1.

18 See: https://pulseofeurope.eu (accessed 21 May 2019) – After the French elections of 2017 the activities of Pulse of Europes lowed down for a while, but new momentum was found in 2019 with a view to the European elections.

depression must have an end and that our common future is a future within and not without the European Union. Polls showed that approval of the EU were rapidly increasing since June 2016, with increases of 18% in Germany, 15% in the Netherlands and 12% in Spain.[19] In this sense, the outcome of the elections in Austria, the Netherlands and France, and perhaps even that of the 2017 elections in the UK indicate that neither the disintegration of Europe nor a hard Brexit or, perhaps, any Brexit at all, is what people in Europe ultimately want to see. If this is true, the Brexit process has so far proved to not only be an exercise of democracy, but even stimulated democracy far beyond the UK.

II. The Brexit Process as a Challenge to Democracy

At the same time, however, certain aspects and effects of the Brexit process raise critical questions and must be understood as a challenge to democracy. Four issues that seem to require special reflection will be discussed below in order to stimulate further thought: the role of the citizens (infra A.); the role of lying and voters' manipulation (infra B.); the effects of a consultative referendum (infra C.); and the specific role of the judiciary (infra D.).

A. Union Citizens who have made use of their fundamental Freedoms

If democracy is a mode of citizen's self-determination and means that citizens of a polity shall participate in the process of decision making on matters that directly or indirectly affect them, then the question already mentioned of participation of Union citizens who have established their residence in a Member State that decides to leave the Union, or the role of the

19 See Hans-Jürgen Schlamp, 'Zustimmung zur EU wächst. Danke Frau May, danke Herr Trump. Keine Lust mehr auf EU? Das war einmal – zumindest laut einer neuen Studie: Demnach steigt die Zustimmung der Europäer zur Union. Mit einer Ausnahme', in: Spiegel Online 20 June 2017, at: http://www.spiegel.de/politik/ausland/europaeische-union-zustimmung-steigt-dank-brexit-studie-a-1152927.html (accessed 22 August 2017). Similarly: European Parliament, 'Aktuelles', of 28 April 2017: 'Meinungsumfrage Eurobarometer special des Europäischen Parlaments: Zustimmung zur Europäischen Union steigt wieder', at: http://www.europarl.europa.eu/news/de/press-room/20170427AVI72828/zustimmung-zur-europaischen-union-steigt-wieder-laut-eurobarometer (accessed 22 August 2017).

citizens of this State who have made use of the freedoms offered by the Treaties with regard to such decisions, is a question of democracy.

1. Decisions with no Voice for those affected

In the case of the UK, the problem was clear: When the British people voted for Brexit, and when the British Parliament decided that the UK would leave, Union citizens from other Member States had no voice, nor representation; they were just ignored in what is for them a very existential matter. Similarly, and perhaps even more strikingly, even British citizens who have chosen to make use of their freedom to move to another Member State and who have been established there for a certain number of years already, as well as UK nationals who have been working in the European institutions and therefore live in Belgium or another Member State for more than fifteen years, are excluded from participating both in the referendum and in the UK elections.[20]

In an early reaction to the referendum, Francesca Strumia not only stresses the damage of these consequences for the very concept of EU citizenship, but also very clearly describes the effects if this popular vote from the 'democratic perspective':

> 'The problem is that, for the significant minority that opposed Brexit with their vote, it is the voice of others that forces exit. This is, of course, the regular course of democracy: winner takes all. In this case, however, the winner takes away from all, winners and losers, part of the political self that supranational citizenship entails: voice in the European Parliament, and for migrant British citizens, voice in local elections in other Member States. Any supranational loyalties that some British citizens may have developed together with such political self are going to be automatically disabled.'[21]

---

20 After fifteen years of residing outside Britain it seems that British citizens no longer have the right to vote: see Gov.UK, 'Voting when you're abroad', at: https:/ /www.gov.uk/voting-when-abroad (accessed 22 August 2017); see also Section 2 (1) of the European Union Referendum Act 2015, together with Section 1 (2–4) of the Representation of the People Act 1985.

21 Francesca Strumia, 'Brexiting European Citizenship through Voice of Others, in: 17 *German Law Journal* (2016), Brexit Special Supplement, p 109, 111, at: https:// www.cambridge.org/core/services/aop-cambridge-core/content/view/9E93BD73EF 9A007BFD13C1BEC1E77119/S2071832200021805a.pdf/brexiting_european_citiz enship_through_the_voice_of_others.pdf (accessed 22 May 2019).

These consequences seem to be at odds with the principle of democracy if it means self-determination. The problem is all the more serious as these citizens risk losing their rights automatically as soon as the withdrawal takes effect, unless an agreement is reached under Article 50 TEU to protect these rights and to ensure the continuing role of the ECJ giving effect to this protection.

2. *The Principle of loyal Cooperation as a negotiation Guideline*

Yet, for both, EU citizens in the UK, and UK citizens in other Member States, the loss of all their rights of European citizenship can be understood as a simple consequence of the constitutional principle of voluntariness. Thus, a democratic justification can be found in the fundamental decision to accept the Union Treaties including Article 50 TEU. But this provision cannot be read in isolation, it must be applied in accordance with other general principles of the EU and, in particular, with the principle of loyal cooperation (Article 4 (3) TEU). Triggering the Article 50 TEU-process would, thus, not be a simple reset – in a situation as it was prior to the accession to the EU, but rather an engagement of finding a just and sustainable solution through a (re-)negotiation of the respective rights of the citizens. Voluntariness, or the freedom to be or not to be a Member State, is coupled with a constitutional duty of cooperation and respect. In cases where people of a Member State do not feel comfortable any more with their membership in the EU, thus, the Treaty provides for a meaningful procedure, including the two-year period as a deadline for the negotiation of a suitable arrangement.

This constitutional duty of cooperation is, in some way, a compensation and guaranty for the citizens having made use of their rights under the Treaties. During the period of negotiation, which may even be extended if necessary, the principle of loyal cooperation under Article 4 (3) TEU fully applies and compels all sides to make every possible effort to find appropriate arrangements regarding all interests involved including, as a priority, to fully protect the *droits acquis* of the citizens. It is a constitutional duty of both sides at the negotiation table, the EU and the UK during the period of Article 50 TEU. The agreement to be reached has to respect the fundamental rights and freedoms of the citizens who have trusted in these guaranties; the full respect and protection of these rights must also play a key role when the Council, the European Parliament and the UK are taking their respective decisions in the ratification process.

Democratic self-determination, thus, goes hand in hand with the respect of the other and, in the case of withdrawal of a Member State from the EU, of the other's rights and interests. The EU institutions have a specific responsibility for making sure that these rights are protected.

3. *Exclusion of Nationals in other Member States from the Vote*

The case of UK citizens who have established themselves in other Member States raises specific questions. These people find themselves in a trap. First, they have been invited to make use of their rights offered by the Treaties, particularly since the internal market would not have become a reality without people moving from one country to another; and second, they are likely to suffer most from a decision taken by people (at home) who have not even had any experience of residing in another EU country. British citizens, therefore, having made use of their right to free movement within the EU for more than 15 years, or having served as a European civil servant in one of the EU institutions, are deprived of their democratic rights in Britain and had no voice in matters directly concerning them.[22]

Democracy goes along with rights. If there is a general practice among States to exclude their nationals from participating in a vote after they have lived abroad for a longer period and are far away from the daily political developments at home, a sufficient explanation may be that these citizens would be no longer affected by the internal politics of their country.

This reasoning, however, does not satisfy the case in point. The Brexit referendum deeply affects the rights of these citizens abroad, much more than it affects the general public in Britain. Not to include them in the vote, therefore, is not only a serious challenge to the principle of democracy but also serves as a punishment for having exercised the rights given by the Treaties to the Union's citizens and thus, would emerge as an indirect barrier to the freedom of movement contrary to Articles 21 and 45 TFEU.

It is, primarily, a matter for each Member State to devise specific provisions including these citizens in decision-making processes. If Union citizenship is the fundamental status of the citizens of the Member States of the Union, as the ECJ confirms in its established case law,[23] to exclude

---

22 Ibid.

23 ECJ Case C-184/99 – *Grzelczyk* (2001) ECR I-6193 ECLI:EU:C:2001:458, para 31, and Case C-34/09 – *Ruiz Zambrano* (2011) ECR I-01177 ECLI:EU:C:2011:124, para 41. See also Christian Calliess, 'The Dynamics of European Citizenship: From Bourgeois to Citoyen', in: Allan Rosas, Egils Levits and Yves Bot (eds.), *The*

those who have made use of their rights under the Treaties from participating in the making of national decisions withdrawing these rights in accordance with Article 50 TEU would compromise this very constitutional status.[24]

4. *The European Parliament and the Union Citizens' Rights*

The protection of the rights of Union citizens on both sides, in the event of a withdrawal of a Member State from the Union, thus, is one of the major tasks particularly of the Commission to implement when negotiating an arrangement with the UK under Article 50 TEU; not only the – transitional – Withdrawal Agreement, but also an agreement on the future relationship between the UK and the EU must provide for the safeguard of these rights. In performing this task, the Commission is under the control of the European Parliament, which directly represents the citizens of the Union – those of the UK as well as those of the other Member States. As long as the UK is a Member State, this representation therefore extends to all Union citizens, including the British. Hence, also the European Parliament plays a particularly important democratic role in the negotiation process with the UK. If no satisfactory solution is found to protect the rights of all the citizens – who have exercised their fundamental freedoms under the Treaties – the European Parliament has a responsibility to refuse ratification of any arrangement under Article 50 (2) TEU.

If it is true that without an agreement the situation of the citizens affected by the withdrawal might be worse than what they would have with the agreement, adequate remedies would have to be found by the EU and the UK outside the Article 50 process.

Court of Justice and the Construction of Europe. Analyses and Perspectives on Sixty Years of Case-law (T.M.C. Asser Press, The Hague 2013), pp 425, 429–32.

24 For the short description of the general rule see Koen Lenaerts/Piet Van Nuffel, *European Union Law* (3rd ed Sweet & Maxwell, London 2011), 8–008: 'Art. 21 TFEU opposes national legislation which places at a disadvantage certain of the nationals of the Member States concerned simply because they have exercised their freedom to move and to reside in another Member State'.

5. *Protection of acquired Rights by the Countries of Residence?*

Is it for each of the other Member States individually, in the event that the negotiations do not result in a satisfactory solution and, in particular, in case of a 'hard Brexit', to protect the 'rights' of these (ex-)EU citizens 'as if' the UK was still a member of the EU – and for the UK to protect the rights of the EU citizens in the UK? While, formally, there is no reason for them to do so, it is difficult to imagine that the 27 could seriously stop treating UK citizens as Union citizens, and of the UK to act accordingly. Solutions have to be found under national law, at least to maintain the *status quo* for those who have established residence in these countries before the withdrawal of the UK takes place. They may be based upon principles like the principle of legitimate expectation or the protection of acquired rights. Yet, there is no secure guarantee for what had been achieved under the rule of 'national treatment'. For there is no such legal duty under EU law, and the ECJ would have no competence to judge upon preliminary questions of national courts on this issue.

Similarly, should no suitable arrangement be reached with the UK on the issue of EU civil servants and employees coming from the UK, the Council of the 27 would have to find an appropriate solution protecting their acquired rights according to the general principles of Union law.

B. *Lies and Democracy*

There was a lot of lying during the Brexit campaign. Apparently, lies were told at all sides in the campaign: Claims that could not stand. A fact check by The Telegraph led to the conclusion:

> 'This is now particularly important: some of these claims have helped swing the UK to Brexit, and now the country must face the consequences'.[25]

Is lying undemocratic; is it a challenge to democracy? And is it perhaps particularly undemocratic when lies and fake news are distributed and advertised through social media and other IT-based mechanisms? What if

25 See Ashley Kirk, 'EU referendum: The claims that won it for Brexit, fact checked', in: The Telegraph 13 March 2017, at: http://www.telegraph.co.uk/news/0/eu-referendum-claims-won-brexit-fact-checked/ (accessed 14 June 2017). With an impressive list of lies see also Brexit Lies at: http://brexitlies.com/.

such news and disinformation are distributed on a massive scale through botnets in social networks? Is there a specific challenge in the case of targeted propaganda based upon big data analysis, such as that offered by undertakings like Cambridge Analytica?[26] If lies alone are not a challenge to democracy, any attempt to use information technology and services to individualise people's personal data and, on this basis, manipulate voters with wrong information in elections or a referendum certainly can be. This seems to have been the case both in the Trump and in the Brexit campaigns 2016.[27] And Steve Bennon, one of the key election campaign aids of Donald Trump, supported by secretive hedge fund billionaire Robert Mercer, is reported actually to continue his activities in Europe aiming to build up a right-wing eurosceptic front for the EU elections.[28]

---

26 See the alarming confession of Michal Kosinski, reported by Hannes Grassegger and Mikael Krogerus, 'Ich habe nur gezeigt, dass es die Bombe gibt', in: Das Magazin no 48 of 3 December 2016, available at: https://www.dasmagazin.ch/2016/12/03/ich-habe-nur-gezeigt-dass-es-die-bombe-gibt/ (accessed 16 June 2017). See also Jamie Doward and Alice Gibbs, 'Did Cambridge Analytica influence the Brexit vote and the US election?', in: The Guardian 4 March 2017, available at: https://www.theguardian.com/politics/2017/mar/04/nigel-oakes-cambridge-analytica-what-role-brexit-trump (accessed 16 June 2017). After heavy critiques Cambridge Analytica does not seem to have maintained its claim, see: Patrick Beuth, 'Die Luftpumpen von Cambridge Analytica', in: Zeit Online of 7 March 2017, available at: http://www.zeit.de/digital/internet/2017-03/us-wahl-cambridge-analytica-donald-trump-widerspruch (accessed 16 June 2017).

27 See Carole Cadwlladr, 'The great British Brexit robbery: how our democracy was hijacked', The Guardian 7 May 2017, at: https://www.theguardian.com/technology/2017/may/07/the-great-british-brexit-robbery-hijacked-democracy (accessed 24 March 2019).

28 See Markus Becker, 'Rechte Front in Europa. Wer hat Angst vor Steve Bennon', Spiegel online, 25.7.2018, at: http://www.spiegel.de/politik/ausland/stephen-bannon-will-die-rechtspopulisten-in-der-eu-einen-a-1220011.html; Jamie Doward, 'Steve Bannon plans foundation to fuel far right in Europe', in: The Guardian 21. Juli 2018, at: https://www.theguardian.com/us-news/2018/jul/21/steve-bannon-plans-foundation-to-fuel-far-right-in-europe; more on this: Jan Sternberg, 'Steve Bannons Netzwerk gegen Europa', in: Hannoversche Allgemeine v. 13. Nov. 2018, at: http://www.haz.de/Nachrichten/Politik/Deutschland-Welt/Steve-Bannons-Netzwerk-gegen-Europa (all accessed 28 December 2018). For the situation one week before the European elections see: Holly Ellyatt, 'Steve Bannon is in Europe ahead of elections. And he's upsetting the locals', CNBC of 21 May 2019, at: https://www.cnbc.com/2019/05/21/steve-bannon-is-in-france-ahead-of-european-parliament-elections.html (accessed 21 May 2019). But: Henry Samuel, 'Marine Le Pen denies Steve Bannon has role in her EU election campaign as he sets up camp in Paris', in: The Telegraph, 20 May 2019, at: https://www.telegraph.co.uk/news/2

With regard to lies, disinformation and manipulation and their effects on democratic decision making a distinction should be drawn between the functioning of representative democracy with parliamentary elections (infra 1.) and direct democracy with referendum on specific political questions with irreversible effects, such as in the case of Brexit (infra 2.).

1. *Parliamentary Democracy and Systemic Lying: Trust and Distrust*

Representative democracy, where people vote for a party or for someone to be a member of Parliament, is based upon trust. The elected representatives are given a mandate to determine the future policies of the country. Yet, their promises in election campaigns will be measured against their action taken in reality. Such accountability and the risk of not being re-elected if people understand that they were misled in the election campaign serve as a remedy against lies. Trust is lost when lies are discovered, and another candidate or party may be elected. In this regard, democracy can also be described as the institution of distrust. It inherently provides a remedy or sanction in the case of failure of a party or policy-maker to honour a pledge. Lies, therefore, do not seem to be undemocratic *per se*.

However, the red line is crossed when lies become systemic, and when they turn into a subtle manipulation of the electorate as in the case of psychographic targeting on a mass scale, with the effect that trust is lost not only in individual candidates or parties but in the entire system. This might be the reason why following the 2016 presidential elections in the United States of America, the threats of foreign hacking (*Hillary Clinton's* e-mails) disinformation campaigns, as well as psychographic targeting became, and continues to be, one of the major political topics in the country, in the EU and beyond.[29] And rightly so: Systemic lying entails an erosion of the democratic system and is a major challenge to democracy.

The threat to democracy is becoming even more serious when the manipulation is coupled with illegal and in-transparent funding from (foreign) governments or organisations as it was reported being the case in the

019/05/20/marine-le-pen-insists-steve-bannon-has-no-part-eu-election-campaign/ (accessed 21 May 2019).

29 See Ingolf Pernice, 'Protecting the global digital information ecosystem: a practical initiative', *Internet Policy Review* 5 March 2019, at: https://policyreview.info/articles/news/protecting-global-digital-information-ecosystem-practical-initiative/1386 (accessed 25 March 2019).

Brexit campaign.[30] Targeted subversive advertising with fake news through social media of this kind is about to undermine the openness and fairness of the public discourse as a fundamental condition of the democratic process, and such experience call not only for a special responsibility of the online platforms operating such social media, but also for regulation and law enforcement. The President of Germany, Frank Walter Steinmeier, rightly warned at re;publica 2019: 'those who create an online forum for political discourse also carry responsibility for democracy – whether they like it or not!';[31] while France has already taken legislative action to turn this responsibility into concrete duties.[32]

2. *Direct Democracy: the Risks of irreversible Decisions*

Trust seems to play a different role in the case of direct democracy with popular voting. Direct democracy suggests that mature and informed people are taking their future into their own hands. A mechanism of accountability and 'repair', as in the system of 'time-limited entrustment of power', does not exist. Once the vote is given in a referendum, there is no need

---

30 Carole Cadwalladr, Facebooks role in Brexit – and the threat to democracy, TED talk of 16 April 2019, at: https://www.ted.com/talks/carole_cadwalladr_facebook_s_role_in_brexit_and_the_threat_to_democracy (accessed 8 May 2019).

31 Frank Walter Steinmeier, Introductory Speech at Re;publica, 6 May 2019, p 5, also calling for transparency: 'as long as casual lies and reputable news reports, as long as checked facts and mere opinion, as long as reason and hate speech appear one after another in people's newsfeeds, with nothing to distinguish between them, demagogues will have it far too easy. We need the sources of our information to be crystal clear, particularly when political ads are concerned. Those who target tailored political messages at specific audiences must be forced by the site operators – and where necessary by law – to show their face, to reveal who exactly sent the ad, who financed it, and what other ads this person or organisation is sending. In other words, they must make transparent whose game are they playing – and how we can opt out of the game', at: https://www.bundespraesident.de/SharedDocs/Downloads/DE/Reden/2019/05/190506-Republica-Englisch.pdf ;jsessionid=729867EFFF010CC0C0CFF783B1A0E7A8.1_cid378?__blob=publicationFile (accessed 8 May 2019).

32 See the French law on the combat of manipulation of information: LOI n 2018–1202 du 22 décembre 2018 relative à la luttecontre la manipulation de l'information, JORF n 0297 du 23 décembre 2018, at: https://www.legifrance.gouv.fr/affichTexte.do?cidTexte=JORFTEXT000037847559&categorieLien=id (accessed 8 May 2019).

for accountability. Nobody voting 'yes' or 'no' can be checked and nobody – except campaigners – has to fear a sanction for misbehaviour or a wrong decision. All the citizens, whether they have participated in the vote or not, equally bear the consequences of the 'decision of the people'. Yet, correct information regarding the background and the implications of the vote, a serious public debate and a keen sense of responsibility on the part of the people voting are conditions for the functioning of direct democracy.

In the case of a *binding* referendum, the outcome is not subject to any other political check. People who find themselves misled upfront of the vote would not accept the result as legitimate and binding, however, if the campaigns for or against the issue at stake were poisoned by lies and manipulation. The loss of trust affects the legitimacy of the system as such, and is particularly serious in cases of irreversibility. The decision to trigger the process of Article 50 TEU is a case in point.

An *advisory* referendum, in contrast, leaves full responsibility for the final decision to the Parliament. It remains for each MP individually to make her independent and responsible judgement upon what the outcome of the referendum would mean to her, and what decision to take. This choice has to be made by each party and each individual MP, well conscious of the implications for the policies they may adopt subsequently; the MP's remain fully accountable to the scrutiny of the voters of their constituency at the next election. Thus, as long as a referendum is not binding – and MP's are taking their responsibilities seriously – the democratic system as such is not more challenged by lying and manipulation than in the case of any other parliamentary vote in a representative democracy.

C. *'Advisory' Referendum?*

Was the British referendum on Brexit binding or advisory only? The European Union Referendum Act 2015 does not specify that it should bind either the Government or the Parliament.[33] Given the sovereignty of Parliament, a referendum in Britain is not binding, as a rule, except if expressly

33 Section 1 of the European Union Referendum Act 2015 reads: 'A referendum is to be held on whether the United Kingdom should remain a member of the European Union', available at: http://www.legislation.gov.uk/ukpga/2015/36/contents/enacted/data.htm (accessed 15 March 2019).

specified in the parliamentary Act.[34] The UK Supreme Court has confirmed this view.[35] Nonetheless, the distinction becomes doubtful in this specific case. Neither the new British Government, nor the great majority of the Members of the UK Parliament seem to have taken the Brexit referendum as a simple expression of the opinion of the voters just to guide their independent consideration of all relevant factors for their own position. Rather, it was suggested that there was a democratic imperative to follow the outcome of the referendum without further ado.

Be it as it may, there was a little critical analysis of the circumstances leading to the referendum's surprising result. Did the MPs who simply followed it as 'the command of the people' take their personal responsibility seriously, being elected representatives of their respective constituency, to follow their own conscience in taking a responsible decision? Though – prior to the referendum – the majority of the Parliament had been in favour of 'remain', what were the reasons for the change of mind after the referendum? It was as if the fact that the people had been misled by lies and fake information was ignored. Even the opposition, the Labour Party, ordered their MPs to vote in favour of Brexit when the Parliament had to decide upon authorising the government to trigger the procedure of Article 50 TEU.[36] The only explanation is that the referendum, which was not meant to be legally binding, was nevertheless understood, politically, to have a binding effect. For Vernon Bogdanor it was

> '… the first time in British history Parliament is enacting a policy in which it does not believe. The majority of MPs and peers are Remainers. So also are the majority of members of the Cabinet. They believe that they have been instructed by the British people. The sovereignty

---

34 See explanations by Haroon Siddique, 'Is the EU referendum legally binding? Parliament is sovereign and, if Brexit wins, Cameron will not be legally obliged to invoke the Lisbon treaty to start an EU exit', in: The Guardian 23 June 2016, at: https://www.theguardian.com/politics/2016/jun/23/eu-referendum-legally-binding-brexit-lisbon-cameron-sovereign-parliament (accessed 25 March 2019).

35 See the convincing argument in the Judgment (2017) UKSC of 24 January 2017, *Miller*, paras 116–125, at: https://www.supremecourt.uk/cases/docs/uksc-2016-0196-judgment.pdf (accessed 21 August 2017).

36 The decision was taken by a majority of 498 against 114 votes. Nonetheless, 20% of the Labour Party MPs, including 13 serving front benchers, were 'defying the whip', see: 'MPs vote to give May power to trigger Article 50 – as it happened', in: The Guardian of 1 February 2017, at: https://www.theguardian.com/politics/blog/live/2017/feb/01/article-50-debate-vote-bill-pmqs-theresa-may-jeremy-corbyn-ivan-rogers-to-give-evidence-to-mps-about-why-he-quit-as-uks-ambassador-to-eu-politics-live (accessed 25 March 2019).

of the people, therefore, has overcome the sovereignty of Parliament – a very significant constitutional event!'[37]

In such circumstances lies and manipulative practices are a challenge to democracy even if the referendum is formally consultative. At least, it is difficult to understand why the MPs did not use the opportunity created for them by the Supreme Court to take an independent decision. Was it the fear that their constituencies would rebuke them if they deviated from the decision taken by 'the people'?

Least to say, the history of the referendum and the irritations it caused for many of the MPs may be an explanation for the almost chaotic dealing of the Parliament with the Withdrawal Agreement and its incapability to take any positive decision on the conclusion of the Brexit process at all. With the second extension of the Article 50 deadline until 31 October 2019, there is time for finding a solution. In a desperate attempt to find agreement in the House of Commons on the Withdrawal Agreement -fourth time after three failures – Theresa May has announced the 21st of May 2019 to include in the bill on the Withdrawal Agreement a referendum to be held on yes or no to ratify it after the Parliament has voted for it.[38] Not much, however, seems to justify the expectation that this initiative will allow the Parliament to accept the proposed 'new deal'.[39] It is difficult to see that the Parliament will come to any common position at all and, thus, deliver on its democratic responsibilities.[40] These difficulties may have led to the major shifts away from the two leading parties in the local

---

37 Vernon Bogdanor quoted in a comment of Antony G Gordon (12th December 2018) at Research Gate: 'Is the EU referendum vote legally binding?', at: https://www.researchgate.net/post/Is_the_EU_referendum_vote_legally_binding (accessed 25 March 2019).

38 'Theresa May makes statement on "new Brexit deal"', speech of 21 May 2019 at: https://www.youtube.com/watch?v=z6Il96yzu2I (accessed 21 May 2019), with a 10 points offer to the MPs regarding changes to the Political Declaration, to reflect her 'new deal'. The speech, however, is broadly understood as containing little new ideas, except for the second referendum, and would not bring about a positive decision of the House of Commons, see Chris Morris, 'Brexit: Is there anything new in Theresa May's "new deal"'?, at: https://www.bbc.com/news/uk-48359350 (accessed 21 May 2019).

39 See Chris Morris (n 38).

40 More optimistic still the analysis of Christos Katsioulis, 'The House of the Rising Sun', IPG 28.3.2019, at: https://www.ipg-journal.de/regionen/europa/artikel/detail/the-house-of-the-rising-sun-3358/ (accessed 21 May 2019).

elections of 2 May 2019,[41] and they could well end in a serious crisis of the British democracy.

The referendum, as it is envisaged here, might even not offer people to rethink Brexit as such, but only give the choice between Brexit with the Agreement or without it. Would such a referendum really allow the Parliament to take up its constitutional responsibilities – or, contrarily, be an expression of a definitive abandon of democratic control?

D. *Courts and Democracy*

Following the referendum, it was only through the intervention of the High Court and the Supreme Court that the authorisation to trigger Article 50 TEU was put to the Parliament at all. Without going into details of the intense debate on the respective prerogatives of the executive and the Parliament in this case, it was the judiciary who insofar had saved the specific form of democracy existing in Britain: A representative democracy based upon the sovereignty of parliament as a fundamental principle. As a result of an impressive constitutional analysis, the Supreme Court made it clear that the Prime Minister could not trigger Article 50, as she had intended to do, without an act of Parliament authorising this step.[42] If the intention was to challenge the existing British democratic system, it was commendable of the Courts to stop Theresa May.

But what does this mean for the concept of democracy? If the parliament is supreme or sovereign, why is it necessary for courts to intervene? Is it a challenge to democracy if courts take on this role?

The answer is no, at least from a German constitutional law perspective. Democracy is a basic constitutional principle, but it is a constitutional principle and neither the only one nor absolute. Without the rule of law, without respect for the fundamental rights of the individual, without the division of powers laid down in the Constitution – written or not – democracy could not function. Courts, acting as the guardians of the Constitution, are therefore not a challenge but a constituent part of the system and a safeguard of democracy.

41 See BBC News on ‚England localelections 2019‘, at: https://www.bbc.com/news/topics/ceeqy0e9894t/england-local-elections-2019 (accessed 21 May 2019): ‚the two main parties have suffered significant losses… The Lib Dems were the biggest winners on the night….‘

42 UKSC (n 35), in particular paras. 43–83.

In some way, the Supreme Court confirms this specific task of the judiciary in the constitutional system of the UK:

> 'By the end of the 20th century, the great majority of what had previously been prerogative powers, at least in relation to domestic matters, had become vested in the three principal organs of the State: the legislature (the two Houses of Parliament), the executive (ministers and the government more generally) and the judiciary (the judges)'.[43]

With a clear reference to the rule of law, it emphasises that

> 'the role of the judiciary is to uphold and further the rule of law; more particularly, judges impartially identify and apply the law in every case brought before the courts. That is why and how these proceedings are being decided'.[44]

This important constitutional role is not necessarily contrary to the principle of sovereignty of the UK Parliament, for the UK Parliament preserves the right at any time to set aside judgments of the judiciary by an express act of abrogation.

III. Lessons learned: Democracy in the EU

Given the subsequent developments in European politics after Brexit, at least four lessons can be learned from the Brexit process as it stands today. They are about lies, democratic dynamics, transborder effects of national policies and the important role of the citizens.

A. Lies have short Legs.

'Lügen haben kurze Beine': This is a German saying meaning that lies have short legs. They cannot go very far. Shortly before the election day – June 8 2017 – a song entitled 'She's a liar, liar' came out. As the Guardian reported: 'Remix by anti-austerity band Captain Ska mocking May's claims of 'strong and stable leadership' tops Amazon UK downloads'. The title of the article was: ' "She's a liar, liar": anti-Theresa May song heads to top of

---

43 Ibid., para. 41.
44 Ibid., para 42.

charts'.[45] More than a million downloads had been counted a few days later. The song seems to reflect feelings shared by more and more people in the UK and beyond.

British people were waking up and walking away from Brexit. Already the negotiation guidelines adopted by the European Council on 29 April 2017[46] showed that the EU had certain top priorities difficult to reconcile with the promises made by the Brexit campaigners and, in particular, by Nigel Farage and Boris Johnson. The first and most important of these priorities was the determination to 'safeguard the status and rights derived from EU law at the date of withdrawal of EU and UK citizens, and their families, affected by the United Kingdom's withdrawal from the Union'. Another is that the financial settlement should 'cover all commitments as well as liabilities, including contingent liabilities', which means that Brexit, at least for a while, would fall far short of allowing Britain substantial financial relief.[47] Apart from all the other difficulties and burdens that will gradually emerge, could the result of the June 2017 elections be understood as a reaction of people who feel that they have been fooled? If so, this disaster for the Tories may be the first bill Theresa May had to pay. What other claims might be made?

What seems to be more important is how people will react given the insight that expectations about positive effects of Brexit on their lives were based upon misleading or false information.

B. Dynamics of Democracy: What if Brexit loses Support?

The outcome of the June elections was unexpected and a clear 'no' to the declared strategy of the Prime Minister. Yet immediately after the elections Theresa May confirmed that she would ensure stability in the country. This is perhaps what the country needs most in a situation that looks any-

45 See: The Guardian of 31 May 2017 https://www.theguardian.com/politics/2017/may/31/liar-liar-anti-theresa-may-song-heads-to-top-of-charts; for the song: https://www.youtube.com/watch?v=danwAOT_WDU (accessed 16 June 2017).

46 Available at: http://www.consilium.europa.eu/en/press/press-releases/2017/04/29-euco-brexit-guidelines/ (accessed 16 June 2017).

47 According to some estimates, Britain will have to pay as much as 100 billion euros, while Boris Johnson seems to expect that the EU will pay large sums to Britain. For a legal assessment of the financial modalities of Brexit see: Steffen Hindelang, 'The Brexit Bill – Großbritanniens Welt der alternativen Fakten', in: 70 ifoSchnelldienst 11/2017 of 8 June 2017, p 12–5.

thing but stable. It includes a lack of clarity about the objectives Britain would want to achieve in the Brexit negotiations that had started on Friday 19 June 2017. Given the failure of the Prime Minister's attempt to get stronger backing in the elections for her 'hard Brexit', a clear parliamentary vote against it and the repeated rejection in March 2019 of the Withdrawal Agreement signed in November 2018 by the Parliament, it remains an open question what Britain will finally strive to achieve and what deal, if any, people will accept.

The Brexit process so far has shown that a 'democratic' decision made yesterday does not necessarily mean a lot for today and the future. A more flexible position, particularly with regard to the rigidities a hard Brexit would bring about for Northern Ireland, seems to be the order of the day. If the May government did not end in June 2017, it was thanks to a conservative group of MPs from Northern Ireland that after the promise of new financial support for their region, allowed the government not to lose its majority.[48]

The next test was the vote in the UK Parliament on the 'European Union (Withdrawal) Bill' providing for the repeal the European Communities Act 1972 'on exit day' (section 1), while retaining substantive EU law applicable in the UK until it is amended through executive regulations concerning 'deficiencies arising from withdrawal', international obligations or the implementation of the withdrawal agreement.[49] It was aiming at 'constitutional change and legal continuity'.[50] But without the European Commission watching the full application of EU law and without the European Court of Justice judging upon questions of interpretation and validity Union-wide, there is no 'legal continuity' after Brexit. And 'implementing the withdrawal agreement' (section 9) presupposes that, in fact, there is such an agreement – which is still not the case three years after the referendum.

---

48 See Jack Maidment, 'DUP agrees £1bn deal with Conservatives to prop up Theresa May's minority Government', in: The Telegraph, 26 June 2017, at: http://www.telegraph.co.uk/news/2017/06/26/arlene-foster-meet-theresa-may-finalise-dup-deal-prop-tory-minority/ (accessed 22 August 2017).

49 Official Publication at: https://publications.parliament.uk/pa/bills/cbill/2017-2019/0005/18005.pdf (accessed 23 August 2017).

50 See Jack Simson Caird, 'The European Union (Withdrawal) Bill: constitutional change and legal continuity', in: The Constitutional Unit, 18 July 2017, at: https://constitution-unit.com/2017/07/18/the-european-union-withdrawal-bill-constitutional-change-and-legal-continuity/ (accessed 22 August 2017).

There are reasons to believe that if, after the extension of the Article 50 deadline and, probably further 2 or more years of negotiations, there is any agreement at all, or the agreement will be rather close to what the law is today. People asked to ratify such an agreement on the future relations of the UK with the EU may then rightly ask the question of whether or not it is worth approving Brexit; they might refuse the ratification of the agreement because Britain's situation would be much worse than it is today. While the estimated aggregated cost of 'hard Brexit' for Britain are up to € 57 bn yearly, with welfare going down by 2.39%, the costs of 'soft Brexit' would be lower, but still around € 32 bn, with a welfare decrease of 1.34%.[51] More importantly, given the fact that the EU has been created for achieving goals that States alone would be unable to achieve on their own, British people may understand that Brexit would mean a real loss of sovereignty instead of the promised gain.[52]

In such conditions – and given the clear interest of the ever-growing body of young voters striving to remain – there is a good chance, finally, of there being a majority for remaining in the EU. As a result, even after a ratification of the Withdrawal Agreement and years of further negotiations on the future relationship between the EU and the UK, Brexit may not be the choice of the then majority of the British people.

Yet, as no valid agreement was reached until 29 March 2019, and if even after the end of the extended deadline – the 31 October 2019 – the Withdrawal Agreement is not ratified, a hard Brexit will be the automatic consequence of the notice given under Article 50 TEU. This would be the worst scenario for all sides. Paul Craig has argued that the notice can be

---

51 See: Bertelsmann Stiftung (ed), 'Estimating the impact of Brexit on European countries and regions. Policy Paper, 2019, introduction and the comparative tables showing losses per country, at: https://www.bertelsmann-stiftung.de/fileadmin/files/user_upload/EZ_Estimating_the_Impact_of_Brexit_2019_ENG.pdf; outside the UK the losses are estimated considerably lower, with the highest rates for Ireland and some limited gains for the U.S., China, and India (p 11 and 18).

52 For more details: Ingolf Pernice, 'European Constitutionalism and the Constitutions of the Member States. Implications for Brexit', in: 2017 Boletin da Faculdade de Direito XCIII Tomo I, p 211, 239–241. On the terms of 'European Sovereignty' coined by the French President Emmanuel Macron, in this sense see also Tom Eijsbouts, 'European Sovereignty', editorial European Constitutional Law Review2018, p 4–6, furthermore id, 'Germany's Grand and Growing European Sovereignty' in Hardt, Sacha, Heringa, Aalt Willem, and Waltermann, Antonia: Bevrijdende&Begrenzendesoevereiniteit (Den Haag, Boom juridisch, 2018), pp 10, 28–31, and id., 'Sovereignty the European Way', in this volume.

withdrawn.[53] Doubts on this view[54] have been rejected by the ECJ in 2018,[55] and so the door still remains open for a quick end of the Brexit process until the definitive closure of the Article 50 deadline.

More than a million people participated at the 'put it to the people march' of 23 March 2019 in London, with the aim to stop Brexit through a second referendum. It was perhaps one of the greatest demonstrations in British history.[56] And more than 5, 6 Million people have signed the petition 'Revoke Article 50 and remain in the EU' to the UK Parliament by 25 March 2019.[57] The Parliament said that it would consider the petition, and people would no doubt appreciate if upcoming votes on the steps to be taken until October 31 did not ignore what could develop to an even broader public support for reconsidering the former policies.

One test was the European elections on 23–26 May 2019. With the polls giving the new Brexit Party of Nigel Farage around 34% of the votes and with its clear choice for a hard Brexit, the political divide of the country may be growing stronger, and so is the challenge to the UK Parliament in the days to come in its task to keep the country together. Its way to deal with the Brexit process so far may feed concerns about the functioning of the democratic system in Britain; preference given by MPs to their position in an internal political power game around the Brexit instead of a concern for the future of their country, as can be observed, seems to result in a real challenge to democracy.

C. *Growing Awareness of the Externalities of national Politics*

The developments in the UK received an unknown public attention in the other Member States. Media keep busy in reporting and discussing day by day the news from the UK, and rightly so since what is decided that will deeply affect people in and of all the other Member States. Organisations like Pulse of Europe are demonstrating their sympathy for and support of

53 Craig, Brexit (n 7) pp 464–65.

54 Pernice, 'European Constitutionalism' (n 52), p 235–6.

55 ECJ case C-621/18 – *Wightman* (n. 3).

56 See: Tim Adams, 'Put it to the People march: a formidable sea of humanity and powerful strength of feeling. They came to London from across Britain and Europe, filled with enthusiasm for the new three Rs: revoke, remain, reform', The Guardian 23 March 2019, at: https://www.theguardian.com/politics/2019/mar/23/put-it-to-the-people-march-against-brexit-london-revoke-remain-reform.

57 See the Website at: https://petition.parliament.uk/petitions/241584.

the UK movements fighting against populist-nationalists who strive at the destruction of the European venture. They do so as well, actually, in other Member States with a view to the European elections of May 2019. This grassroot movement is an excellent example of exercise of democracy related to, or even triggered by the Brexit process.

What we learn from the Brexit-process, more generally, is that within the EU political developments in one country are of highest relevance to people in other Member States as well. Brexit isn't but one striking example. The great success of *Macron* in the French elections 2017 was another. Both have the potential to change the EU considerably – in different directions – and so to change the life of millions of Union citizens in all the Member States.

What does this mean for democracy? If politics in one Member State, and even the vote of individuals in national elections, have an impact on people and politics in other Member States, such possible implications on others must seriously be taken into account in each Member State. This connectivity of what I call the European 'Verfassungsverbund'[58] entails externalities and horizontal effects and explains why the media and citizens in one Member State have a legitimate cross-border interest in political processes in other Member States. Accordingly, the shock of the Brexit referendum was felt to be a disaster in all other Member States. Similarly, recent political developments in Hungary and Poland are felt as a threat to democracy in Europe at large. The citizens of the Union do not feel neutral on such developments. They have a stake, even if they have no voice.

Yet, things have begun to change in the wake of these shocks. People from all Member States are taking part in a European-wide public discourse on the shaping of our common future, and this includes national election campaigns and referenda. Thanks to the internet, rapid information can easily be gathered from all Member States, and arguments can be exchanged within social networks, through blogs and at discussion platforms, thus allowing discourses beyond borders and languages.[59] While

58 For the concept: Ingolf Pernice, Bestandssicherung der Verfassungen: Verfassungsrechtliche Mechanismen zur Wahrung der Verfassungsordnung, in: Roland Bieber / Pierre Widmer (Hrsg.), *L'espace constitutionnel européen. Der Europäische Verfassungsraum. The European Constitutional Area* (Zürich, Schulthess 1995), p 225–264, more recently id, 'European Constitutionalism' (n 52).

59 See also Ingolf Pernice, 'E-Government and E-Democracy: Overcoming Legitimacy Deficits in a Digital Europe?', in: Lina Papadopoulou/Ingolf Pernice/Joseph H.H. Weiler (eds), *Legitimacy Issues of the European Union in the Face of Crisis. Dimitrios Tsatsos in memoriam* (Nomos, Baden-Baden 2017) p 287, 305–7.

participation in national elections or referendums remain reserved for nationals of each country, views and experience from foreign stakeholders can have a considerable impact and increasingly do so.

D. People and Citizens of Member States acting as Citizens of the EU

After all, the Brexit process is perhaps not only a challenge to, and an exercise of democracy; but more than this: it also triggers a new step in developing democracy in the EU. It has led to a growing awareness of the values and benefits of the EU; people are becoming more responsible for their common European future and they are increasingly viewing the EU as their vehicle to secure peace, freedom and prosperity in Europe, and as a common instrument for securing the effective participation of our countries and, thus, of the EU citizens, in the shaping of globalisation.

Conclusion

The Brexit process was first considered to be a serious threat to the idea of European integration. Whether or not it will, ultimately, bring the EU back to 27 Member States, it seems to have a positive side too. Little more than from one year after the referendum up to now, reasons are given to assume that it has a potential to give a beneficial impulse to the European project. Together with the surprising outcome of the American election in 2016 it has raised awareness throughout Europe of the fundamental values the EU represents and has mobilised new citizens' movements determined to make the European Union more democratic and effective. This unexpected positive effect may be understood as one that is impelling people to take ownership of the Union and push it towards a democratic reform that brings it in conformity with their hopes and expectations.

Whatever the outcome of the Brexit process might be, the withdrawal of the UK on the basis of a fair agreement on the future relationship with the EU, hopefully a „do-not-harm Brexit", as Kalypso Nicolaidis thoughtfully calls for,[60] or the revocation of the Article 50 notice as a consequence of a second referendum, the experiences and lessons learned from the process – in spite of the costs it has caused – are important for the upcoming discussions on the reform of the EU. With the completion of the internal mar-

60 Nicolaidis, Exodus (n 16), p 2, 188.

ket, including tax harmonisation, with a stronger role of the national Parliaments in the control of subsidiarity regarding the exercise of EU competencies and better parliamentary oversight of the European policies and, in particular, with new provisions for the enhanced involvement and participation of both, the European and national Parliaments, in the shaping and control of the common economic and fiscal policies of a reformed EMU, the EU could become closer to what *David Cameron* may have had in mind when in his Bloomberg speech of 23 January 2013 he called for an "updated European Union".[61] And a future can be envisaged „where a transformed UK rejoins a transformed EU",[62] ultimately, as an expression of democracy both sides.

61 David Cameron, EU speech at Bloomberg, 23 January 2013, at: https://www.gov.uk/government/speeches/eu-speech-at-bloomberg (accessed 25 March 2019).
62 Nicolaidis, Exodus (n 16), p. 189.

Part II
The Future of the Internal Market and its Social Dimension

Internal Market and Brexit

Paula Vaz Freire

Abstract

The economic effects of Brexit in the UK and in the EU are still uncertain. Although immediately after the referendum British GDP growth had not declined dramatically, neither did firms and consumers drastically changed their behaviour in advance of future scenarios. In the long run it's safe to say there will be reductions in trade and foreign direct investment, which will low UK living standards. In fact, living standards were already affected by Brexit, as it caused the value of the pound to decline and that in turn led to the depreciation of the terms of trade to higher inflation and to a lower real wage growth.

For the EU, as a whole, the economic effects of UK's exit may not be very significant, but they surely are very relevant to some European economies. That aspect, as well as the strategic and political importance of the UK, recommends the definition of a close economic cooperation that, nevertheless, cannot be conceived as a 'soft version' of EU's internal market.

I. Internal Market and the UK

As it is well known, since the mid 90's, the UK's development model evolved towards specialization in services, in particular, financial services. A prosperous financial hub was formed as "the financial sector has a natural tendency to form clusters and London – where English is spoken, the legal system is efficient, labour markets are flexible, and the regulatory regime is relatively streamlined – offered substantial advantages'.[1]

The financial market's success is inextricably linked to the UK's EU membership. Actually, the concentration of many types of wholesale financial services in the City of London began with the capital movements liberalization (under the internal market program, in the 1990s), and was

1 Daniel Gros, 'The Economics of Brexit: It's not about the Internal Market', *CEPS Commentary* (2016), at https://www.ceps.eu/publications/economics-brexit-it's-not-about-internal-market.

fostered by the common currency, combined with the elimination of obstacles to cross-border capital flows and a global credit boom. Additionally, the European 'passporting' system – further assessed below – enabled London-based banks to sell their services directly throughout the EU.

The expansion of the financial services industry was one of the major economic benefits of the UK's EU membership but at the same time led the British to reject the European project. In fact, the financial industry created few very highly paid jobs, contributing to raise income inequality, in a much more pronounced way than elsewhere in the EU; and inequality helped to fuel Brexit, by creating a widespread frustration towards globalization and the so-called 'establishment elites'.

II. Economic Impacts of Brexit

Official institutions and independent economists have produced a considerable amount of economic studies on the consequences of Brexit.[2]

These studies cover a wide range of legal scenarios in the optimistic-pessimistic spectrum, but from them it can be concluded that for the EU 27 the losses are virtually insignificant (averaging between 0.11% and 0.52% of GDP for the optimistic versus pessimistic scenarios respectively); on the other hand, for the UK the losses average between 1.31% and 4.21 % of GDP for the optimistic and pessimistic scenarios respectively, or 0.13% to

2 Ian Begg & Fabian Mushövel, 'The economic impact of Brexit: jobs, growth and the public finances', The London School of Economics and Political Science, European Institute, London, UK (2016), at https://www.lse.ac.uk/europeanInstitute/LSE-Commission/Hearing-11--The-impact-of-Brexit-on-jobs-and-economic-growth-sumary.pdf; Ian Begg, 'Making sense of the costs and benefits of Brexit: challenges for economista', *Atlantic Economic Journal* (2017), at https://core.ac.uk/download/pdf/84310352.pdf; R. Kierzenkowski et al., 'The Economic Consequences of Brexit: A Taxing Decision', *OECD Economic Policy Papers*, No. 16, (OECD Publishing, Paris 2016), at https://doi.org/10.1787/5jm0lsvdkf6k-en; Guntram B. Wolff, 'The implications of a no-deal Brexit: is the European Union prepared?', Policy Contribution Issue n° 2 (2019), at http://bruegel.org/wp-content/uploads/2019/01/PC-2019-02-140119.pdf.

0.41% of GDP annually.[3] As an example, one of those analysis estimates that as a result of Brexit the UK may end up losing 2–3% of its GDP.[4]

The mentioned economic effects upon British economy result, mainly, from the fact that Brexit will strongly affect *foreign direct investment* (FDI) in the UK.[5] Nevertheless, some factors will cushion the negative effects of Brexit, such as a probable depreciation of the national currency that will likely increase export competitiveness, and the strong commercial relation with non-EU markets.

As it is well known, UK's features have long made it a very important destination for FDI. The UK is a big and rich market, characterized by a strong rule of law, flexible labour markets and a highly educated workforce and all these aspects make it an attractive FDI location. Additionally, for non-EU firms the fact that the UK was fully in the internal market made it a very interesting export platform for the rest of the European countries.

After Brexit trade costs, coordination costs and compliance costs with different regulations will certainly increase, diminishing UK's attractiveness. Accordingly, some studies estimate that Brexit is likely to reduce FDI inflows to the UK by about 22%; as a consequence, it can also be expected a decrease in productivity and a fall in real income.

Two of the most important sectors in British economy will be affected: car industry and financial services industry.

The UK is now the world's fourth largest car producer but without the internal market the worst-case scenario predictions estimate a production fall of 12% (almost 180,000 cars per year) and prices faced by UK consumers raised by 2.55%, as the cost of imported cars and their components increase. This is mainly because European car manufacturers such as BMW will most probably move some production away from the UK, as it is ex-

---

3 Michael Emerson, Matthias Busse, Mattia Di Salvo, Daniel Gros & Jacques Pelkmans, '*An Assessment of the Economic Impact of Brexit on the EU27*', European Parliament, Directorate General for Internal Policies, Policy Department A: Economic and Scientific Policy (2017), p. 8.

4 The estimated losses are a consequence of the exit from the single market; if the exit turns out to be a ten-year process, the losses would be borne gradually over that period, costing the UK about 0.2 – 0.3% of GDP per year, on average, see Daniel Gros, 'The Economics of Brexit: It's not about the Internal Market', *CEPS Commentary* (2016), https://www.ceps.eu/publications/economics-brexit-it's-not-about-internal-market.

5 Swati Dhingra, Gianmarco Ottaviano, Thomas Sampson & John Van Reenen, 'The impact of Brexit on foreign investment in the UK', Centre for Economic Performance, London School of Economics and Political Science (2016).

pected an increase in trade costs and coordination costs between headquarters and British located production plants (transfers of key staff within the firm may be harder because of migration controls; different regulatory standards can make engineering, R&D and consultancy services more difficult and expensive).[6]

Financial services have the largest stock of inward FDI in the UK (45%), constitute 8% of its GDP and generates 12% of tax receipts. In this domain, the effects of Brexit are difficult to predict, and they can't hardly be offset by expanding to other markets since there is no evidence that European regulations were a burden that hindered the UK's ability to trade with countries outside the EU. On the contrary, the negative effects of becoming a non-EU Member State seem to be significant as there is a consensus that the City became a financial hub while being in the EU. Europe is actually the world's largest exporter of financial services (making up for a quarter of world financial services exports) and half of the cross-border lending in the world is originated within the EU.[7]

A part of the financial flows – once in London – will shift to other financial centres such as Paris or Frankfurt, but it is safe to say that – probably with less vigour – London's financial services industry will survive Brexit.[8] Many of the advantages that have made London a financial services hub will remain after Brexit, and the loss of passporting might be partially offset by the creation of subsidiaries or bridgeheads within the EU or by the principle of equivalence.[9]

The internal market for financial services is based on the EU 'passporting' system for banks and financial services companies which allows a

---

6 Aimin Zhang & Ran An, 'The Impact of Brexit on Motor Industry in UK', *Advances in Economics, Business and Management Research* (AEBMR), Vol. 37 (2017), 643–653. David Bailey & Lisa De Propris, 'Brexit and the UK Automotive Industry', *NIER* (2017), at https://research.aston.ac.uk/portal/files/23922060/Bailey_De_Propris_final_author_copy_NIER_Nov_2017.pdf.

7 On the impact of Brexit on UK financial markets: Welfens, Paul J. J. & Fabian J. Baier (2018), 'Brexit and FDI: Key Issues and New Empirical Findings', Discussion Paper No. 241, Wuppertal: Universitätsbibliothek Wuppertal; Sapir, André; Dirk Schoenmaker & Nicolas Véron (2017), 'Making the Best of Brexit for the EU-27 Financial System', Peterson Institute for International Economics No. 17–8. Bruegel: Bruegel.

8 That will probably determine some changes in UK's growth model, perhaps through a revival of manufacturing, which has experienced decades of decline.

9 A Duvillet-Margerit, M. Magnus, B Mesnard & A Xirou, *Third-country equivalence in EU banking legislation*, European Parliament, Directorate General for Internal Policies (2017).

bank based in one member of the EU to set up a branch or provide cross-border financial services in another (or in the European Economic Area (EEA)), while being regulated by authorities in the home country (home state authorization). 'Passporting' means that a UK bank can provide services across the EU from its UK home. It also means that a Swiss or an American bank can do the same from a branch or subsidiary established in the UK.

Loosing access to the passporting system is a huge change for Great Britain's financial firms. As it was explained, EU internal market offers the possibility to provide regulated financial services across borders under simplified conditions: companies can apply only once for a license within the EU and then offer their services in the entire Union without additional national permits ('EU passport').[10] Passporting is a tool for a more efficient functioning and integration of financial markets, since it reduces supervisory and compliance burdens, as well as ensure that investors—especially retail investors— all over the EU are protected in the same way.

However, without a special agreement, EU passports like all European legislation cease to apply for business activities between UK and EU jurisdictions after Brexit. In a scenario of no-deal Brexit, the UK becomes a 'third-country', regarding its relationship with the EU, and could eventually benefit from a specific regime. These so called third-country regimes give companies from countries that are not Members of the European Economic Area (EEA) uniformly regulated access to EU markets, so that cross-border transactions can be concluded more securely and efficiently. The most common third-country solution are so-called 'equivalence regimes'.[11]

10 EU passports can be granted for market participants (e.g., banking permit), products (e.g., securities prospectus) or services (e.g., marketing a fund).

11 'Equivalence' refers to a process whereby the European Commission assesses and determines that a third country's regulatory, supervisory and enforcement regime is equivalent to the corresponding EU framework. That recognition makes it possible for the competent authorities in the EU to rely on third country entities' compliance with the third country framework which has been deemed 'equivalent' by the Commission. Equivalence decisions can include conditions or limitations, to better cater for the objectives of granting equivalence (...). Equivalence is primarily used to reduce overlaps in terms of regulatory and supervisory compliance in the interest of EU financial institution or market participants": J Deslandes, C Dias & M Magnus, 'Third Country Equivalence in EU Banking and Financial Regulation', European Parliament (2019), p. 1.
http://www.europarl.europa.eu/RegData/etudes/IDAN/2018/614495/IPOL_IDA(2018)614495_EN.pdf.

Equivalence is a condition that allows third-country firms to access the EU markets, if the third-country regulation meets the essential requirements of the EU regime:

> 'equivalence is not a vehicle for liberalizing international trade in financial services, but a key instrument to effectively manage cross-border activity of market players in a sound and secure prudential environment with third-country jurisdictions that adhere to, implement, and enforce rigorously the same high standards of prudential rules as the EU'.[12]

Equivalence aims at reducing the risks of contagion from non-EU jurisdictions or protecting the domestic market against financial crises outside the EU. But this system involves a process of recognizing 'equivalence' by the European Commission and such decisions on equivalence may be revoked at short notice, that is to say, 'equivalence' regimes for third countries may be discretionarily activated or revoked by the Commission. This, indeed, does not offer a good amount of certainty and legal continuity for market participants.

Due to the political uncertainty concerning the Brexit process, some temporary measures have been taken in order to minimize the chaotic outcomes from a no-deal exit. In this context, the UK Government announced a temporary permissions regime (TPR) for inbound passporting EEA firms and funds that will come into effect in the event of a hard Brexit.[13] The TPR is only relevant for firms that passport into the UK and the European Commission has so far not reciprocated with a similar regime.[14]

Additionally, some EU countries have taken their own measures in this area. One of the most relevant transitory regimes was created by Germany. German Parliament has adopted a bill which, *inter alia*, sets out a national

---

12 Commission Staff Working Document, 'EU equivalence decisions in financial services policy: an assessment' SWD (2017) 102 final, 5.

13 In order to take advantage of the TPR firms and funds need to make a notification to the UK Financial Conduct Authority (FCA) or UK Prudential Regulation Authority (PRA).

14 Instead the EU continues to push for UK firms to submit an application for authorisation in the relevant Member State where they wish to conduct business. In particular, the "no-deal" Contingency Action Plan of the European Commission deliberately provides for a limited number of contingency measures only (including temporary and conditional equivalence regimes for UK central counterparties and UK central depositaries): Bank of England, "Temporary permissions regime", at https://www.bankofengland.co.uk/eu-withdrawal/temporary-permissions-regime.

transition regime for regulated market participants from the UK in case of a hard Brexit.[15] The German regulator (Federal Financial Supervisory Authority, 'BaFin') is empowered to allow the UK entities[16] covered by the transitional regime, that have operated in Germany under the European passport regime so far, to continue providing certain services without a German license, for a period up to 21 months following a hard Brexit. In synthesis, the bill empowers 'BaFin' to treat UK banks and investment firms currently providing banking and investment services under the European passport regime as if they continued to hold an EU passport post-Brexit.

III. Legal Framework for UK'S 'Access to the EU Single Market'

Brexit also means uncertainty, which has always a negative impact. The British Government is planning to conclude a free trade agreement with the EU, but such an agreement can take several years and as a result, companies in the UK and Europe will lack certainty about the conditions under which they will be able to trade with and invest in the future.

The degree of co-operation with the EU27 can range from two extreme scenarios: (i) the UK would accede to the European Economic Area (EEA), or (ii) the UK would have no preferential trade relationship with the EU, with only their common membership of the World Trade Organization (WTO). In the middle ground, that relation can be similar to other bilateral agreements that exist between the EU and third countries: customs unions, free trade agreements, association agreements, stabilization and association agreements, partnership and cooperation agreements, etc.[17]

---

15 It seeks to avoid market distortions and risks to financial stability and will enter into force only in the event that the EU and the UK do not enter into a Withdrawal Agreement. Given the tax-related provisions also included, the bill is entitled "Tax Act relating to Brexit" (*Brexit-Steuerbegleitgesetz* – Brexit-StBG) http://dip21.bundestag.de/dip21/btd/19/073/1907377.pdf.

16 The Brexit-StBG introduces transitional rules for regulated market participants and trading venues that target the German market from the UK, namely, credit institutions, investment firms, insurance undertakings, payment institutions and electronic money institutions, regulated markets, multilateral trading facilities (MTFs) and organised trading facilities (OTFs).

17 Michael Emerson, Matthias Busse; Mattia Di Salvo, Daniel Gros & Jacques Pelkmans, *An Assessment of the Economic Impact of Brexit on the EU27*, European Parliament, Directorate General for Internal Policies, Policy Department A: Economic and Scientific Policy (2017).

The shape of the agreement between the EU and the UK is still to be defined but the 12-point plan for the UK's exit, presented by British Prime Minister,[18] has established some boundaries and features for future relations. Theresa May established as an objective for Brexit: '*8. Free trade with the EU: The United Kingdom is seeking the greatest possible access to the EU single market for goods and services. It is willing to make financial contributions to the EU.*' But according to the same speech, the relation with the EU is also determined by other objectives: '*2. Control over legislation: The laws applicable in the United Kingdom will be made in the UK and interpreted only by UK courts, no longer by the European Court of Justice*' and '*5. Control of immigration: The United Kingdom intends to control the number of immigrants from the EU.*'

As the internal market represents a 50 per cent share of British trade (the other 50 per cent is divided up between various trading partners such as China, India, Japan, Canada and USA), it's in the UK best interest to establish a free trade agreement guaranteeing the 'greatest possible access' to the European markets.

The internal market for *goods* is far less significant for the UK today than it was in the mid 1990s, not only because since then British economic development model shifted towards a specialization in services, but also because of a rise in Britain's non-EU exports (especially to Asia). Regarding goods, the fact that UK relies more heavily on access to world markets than on access to the EU's internal market it's accompanied by the conviction that the country can secure privileged access to those markets on its own rather than as part of the EU, because trade deals will be much easier to negotiate[19]. However, the UK will have less leverage in negotiations than the EU does, especially in dealing with large emerging economies.

As for the internal market for *services* things can be different, because services exported to the EU account for about 40% of the UK total[20]. If the UK adopted a relation as the one covered by the *Treaty on the European Eco-*

---

18 Theresa May's speech delivered on 17 January 2017 at https://www.gov.uk/government/speeches/the-governments-negotiating-objectives-for-exiting-the-eu-pm-speech.

19 Nevertheless, some political declarations state that Brexit is the opportunity for the UK to be the global leader in free trade, to build a new Prosperity Zone (with countries such as New Zealand, Singapore and Australia, who are all committed to free trade), to engage in a US-UK trade deal or in a Continental partnership.

20 Regarding financial services, the effects of Brexit can be significant, as they account for about one-third of Britain's total services exports and two-thirds of the overall services surplus that the UK needs to pay for its deficit on goods. David Blake, *Brexit and the City*, Cass Business School (2017) at

nomic Area (EEA)[21] it would have an extensive access to the EU internal market. Companies based in the EEA can export goods to the EU, duty free or at reduced rates of duty, and offer services, including financial services, throughout the EU without having to set up an EU subsidiary ('EU passporting'). As there is no obligation of complying with a common economic policy, British Government could conclude its own free trade agreements. But this model of economic relation is incompatible with the UK's claims for full control over legislation and over immigration. Actually, EEA countries are obliged to accept all EU rules relating to the internal market (without any involvement in drafting them) and are subject to the jurisdiction of the EFTA (European Free Trade Association) Court that in turn has to base its decisions on the case law of the European Court of Justice (ECJ) (Article 3 of the Treaty establishing an EEA Court). Conversely, by accepting all the *acquis* related to the internal market EEA countries have to respect all four freedoms of the EU, including the freedom of movement.

Another way of designing the economic relationship between Europe and the UK could be based in the 'Swiss model' or EFTA model, in which the access to the EU internal market only applies to certain sectors. Considering that financial services have been almost completed excluded from market opening,[22] this will not be a good solution for the UK.

A *Comprehensive Economic and Trade Agreement* (CETA), such the one EU has concluded with Canada, would provide free trade without free movement, but it doesn't provide the necessary framework for a close cooperation with the EU on foreign and defence policy as well as on combating crime and terrorism.

---

https://static1.squarespace.com/static/58a0b77fe58c624794f29287/t/58ca91f8e58c62741806e682/1489670684557/Brexit-and-the-City.pdf.

21 Since 1992, with Norway, Iceland and Liechtenstein.

22 "The main argument against the 'Swiss Model' though is the fact that the United Kingdom wants to restrict free movement. Since 2002, an agreement on free movement has been in place between the EU and Switzerland. This states that free movement can only be restricted in exceptional cases by mutual agreement. If Switzerland were to terminate the agreement on free movement in order to implement the popular initiative 'against mass immigration', this would result in the automatic termination of all bilateral agreements between Switzerland and the EU ("Guillotine Clause")': Urs Pötzsch & Bert Van Roosebeke, '"Ukraine Plus" as a model for Brexit', cep Adhoc, (2017) p 4, at http://www.cep.eu/fileadmin/user_upload/cep.eu/Studien/cepAdhoc_Brexit/cepAdhoc_Ukraine_Plus_as_a_model_for_Brexit.pdf.

The Association and Free Trade Agreement that the EU concluded with the Ukraine (*Deep and Comprehensive Free Trade Area* (DCFTA)) seems to correspond to the British objectives: it guarantees a substantial market access without requiring the application of EU law or the compliance with the ECJ case law; it doesn't provide for free movement and allows free trade agreements with third countries. It also provides for collaboration on foreign and defence policy, as well as in combating crime and terrorism. Nevertheless, the 'Ukraine Model' contains numerous restrictions on market access particularly for cross-border services, incompatible with interests of the British finance industry.

IV. Financial Contribution

The United Kingdom has been the third largest net payer into the EU, behind Germany but almost equal to France, and it is pointed by some British politicians that one of the "advantages" of Brexit is that, being no longer a member of the single market, the UK will not be required to contribute with huge sums to the EU.

With the UK's withdrawal, the EU is likely to face a € 9 billion 'hole' in its annual budget, but at the same time, the UK declared that in exchange for the access to the EU single market it is willing to make financial contributions.

All Member States are interested in keeping the gap, caused by Brexit in the EU-finances, as small as possible because otherwise national contributions would have to increase or European expenditures be reduced. Receiving a financial contribution in connection with a trade agreement is particularly relevant for Germany and France, the two biggest net payers into the EU budget but also the countries that have a significant trade surplus *visà vis* the UK. Therefore, British willingness to pay is an additional very interesting incentive especially for those countries as they "have an interest, both fiscal and trade related in a comprehensive free trade agreement paid for with a substantial financial contribution from the United Kingdom"[23].

The amount of that contribution as a condition for a comprehensive free trade agreement can also be estimated: taking as reference amount the

23 Urs Pötzsch & Bert Van Roosebeke, '"Ukraine Plus" as a model for Brexit', cep Adhoc (2017), p 7, at http://www.cep.eu/fileadmin/user_upload/cep.eu/Studien/cepAdhoc_Brexit/cepAdhoc_Ukraine_Plus_as_a_model_for_Brexit.pdf.

contribution that Norway makes, scaled up for the size of the UK economy, this gives about € 3.5 billion. On the other hand, if the UK has simply a WTO-based relationship with the EU, then the European budget would receive additional tariff revenues, estimated at € 4.5 billion. Either way the EU will recuperate around a third to half of its loss of UK contributions.[24]

Conclusive Remarks

Any agreement must reasonably balance the interests of all sides, and the scenario of a close economic cooperation is of course the one with larger mutual benefits.

The UK needs to preserve its relationship with the EU; but it is also very important for companies in the EU to retain the greatest possible access to the British market, as in 2015, the EU's trade surplus with the UK amounted to almost 80 billion euros.

Although the advantages of economic cooperation are huge, it cannot be ignored the UK's will to terminate being a participant in the most developed economic integration project in the world. A project of free trade and free movement, based on non-discrimination, characterized by its coherence, which justifies the EU Heads of State and Government, repeated emphasis that 'access to the single market' after Brexit will be linked to the continuation of 'free movement'.

In our view, this is the correct perspective as internal market is a 'global reality' that cannot be fragmented, and the European project is not compatible with a kind of 'differentiated integration' outside the EU legal and institutional framework.

---

24 Additionally, there also the issue of 'legacy costs' of the divorce with figures in the range of € 20–40 billion; there has been so far no listing of the EU's assets and liabilities, including contingent liabilities such as loan guarantees, nor explanation of the legal basis for this claim.
Michael Emerson, Matthias Busse, Mattia Di Salvo, Daniel Gros & Jacques Pelkmans, *An Assessment of the Economic Impact of Brexit on the EU27*, European Parliament, Directorate General for Internal Policies, Policy Department A: Economic and Scientific Policy (2017).

Brexit and EU Citizen's Social Rights – the Commission v. United Kingdom [*UK child benefit or child tax credit*] and the CJEU case law on social rights

Rui Lanceiro

Abstract

Since its creation, the concept of EU citizenship, as well as the rights and duties it entails, have evolved greatly, notably in the area of social rights. The CJEU case-law broadened non-national EU citizens' rights to claim social benefits while narrowing Member States' scope to restrict their access to national welfare systems. However, the recent Dano, Alimanovic, and García-Nieto judgments present a striking shift in relation to the previous case-law, establishing limits on the right of EU citizens to social assistance in host Member States. The UK child benefit or child tax credit case provides proof that this evolution of the CJEU case-law is emerging as a general trend leading to possible changes in EU law but, especially, to the emergence of a restrictive view of the social dimension of EU citizenship. The right to reside in another Member State appears to be made dependent on the worker status of the citizen, in order to avoid becoming 'an unreasonable burden on the social system of the host Member State'. Several questions remain. Were these decisions an attempt to address the debate on 'welfare tourism' namely during the Brexit referendum? What will be left of the previous jurisprudence?

I. Introduction: the current debate on non-national EU citizens social rights in a host State

In the European Union (EU) a growing tension between a strong centralized enforcement of EU citizen's rights, enshrined both in the Treaties and in the Charter of Fundamental Rights, and a more decentralized approach, concerned with Member States autonomy can be observed and is central to Jirí Zemánek's text «*The Future of the Protection of Fundamental Rights after Brexit*».

One of the most important areas in that debate, which was also of great importance in the Brexit debate, is the freedom of movement and of residence within the Member States of the EU by Union citizens. In fact, EU citizenship, which is additional to national citizenship of a Member State and affords a set of rights, is at a crossroads. This is especially felt in terms of its implementation by the Member States and its relation to fundamental rights, namely social rights, and the principle of non-discrimination.

The concept of citizenship of the EU, which is a novel experiment[1] established by the Maastricht Treaty, and recognised in the Treaty of the EU (TEU) and the Treaty on the Functioning of the EU (TFEU), as well as the rights and duties it entails, have evolved greatly, much due to the case-law of the Court of Justice of the European Union's (CJEU). The rights of freedom of movement and of residence of EU citizens, as developed by the CJEU case law, are closely connected with the development of EU integration.

The development of Union citizenship by the CJEU case-law was especially notable in the area of the free movement and residence of EU citizens and their access to social benefits. The Court's case-law has been central for the guarantee of an effective freedom of movement of citizens within the territory of the Member States, recognised in the TEU as one of the fundamental freedoms on which the Union is based, especially when interpreted together with the principle of prohibition of discrimination on grounds of nationality (Article 18 TFEU).[2] According to Article 3(2) TEU, '*The Union shall offer its citizens an area of freedom, security and justice without internal frontiers, in which the free movement of persons is ensured*'. The right of every citizen of the Union '*to move and reside freely within the territory of the Member States, subject to the limitations and conditions laid down in the Treaties and by the measures adopted to give them effect*' is also recognised (Ar-

1 E Gild / C Gortázar Rotaeche / D Kostakopoulou, *The reconceptualization of European Union citizenship* (Leiden, M. Nijhoff, 2014).

2 On the expansive interpretation by the Court of the EU citizenship in relation to the principle of equality, v., *v.g.*, C Barnard, 'EU citizenship and the principle of solidarity' in M Dougan / E Spaventa (eds.), *Social welfare and EU law* (Oxford, Hart Publishing, 2005) 157–180; G Davies, 'The humiliation of the state as a constitutional tactic' in F. Amtenbrink / P.A.J. van den Berg (eds.), *The Constitutional Integrity of the European Union* (The Hague, Asser Press, 2010) 147; M Dougan / E Spaventa, 'Wish you weren't here...: new models of social solidarity in the European Union', in M Dougan / E Spaventa (eds.), *Social welfare and EU law* (Oxford, Hart Publishing, 2005) 181–218; S Giubonni, 'Free movement of Persons and European solidarity' (2007) 13 3 *European Law Journal* 360–379; C O'Brien, 'Real links, abstract rights and false alarms: the relationship between ECJ's 'real link' case law and national solidarity', (2008) 33 5 *European Law Review* 643–665.

ticle 21 TFEU).[3] The relation between freedom of movement, freedom of residence, and the prohibition of discrimination is implemented by the Citizens' Directive.[45]

In the *Grzelczyk* case, the Court established one of the cornerstones of the EU citizenship case-law: that '*Union citizenship is destined to be the fundamental status of nationals of the Member States, enabling those who find themselves in the same situation to enjoy the same treatment in law irrespective of their nationality, subject to such exceptions as are expressly provided for*'.[6]

The CJEU recognised the direct effect of the right of residence of Union citizens[7] and has consistently extended the prohibition of discrimination and the principle of equality, while interpreting Articles 18, 20 and 21 TFUE, namely to EU citizens who reside lawfully in a Member State but are economically inactive.[8] The Court was especially important in the building of a notion of EU citizenship which was not connected with the need to have an economic link to a certain Member State and which granted access to a wider range of rights.[9] It developed its case-law according to

---

3 J Cunha Rodrigues, 'Liberdade de Circulação e Permanência' in A. Silveira / M. Canotilho (eds) *Carta dos Direitos Fundamentais da União Europeia Comentada* (Coimbra, Almedina, 2013) 522–523; *Idem*, 'A proposEuropeancitizenship: theright to move and reside freely' in P Cordonnel/ A Rosas / N Wahl (eds) *Constitutionalisingthe EU judicial system: essays in honourofPernillaLindh* (Oxford, HartPublishing, 2012) 206.

4 Directive 2004/38/EC of the European Parliament and of the Council of 29 April 2004 on the right of citizens of the Union and their family members to move and reside freely within the territory of the Member States amending Regulation (EEC) No 1612/68 and repealing Directives 64/221/EEC, 68/360/EEC, 72/194/EEC, 73/148/EEC, 75/34/EEC, 75/35/EEC, 90/364/EEC, 90/365/EEC and 93/96/EEC [2004] OJ L 158.

5 For a comprehensible analysis, v. E Guild / S Peers / J Tomkin, *The EU citizenship directive: a commentary* (Oxford, Oxford University Press, 2014).

6 Case C-184/99 *Grzelczyk* ECLI:EU:C:2001:458, para. 31.

7 V., *v.g.*, Case C-413/99 *Baumbast* ECLI:EU:C:2002:493, para. 84, and Case C-456/02 *Trojani* ECLI:EU:C:2004:488, para. 32.

8 V., *v.g.*, Case C-85/96 *Martínez Sala* ECLI:EU:C:1998:217, paras. 61–62.

9 V., *v.g.*, Case C-85/96 *Martínez Sala* ECLI:EU:C:1998:217, paras. 61–62, Case C-184/99 *Grzelczyk* ECLI:EU:C:2001:458, para. 44, Case C-60/00 *Carpenter* ECLI:EU:C:2002:434, para 38, Case C-413/99 *Baumbast* ECLI:EU:C:2002:493, para. 84, Case C-109/01 *Akrich* ECLI:EU:C:2003:491, paras 57–58, Case C-148/02 *Garcia Avello* ECLI:EU:C:2003:539, para 24, Case C-456/02 *Trojani* ECLI:EU:C:2004:488, para. 32, Case C-209/03 *Bidar* ECLI:EU:C:2005:169, para 31, Case C-22/08 and C-23/08 *Vatsouras* ECLI:EU:C:2009:344, paras 38–39, and Case C-34/09 *Ruiz Zambrano* ECLI:EU:C:2011:124, paras 42–44.

which Article 20 TFEU, 'precludes national measures that have effect of depriving citizens of the Union of the genuine enjoyment of the substance of the rights conferred by the virtue of their status as citizens of the union'.[10] The EU citizenship should make a difference and involves a break from merely economic categories, such as '*worker*', which were predominant in the EEC.[11]

However, this case-law was sometimes criticised, namely by some of the Member States, including the United Kingdom of Great Britain and Northern Ireland (UK), for being too broad in recognising the access to benefits while interpreting the Citizens' Directive too extensively.[12] In this debate, at least some of the Member States reject intrusions in their autonomy while the European Commission defends the freedom of movement of persons.[13] The broad interpretation of these rights could interfere with

---

10 Case C-34/09 *Ruiz Zambrano* ECLI:EU:C:2011:124, para 42, quoting Case C-135/08 *Rottmann* ECLI:EU:C:2010:104, para 42.

11 V., *v.g.*, E Spaventa, 'From Gebhard to Carpenter: Towards a (non-)economic European constitution' (2004) 41 (3) *Common Market Law Review* 743–773; N NShuibhne, 'The Resilience of EU Market Citizenship' (2010) 47 (6) *Common Market Law Review* 1597–1628, pp 1605–1609; S Kadelbach, 'Union citizenship' in A von Bogdandy / Bast (ed.) *Principles of European Constitutional Law*, 2nd ed. (Oxford, Hart, 2009) 443–478, pp 445–448; C. O'Brien, 'I trade, therefore I am: legal personhood in the European Union' (2013) 50 *Common Market Law Review* 1643–1684.

12 V., *v.g.*, N Caicedo Camacho, 'La Directiva 2004/38/CE y la jurisprudenciadel TJCE sobre el disfrute de las prestaciones sociales: ¿freno al avance en materia social o adecuación a los intereses de los estados?' (2014) 19 *Revistad'estudis autonòmicsi federals* 96–143; Davies, 'The humiliation of the state as a constitutional tactic', 147–174; Giubonni, 'Free movement of persons and European solidarity', 360–379; *Idem*, 'A Certain Degree of Solidarity? Free Movement of Persons and Access to Social Protection in the Case Law of the European Court of Justice', in M Ross / Y Borgmann-Prebil (eds) *Promoting Solidarity in the European Union* (Oxford, Oxford University Press, 2010) 191–193; I. Lirola Delgado, 'Derecho de residencia de los ciudadanos de la Unión y prestaciones sociales en tiempos de crisis' (2014) 18 (49) *Revista de Derecho Comunitario Europeo* 761–762; F Wollenschläger, 'A New Fundamental Freedom beyond Market Integration: Union Citizenship and its Dynamics for Shifting the Economic Paradigm of European Integration' (2011) 17 *European Law Journal* 1–34.

13 For an overview, v. M Morsa, 'Les migrations internes à l'Unioneuropéennesont-ellesmotivées par un accès à des prestationssociales? Citoyenneté européenne, liberté de circulation et de séjour des inactifs et droits sociaux. La relation entre la coordination européenne et la directive 2004/38' (2014) 1190 *Journal des tribunaux du travail* 245–246; H Verschueren, 'Free Movement or Benefit Tourism: The Unreasonable Burden of Brey' (2014) 16 *European Journal of Migration and Law* 147–179.

the Member States' political choices or the national solidarity on the basis of their welfare systems.[14]

There is a direct relation of this matter with the current debates on access by non-national EU citizens to social security in host Member States, characterised sometimes as '*welfare migration*'[15], '*benefit tourism*'[16] or '*social tourism*'.[17] These are terms used in the context of the perceived threat that a number of economically inactive EU citizens move to a given Member State to benefit from its social welfare system rather than to work. The debate has grown in intensity because of the perceived need to implement budget-cuts on national benefits during the global economic crisis.[18]

The access by non-national EU citizens to social security in host Member States was one of the central questions in the debate of the prospective withdrawal of the UK from the EU. In fact, when then Prime-Minister Cameron called for '*a new settlement for the United Kingdom in a reformed European Union*' in his letter of 10 November 2015 one of the main areas of concern pointed out was immigration and specifically that the UK was not able to '*cope with all the pressures that free movement can bring – on our schools, our hospitals and our public services*' and that it was necessary '*to crack*

---

14 V., *v.g.*, M Dougan, 'The constitutional dimension to the case law on Union citizenship' (2006) 31 *European Law Review*, 613–641, 623; AJ Menéndez, 'European Citizenship after Martínez Sala and Baumbast: Has European Law Become More Human but Less Social?' in M Poiares Maduro / L Azoulai (eds) *The Past and Future of EU Law. The Classics of EU Law Revisited on the 50th Anniversary of the Rome Treaty* (Oxford, Hart, 2010), 391–392.

15 V., *v.g.*, P Larkin, 'The Limits to European Social Citizenship in the United Kingdom' (2005) 68 *Modern Law Review*, 435–447, pp. 440–442; S Mantu / P Minderhoud, 'Exploring the limits of social solidarity: welfare tourism and EU citizenship' (2016) 2(2) *UNIO – EU Law Jounal*, 4–19.

16 H Verschueren, 'Preventing "benefit tourism" in the EU: A narrow or broad interpretation of the possibilities offered by the ECJ in Dano?' (2015) 52(2) *Common Market Law Review* 363–390

17 Term used by Advocate General Geelhoed, and described as "*moving to a Member State with a more congenial social security environment*" (Case C-456/02 *Trojani* ECLI:EU:C:2004:112, Opinion of AG Geelhoed, para 18).

18 V. Editorial Comments, 'The free movement of persons in the European Union: Salvaging the dream while explaining the nightmare' (2014) 51 *Common Market Law Review*, 729–740; J. Shaw, 'Between law and political truth? Member States preferences, EU free movement rules and national immigration law', *Conference paper, UACES 44th Annual Conference*, Cork, 1–3 September 2014, at http://www.uaces.org; I. Lirola Delgado, 'Derecho de residencia de los ciudadanos de la Unión y prestaciones sociales en tiempos de crisis. ¿Hacia un planteamiento casuístico y ambiguo de la solidaridad entre los Estados miembros?' (2015) 49 *Revista de DerechoComunitarioEuropeo*, 733–766, 734–742.

down on the abuse of free movement'.[19] The letter, thus, asked for a limitation of the rights of European citizens who were migrants to receive social benefits in host Member States. This was one of the issues discussed in the negotiation of the package of changes to the UK's terms of membership to the EU and changes to EU rules that came to a conclusion during the European Council meeting on 18 and 19 February 2016.[20] The set of arrangements agreed by the President of the European Council Donald Tusk, and approved by EU leaders of all 27 other Member States in the European Council meeting on 18th and 19th February were spelled out in its Conclusions.[21]

The agreement included as response to the concerns of the UK in these matters is in three declarations of the European Commission as annexes V, VI and VII. In these annexes the Commission agreed to *i)* '*make a proposal to amend Regulation (EC) No 883/2004 of the European Parliament and of the Council on the coordination of social security systems in order to give Member States, with regard to the exportation of child benefits to a Member State other than that where the worker resides, an option to index such benefits to the conditions of the Member State where the child resides*' (annex V); *ii)* '*table a proposal to amend Regulation 492/2011 on freedom of movement for workers within the Union to provide for a safeguard mechanism with the understanding that it can and will be used and therefore will act as a solution to the United Kingdom's concerns about the exceptional inflow of workers from elsewhere in the European Union*' (annex VI); and *iii)* '*adopt a proposal to complement Directive 2004/38 on free movement of Union citizens*' in matters of persons who marry a

19 David Cameron, 'A new settlement for the United Kingdom in a reformed European Union', 10th November 2015, at https://www.gov.uk/government/uploads/system/uploads/attachment_data/file/475679/Donald_Tusk_letter.pdf

20 The negotiations only began following the outcome of the UK General Election in the summer of 2015.

21 V. General Secretariat of the Council (2016–02–19). 'European Council meeting (18 and 19 February 2016) – Conclusions', EUCO 1/16.

Union citizen,[22] abuse of free movement rights[23] and other clarifications[24] (annex VII). The changes were intended to become effective on the date the Government of the UK informed the Secretary-General of the Council that the UK has decided to remain a member of the EU, following a vote in the UK's referendum. Due to the result of the referendum, the changes were never implemented.

The subject of immigration and of access of non-national EU citizens to welfare benefits was also one of the most discussed subjects in the UK 'Remain/Leave' referendum campaign. It was during this campaign that the CJEU issued its decision on the *UK child benefit or child tax credit* case.[25] This decision must be read in the context of a recent change in the CJEU case-law on this subject, that could have profound consequences in the way EU citizen's rights and the freedom of movement are interpreted and implemented.

---

22 The change would be 'in order to exclude, from the scope of free movement rights, third country nationals who had no prior lawful residence in a Member State before marrying a Union citizen or who marry a Union citizen only after the Union citizen has established residence in the host Member State" and clarifying that "the concept of marriage of convenience – which is not protected under Union law – also covers a marriage which is maintained for the purpose of enjoying a right of residence by a family member who is not a national of a Member State'.

23 The change would be to clarify that 'Member States can address specific cases of abuse of free movement rights by Union citizens returning to their Member State of nationality with a non-EU family member where residence in the host Member State has not been sufficiently genuine to create or strengthen family life and had the purpose of evading the application of national immigration rules'.

24 'The Commission will also clarify that Member States may take into account past conduct of an individual in the determination of whether a Union citizen's conduct poses a 'present' threat to public policy or security. They may act on grounds of public policy or public security even in the absence of a previous criminal conviction on preventative grounds but specific to the individual concerned. The Commission will also clarify the notions of "serious grounds of public policy or public security" and "imperative grounds of public security". Moreover, on the occasion of a future revision of Directive 2004/38 on free movement of Union citizens, the Commission will examine the thresholds to which these notions are connected'.

25 Case C-308/14 *Commission v United Kingdom [UK child benefit or child tax credit case]* ECLI:EU:C:2016:436. See also D. Berlin, 'La Cour invite dans le débat sur le Brexit?' (2016) 26 *La Semaine Juridique – édition générale*, 1310.

II. The Recent Evolution in CJEU Case-law on Access to Social Assistance Granted to Non-national EU Citizens

Against this background, a number of recent CJEU judgments present a striking shift in relation to the previous case-law, clarifying the limits of the right to access to social assistance granted to non-national Union citizens in host Member States under EU Law.

In fact, it has been up to the CJEU to largely develop the legal framework and the principles applicable to the connection between the freedom of movement and the non-national EU citizens' access to social rights, and specifically to social benefits, in the host State. The Court developed an approach which was centred on the individual at issue and its subjective case and established that the right of residence and of establishment and the equal treatment principle should not be precluded by lack of resources. For instance, the principle of equality was declared applicable to the rights to maintenance aid for students who are exercising their right of residence, despite the exception established in Article 24 (2) of the Citizens' Directive.[26]

The prohibition of discrimination on the grounds of nationality and the establishment of the EU citizenship were seen by the CJEU as precluding the entitlement to a non-contributory social benefit from being made conditional to non-national legally residing EU citizens being considered as workers when no such conditions would apply to nationals of the Member State. In Judgments such as *Martínez Sala*, *Grzelczyk*, *Trojani*, or *Bidar*, for instance, the CJEU developed a case-law which incrementally broadened non-national EU citizens' rights to claim social benefits while narrowing Member States' scope to regulate or restrict their access to national welfare systems, notably in the case of non-contributory benefits. The Court recognised and accepted that this involved the need for a certain degree of financial solidarity between Member States.[27] However, the Court accepted that in certain cases it was legitimate for a Member State to grant such a benefit only after it has been possible to establish a '*real link*' between the jobseeker and the labour market of that State[28], or a '*certain degree of integration*

26 V., *v.g.*, Case C-224/98 *D'Hoop* ECLI:EU:C:2002:432, paras 30–32; Case C-209/03 *Bidar* ECLI:EU:C:2005:169, para 31.

27 V., *v.g.*, Case C-184/99 *Grzelczyk* ECLI:EU:C:2001:458, para. 44, Case C-209/03 *Bidar* ECLI:EU:C:2005:169, para 56.

28 V., *v.g.*, Case C-22/08 and C-23/08 *Vatsouras* ECLI:EU:C:2009:344, paras 38–39, and Case C-138/02 *Collins* ECLI:EU:C:2004:172, paras 67–69.

into the society of the host State' was demonstrated. [29] Finally, in any case, the Court recognised that the applicant should not become '*an unreasonable burden*' on the public finances of the Member State.[30]

In the *Brey* judgment of September 2013[31] the CJEU stated that the Citizen's Directive '*allows the host Member State to impose legitimate restrictions in connection with the grant of* [social security] *benefits to Union citizens who do not or no longer have worker status, so that those citizens do not become an unreasonable burden on the social assistance system of that Member State*'.[32] This objective to avoid that a citizen becomes an '*unreasonable burden*' was already stated in recital 10 in the preamble to the Directive.[33]

However, the Court interpreted the Directive in light of the Treaty and of general principles of EU law. The result was that '*since the right to freedom of movement is – as a fundamental principle of EU law – the general rule, the conditions laid down in Article 7(1)(b) of Directive 2004/38 must be construed narrowly (see, by analogy, Kamberaj, paragraph 86, and Chakroun, paragraph 43) and in compliance with the limits imposed by EU law and the principle of proportionality (see Baumbast and R, paragraph 91; Zhu and Chen, paragraph 32; and Commission v Belgium, paragraph 39)*'. This meant that EU

---

29 V., *v.g.*, Case C-209/03 *Bidar* ECLI:EU:C:2005:169, para 57; Case C-258/04 *Ioannidis* ECLI:EU:C:2005:559, paras 30 *etseq.*; Case C-158/07 *Förster* ECLI:EU:C:2008:63, para 54; Case C-103/08 *Gottwald* ECLI:EU:C:2009:597, paras 32 *etseq.*

30 V., *v.g.*, Case C-184/99 *Grzelczyk* ECLI:EU:C:2001:458, para. 44; and Case C-75/11 *Commission v Austria [reduced fares on public transport granted to students]* ECLI:EU:C:2012:605, para 60.

31 Case C-140/12 *Brey* ECLI:EU:C:2013:565. Mr Brey and his wife were both German nationals with no other income or assets other than a low sum of pension and benefit payments received in Germany. After moving to Austria in 2011, Mr Brey applied for a compensatory supplement. However, the Austrian authorities refused this because the aforementioned low amounts of pension payments from Germany supposedly did not constitute sufficient resources to establish his lawful residence in Austria.

32 Case C-140/12 *Brey* ECLI:EU:C:2013:565, para 57. For an analysis of the *Brey* case, v., *v.g.*, B Spiegel, 'Anspruch auf Leistungen der sozialen Sicherheit von nichtaktiven Personen – wer fürchtet sich vor 'Sozialtourismus'? Neue EuGH Fälle: C-140/12, Brey, und C-333/13, Dano', (2014) 15 *ERA Forum*, 339–340; D Thym, 'Sozialleistungen für und Aufenthalt von nichterwerbstätigen Unionbürgern' (2014) 23 *Neue Zeitschrift für Sozialrecht*, 81–120; H Verschueren, 'Free Movement or Benefit Tourism' 147–179; A.P. van der Mei, 'Overview of Recent Cases before the Court of Justice of the European Union (October-December 2014)' (2014) 17(1) *European Journal of Social Security*, 102–122.

33 Case C-140/12 *Brey* ECLI:EU:C:2013:565, para 54. It was already stated in the Case C-424/10 and C-425/10 *Ziolkowski and Szeja* ECLI:EU:C:2011:866, para 40.

law precluded the automatic exclusion of an economically inactive citizen of another Member State from receiving a particular social benefit because that exclusion does not enable the competent authorities of the host Member State to *'carry out – in accordance with the requirements under, inter alia, Articles 7(1)(b) and 8(4) of that directive and the principle of proportionality – an overall assessment of the specific burden which granting that benefit would place on the social assistance system as a whole by reference to the personal circumstances characterising the individual situation of the person concerned'*.[34]

The *Brey* test was construed in such a way that the Member State's authorities can only claim that a citizen is an unreasonable burden to their social security system after considering his/her individual personal situation.

Only a year later, in November 2014, the *Dano* case[35] represents the beginning of a different methodology of analysis of the relation between the right to reside and the access to social benefits.[36] In the *Dano* decision, the CJEU made clear that Member States may reject claims to social assistance by EU citizens who have no intention to work and cannot support themselves. It was followed by the *Alimanovic* case[37], which confirmed the new trend and gave the Court the opportunity to clarify the application of this principle.

---

34 Case C-140/12 *Brey* ECLI:EU:C:2013:565, para 77.

35 Case C-333/13 *Dano* ECLI:EU:C:2014:2358. Ms Dano and her son, Romanian nationals, claimed an entitlement to unemployment benefits at the Leipzig Social Court, after being denied by the Jobcenter Leipzig. Ms Dano is currently staying with her son in Germany. She was not seeking employment, nor has she been trained in a profession and, to date, she has never worked in Germany or Romania. They lived with Ms Dano's sister, who provided for them.

36 For an analysis of the *Dano* case, v., *v.g.*, D Guimarães, 'The Right of Free Movement and the Access To Social Protection in the EU: The Economical Dimension. Notes on the Case Elisabeta Dano v Jobcenter Leipzig, C-333/13' (2015) 1(1) *UNIO – EU Law Jounal* 110–120; D Thym, 'The Elusive limits of solidarity: Residence rights of and social benefits for economically inactive Union citizens' (2015) 52 *Common Market Law Review* 17–20; *Id*, 'When Union Citizens turn into illegal migrants: the Dano case' (2015) 40 *European Law Review* 249 ff, 260; AP van der Mei, 'Overview of Recent Cases before the Court of Justice of the European Union (January-June 2015)', 481–496; H Verschueren, 'Preventing 'Benefit Tourism' in the EU' 363–364; F Wollenschläger, 'Keine Sozialleistungen für nichterwerbstätige Unionsbürger?' (2014) 24 NVwZ 1628–1632; and, very critically of the CJEU's new approach: N N Shuibne, 'Limits Rising, Duties Ascending: The Changing Legal Shape of Union Citizenship' (2015) 52 *Common Market Law Review* 889–937.

37 Case C-67/14 *Alimanovic* ECLI:EU:C:2015:597.

At the beginning of the reasoning of the *Dano* decision, the Court repeats the *Grzelczyk* statement that '*the status of citizen of the Union is destined to be the fundamental status of nationals of the Member States*'.[38] However, the CJEU subsequently answered the questions by reference to the Citizens' Directive and Regulation No 883/2004[39], as '*more specific expressions*' of the prohibition of discrimination on grounds of nationality of Article 18 TFEU, and said that '*so far as concerns access to social benefits, such as those at issue in the main proceedings, a Union citizen can claim equal treatment with nationals of the host Member State only if his residence in the territory of the host Member State complies with the conditions of Directive 2004/38*'.[40] In doing so, the Court does a literal interpretation of the text of the Directive without reference to the Treaties – especially to the provisions on EU citizenship and the freedom of movement and of residence.

Adopting this methodology allows the CJEU to state that '*any unequal treatment between Union citizens who have made use of their freedom of movement and residence and nationals of the host Member State with regard to the grant of social benefits is an inevitable consequence of Directive 2004/38*'[41] without having to equate this statement with the general principles of EU law and with the Treaties' rules.

According to the Citizens' Directive, the right of residence for periods longer than three months is subject to the conditions set out in Article 7(1) which distinguishes between (*i*) persons who are working and (*ii*) those who are not. The first group of citizens have the right of residence in the host Member State without having to fulfil any other condition (Article 7(1)(a) of Directive). Persons who are economically inactive are required by Article 7(1)(b) of the Directive to meet the condition that they have sufficient resources of their own. From these provisions, the Court concludes that each '*Member State must therefore have the possibility, pursuant to Article 7 of Directive 2004/38, of refusing to grant social benefits to economically inac-*

38 Case C-333/13 *Dano* ECLI:EU:C:2014:2358, para 58.

39 Regulation (EC) No 883/2004 of the European Parliament and of the Council of 29 April 2004 on the coordination of social security systems, OJ L 166.

40 Case C-333/13 *Dano* ECLI:EU:C:2014:2358, para 69. The Advocate General Wathelet also concluded that EU law did not preclude the national legislature from choosing to exclude nationals of other Member States from entitlement to a special non-contributory cash benefit on the basis of a general criterion, such as the reason for entering the territory of the host Member State, but used the capability of demonstrating the absence of a genuine link with that State, in order to prevent an unreasonable burden on its social assistance system (v. Case C-333/13 *Dano* ECLI:EU:C:2014:341, Opinion AG Wathelet, para 139).

41 Case C-333/13 *Dano* ECLI:EU:C:2014:2358, para 77.

tive Union citizens who exercise their right to freedom of movement solely in order to obtain another Member State's social assistance although they do not have sufficient resources to claim a right of residence'.[42]

No reference to the individual situation of Ms. Dano was made other than that '*in the main proceedings, according to the findings of the referring court the applicants do not have sufficient resources and thus cannot claim a right of residence in the host Member State*'.[43] This, in itself, signified a departure from the *Brey* test described *supra*.

One of the questions referred to the Court were on the application of the Charter of Fundamental Rights to the case. The CJEU, however, stated that it did not have jurisdiction. Its reasoning was that, since the conditions creating the right to the benefits did result neither from Regulation No 883/2004 nor from Directive 2004/38 or other secondary EU legislation, it was thus for the legislature of each Member State to lay down those conditions. According to the Court, while doing so, the Member States are not implementing EU law for the effect of triggering the application of the Charter under its Article 51 (1).[44] In the *Alimanovic* case,[45] one year later, the Court used the *Dano* line of reasoning, confirming that a new paradigm of access of non-national EU citizens to the host State's social benefits had emerged.[46]

---

42 Case C-333/13 *Dano* ECLI:EU:C:2014:2358, para 78.

43 Case C-333/13 *Dano* ECLI:EU:C:2014:2358, para 81.

44 Case C-333/13 *Dano* ECLI:EU:C:2014:2358, paras 87–92.

45 Case C-67/14 *Alimanovic* ECLI:EU:C:2015:597. The case concerns the access of Nazifa Alimanovic and her three German-born children, all possessing the Swedish nationality, to German social welfare benefits. These welfare benefits include *Arbeitslosengeld II*, Germany's subsistence allowance for the long-termed unemployed, and social allowances for beneficiaries unfit to work. In contrast with the *Dano* case, in which the EU citizen in question had never worked and was not seeking work, mother Alimanovic and her oldest daughter did have temporary jobs between June 2010 and May 2011 in Germany. As a result, they received social benefits from 1 December 2011 to 31 May 2012, after which the '*Job Center*', the responsible German authority, withdrew their grant. For an analysis of the *Alimanovic* case, v., *v.g.*, A Iliopoulou-Penot, 'Deconstructing the former edifice of Union citizenship? The Alimanovic judgment' (2016) 53 *Common Market Law Review* 1007–1035; AP van der Mei, 'Overview of Recent Cases before the Court of Justice of the European Union (July-December 2015)', 74–84.

46 This meant not following the Advocate General's opinion. Advocate General Wathelet considered that it was "*contrary to EU law, and more precisely, to the principle of equal treatment affirmed in Article 18 TFEU and clarified in Article 4 of Regulation No 883/2004 and Article 24 of Directive 2004/38, for the legislation of a Member State, such as that at issue in the main proceedings, automatically to exclude a citizen of the Union from entitlement to a special non-contributory cash benefit within the mean-*

The question before the CJEU was if Member States could exclude nationals of other Member States who are jobseekers in the host Member State from entitlement to certain '*special non-contributory cash benefits*' within the meaning of Article 70(2) of Regulation No 883/2004, which also constitute 'social assistance' within the meaning of Article 24(2) of the Citizens' Directive, although those benefits were granted to nationals of the Member State concerned who are in the same situation.[47] The Court reiterated the *Dano* assessment that '*a Union citizen can claim equal treatment with nationals of the host Member State under Article 24(1) of Directive 2004/38 only if his residence in the territory of the host Member State complies with the conditions of Directive 2004/38*'.[48] Only Article 7(3)(c) and Article 14(4)(b) of the Citizens' Directive were considered as able to confer a right of residence on jobseekers in the situation of Ms Alimanovic and her

---

ing of Regulation No 883/2004 (a benefit which, moreover, constitutes social assistance within the meaning of Directive 2004/38) beyond a period of involuntary unemployment of six months after working for less than a year, without allowing that citizen to demonstrate the existence of a genuine link with the host Member State" (v. Case C-67/14 *Alimanovic* ECLI:EU:C:2015:210, Opinion of AG Wathelet, para 110). The Advocate General also stated that in circumstances such as those of the main proceedings, the children of a national of a Member State who works or has worked in the host Member State and the parent who is their primary carer may claim a right of residence there on the sole basis of Article 10 of Regulation (EU) No 492/2011 on freedom of movement for workers within the Union, without such a right being conditional on their having sufficient resources and comprehensive sickness insurance cover in that State (v. Case C-67/14 *Alimanovic* ECLI:EU:C:2015:210, Opinion of AG Wathelet, paras 117–122).

47 In this decision, as in the *Dano* case, the benefits at issue were characterised as 'special non-contributory cash benefits' within the meaning of Article 70(2) of Regulation No 883/2004, *i.e.* benefits which were intended to cover subsistence costs for persons who cannot cover them themselves and that are not financed through contributions, but through tax revenue. The Court considered that, from its case-law, those benefits were also covered by the concept of 'social assistance' within the meaning of Article 24(2) of Directive 2004/38, which refers to all assistance schemes established by the public authorities to which recourse may be had by an individual who does not have resources sufficient to meet his own basic needs and those of his family and who by reason of that fact may, during his period of residence, become a burden on the public finances of the host Member State which could have consequences for the overall level of assistance which may be granted by that State. V. Case C-333/13 *Dano* ECLI:EU:C:2014:2358, para 63, and Case C-67/14 *Alimanovic* ECLI:EU:C:2015:597, paras 43–44.

48 Case C-333/13 *Dano* ECLI:EU:C:2014:2358, para 69, and Case C-67/14 *Alimanovic* ECLI:EU:C:2015:597, para 49.

daughter. The first provision (Article 7(3)(c))[49] only conferred worker status during 6 months after their last employment had ended, a period which had already expired when they were refused entitlement to the benefits at issue. Article 14(4)(b) can be relied upon to establish a right of residence even after the expiry of the period referred to in Article 7(3)(c) of the Citizens' Directive, entitling Ms. Alimanovic and her daughter to equal treatment with the nationals of the host Member State so far as access to social assistance is concerned.[50] However, in that case, the host Member State may rely on the derogation in Article 24(2) of that Directive in order not to grant that citizen the social assistance sought.

The Court addressed the *Brey* case, stating that '*although the Court has held that Directive 2004/38 requires a Member State to take account of the individual situation of the person concerned before it adopts an expulsion measure or finds that the residence of that person is placing an unreasonable burden on its social assistance system (judgment in Brey, C-140/12, EU:C:2013:565, paragraphs 64, 69 and 78)*', no such individual assessment is necessary '*in circumstances such as those at issue in the main proceedings*'.[51] The reason for this conclusion begins with stating that the Citizens' Directive '*itself takes into consideration various factors characterising the individual situation of each applicant for social assistance and, in particular, the duration of the exercise of any economic activity*'. Besides, the Directive does '*guarantee a significant level of legal certainty and transparency in the context of the award of social assistance by way of basic provision, while complying with the principle of proportionality*'. Finally, '*while an individual claim might not place the Member State concerned*

49 This provision establishes that if the worker is in duly recorded involuntary unemployment after completing a fixed-term employment contract of less than a year or after having become involuntarily unemployed during the first 12 months and has registered as a jobseeker with the relevant employment office, he retains the status of worker for no less than six months. During that period, the Union citizen concerned retains his right of residence in the host Member State under Article 7 of the Citizens' Directive. Article 7(3)(b) provides in principle for the unlimited retention of the worker status after employment for more than a year, but in that case the worker would have to have completed an employment contract longer than a year.

50 Article 14(4)(b) stipulates that Union citizens who have entered the territory of the host Member State in order to seek employment may not be expelled for as long as they can provide evidence that they are continuing to seek employment and that they have a genuine chance of being engaged.

51 Case C-67/14 *Alimanovic* ECLI:EU:C:2015:597, para 59.

under an unreasonable burden, the accumulation of all the individual claims which would be submitted to it would be bound to do so'. [52]

Any prospect that these cases did not represent the adoption of a broad new approach of the CJEU to the question of access to social benefits by non-national EU citizens was proven unfounded by the subsequent case that adopts the same methodology.

In the *García-Nieto* case[53] the Court once again addressed the access to '*special non-contributory cash benefits*' within the meaning of Article 70(2) of Regulation No 883/2004, which also constitute '*social assistance*' within the meaning of Article 24(2) of the Citizens' Directive, by quoting the *Dano* and *Alimanovic* cases – '*a Union citizen can claim equal treatment with nationals of the host Member State (...) only if his residence in the territory of the host Member State complies with the conditions*' of the Citizens' Directive.[54] The Court followed the same kind of reasoning, limiting itself to the interpretation of the provisions of the Citizens' Directive. Article 6(1) of the Directive provides that EU citizens have the right of residence on the territory of another Member State for a period of up to three months without any conditions or any formalities other than the requirement to hold a valid identity card or passport. However, in such a case, the host Member State may rely on the derogation in Article 24(2) in order to refuse to grant that citizen the social assistance sought.[55] Hence, the host Member States can exclude economically inactive non-national EU citizens from access to '*social assistance*' as long as they are residing for a period shorter than three

---

52 Case C-67/14 *Alimanovic* ECLI:EU:C:2015:597, paras 60–62.

53 Case C-299/14 *García-Nieto* ECLI:EU:C:2016:114. The unmarried Spanish couple García-Nieto and Peña Cuevas, had lived together in Spain for several years and had a common child. The father also had a son from an earlier relationship. Mother García-Nieto and their common child moved to Germany in April 2012, where she moved in with her mother, registered as a jobseeker and started working in June 2012. The father and his other son joined the family in Germany in June 2012. Until November 2012, the family's living expenses were met from the mother García-Nieto's income. From that moment onwards, the father also started to work in short-term jobs. The case concerned the request for social assistance benefits that the father made for himself and his son in July 2012. The German authorities denied them these benefits for August and September as they had resided for a period shorter than three months in Germany and, during that time, were neither working nor self-employed.

54 Case C-299/14 *García-Nieto* ECLI:EU:C:2016:114, para38, quoting Case C-333/13 *Dano* ECLI:EU:C:2014:2358, para 69, and Case C-67/14 *Alimanovic* ECLI:EU:C:2015:597, para 49.

55 Case C-299/14 *García-Nieto* ECLI:EU:C:2016:114, paras 42–43, quoting Case C-333/13 *Dano* ECLI:EU:C:2014:2358, para 70.

months. No reference to the special status of EU citizen or to the Treaties is made. No consideration is given to the family status of those involved.

The individual personal situation test put forward in *Brey* was replaced by the objective test used in the *Alimanovic* case. In *Alimanovic*, the Court stated that the Citizens' Directive, '*establishing a gradual system as regards the retention of the status of 'worker' which seeks to safeguard the right of residence and access to social assistance, itself takes into consideration various factors characterising the individual situation of each applicant for social assistance and, in particular, the duration of the exercise of any economic activity*'.[56] This reasoning is taken a step further by the Court in the *García-Nieto* case, stating that '*if such an assessment is not necessary in the case of a citizen seeking employment who no longer has the status of 'worker', the same applies a fortiori to persons who are in a situation such as that (…) in the main proceedings*'.[57]

This delivers the *coup de grace* on the *Brey* doctrine – no individual personal situation test is needed; the Court merely applies the Citizens' Directive to the case. However, the Court does so without the admission of abandoning that doctrine, and without a specific reasoning on that subject: it is as if the Court is presenting a mere exception to previous case-law.

III. The evolution of the case-law: the UK child benefit or child tax credit case

This evolution of the CJEU case-law emerged in cases dealing with '*special non-contributory cash benefits*'[58], which were the benefits at issue in the *Dano*, *Alimanovic* and *García-Nieto* cases. However, it appears to be emerging as a general change in the Courts doctrine in the matter of access to

56 Case C-299/14 *García-Nieto* ECLI:EU:C:2016:114, para47, quoting Case C-67/14 *Alimanovic* ECLI:EU:C:2015:597, para 60.

57 Case C-299/14 *García-Nieto* ECLI:EU:C:2016:114, para 48.

58 On this subject, v. T. Guerrero Padrón, 'The scope and instrumentation of the principle of equal treatment regarding social assistance benefits' (2016) I (1) e-Revista Internacional de la Protección Social 87, 89–90.

social benefits, with consequences outside of that field[59] – the *UK child benefit or child tax credit* case provides proof of this change.[60]

In this case the question brought before the CJEU was the implementation of Regulation (EC) No 883/2004 of the European Parliament and of the Council of 29 April 2004 on the coordination of social security systems, and not the Citizens' Directive. This Regulation lays down a series of common principles to be observed by the legislation of the Member States in that sphere so that the various national systems do not place at a disadvantage person who exercise their right of freedom of movement and of residence within the EU. One of the common principles that the Member States must observe is the principle of equality which, in the field of social security, takes the form of prohibiting any discrimination on grounds of nationality.

The UK was requiring a person claiming some social benefits (child benefit and child tax credit) to satisfy the right to reside test in order to be treated as habitually resident in that Member State. Since the Commission took the view that the UK legislation does not comply with the Regulation, because it has added a condition that does not appear in Regulation No 883/2004, it brought an action for failure to fulfil obligations against the UK. According to the Commission, that condition deprives persons

---

59 *E.g.*, Case C-233/14 *Commission v the Netherlands [financial support for travel costs awarded to national students]* ECLI:EU:C:2016:396. This case is about the restricting of access to fares at preferential rates on public transport for students who pursue their studies in the Netherlands to Netherlands students who are registered with a private or public educational establishment in the Netherlands and to students from other Member States who, in the Netherlands, are economically active or have obtained the right of permanent residence.

60 For an analysis of the *UK child benefit or child tax credit* case, v., *v.g.*, C O'Brien, 'The ECJ sacrifices EU citizenship in vain: Commission v. United Kingdom' (2016) 54 *Common Market Law Review* 209–243; *Idem*, 'A failed Faustian pact: Case C-308/14 Commission v UK and the sacrifice of EU citizenship' (2016) 4 *Quaderni costituzionali* 824–827; M D Bollo Arocena, 'Salvaguarda de las finanzaspúblicas, derecho de residencia y obtención de prestaciones de seguridad social en el Estado miembro de acogida. Comentario a la Sentenciadel TJUE (Sala Primera), de 14 de junio de 2016. Asunto C-308/14' (2016) 8–9 *Revista Aranzadi Unión Europea*, 95–102; NN Shuibhne, '"WHAT I TELL YOU THREE TIMES IS TRUE" Lawful Residence and Equal Treatment after Dano', (2016) *Maastricht Journal of European and Comparative Law* 908–936. See also C O'Brien, 'Don't think of the children! CJEU approves automatic exclusions from family benefits in Case C-308/14 Commission v UK' in *EU Law Analysis Blog*, 16 June 2016, available at http://eulawanalysis.blogspot.com/2016/06/dont-think-of-children-cjeu-approves.html.

who do not meet it of cover under the social security legislation of one of the Member States, cover which that regulation is intended to ensure. The condition was, thusly, considered discriminatory and contrary to the spirit of the Regulation since it had regard only to the claimant's habitual residence.[61]

In response to those arguments, the UK, which relied on the *Brey* decision, maintained that the host State may lawfully require that social benefits be granted only to Union citizens who fulfil the conditions for possessing a right to reside in its territory, conditions which are, essentially, laid down in the Citizens' Directive. Furthermore, while acknowledging that the conditions conferring entitlement to the social benefits at issue are more easily satisfied by its own nationals (as they have, by definition, a right of residence), the UK maintains that in each case the condition requiring a right of residence is a proportionate measure for ensuring that the benefits are paid to persons sufficiently integrated in the UK.[62]

In its decision, the Court found, first of all, that the benefits at issue were social security benefits and therefore fell within the Regulation's scope.[63] However, the CJEU, following the Opinion of the AG Cruz Villalón,[64] rejected the Commission's arguments, and concluded that the action was to be dismissed in its entirety.

Firstly, the CJEU addressed the Commission's main argument that the UK legislation imposes a condition supplementing that of habitual residence contained in the Regulation. The Court pointed out that the criterion of habitual residence, within the meaning of the Regulation, was not a condition that must be met to qualify for benefits, but a '*conflict rule*' which was intended to prevent the concurrent application of a number of national legislative systems and to ensure that persons who have exercised their right of freedom of movement were not left without cover. According to the Court, the Regulation does not set up a common scheme of social security, but allows different national social security schemes to exist. It thus does not lay down the conditions creating the right to benefits, because it is in principle for the legislation of each Member State to lay down those conditions.[65]

---

61 Case C-308/14 *Commission v United Kingdom* ECLI:EU:C:2016:436, para 28.

62 Case C-308/14 *Commission v United Kingdom* ECLI:EU:C:2016:436, paras 38–39.

63 Case C-308/14 *Commission v United Kingdom* ECLI:EU:C:2016:436, para 61.

64 V. Case C-308/14 *Commission v United Kingdom [UK child benefit or child tax credit case]* ECLI:EU:C:2015:666, Opinion of AG Cruz Villalón.

65 Case C-308/14 *Commission v United Kingdom* ECLI:EU:C:2016:436, paras 62–67.

This approach to Regulation No 883/2004 seems to ignore that it also establishes some aspects of eligibility, and the principle of equal treatment between persons subject to the Regulation (Article 4). This means that the Regulation does establish some substantive general rules applicable to the different national social security schemes – which could be of importance in this case.[66]

The Court also quotes as the basis for this assessment the *Brey* and the *Dano* cases, stating that '*it is clear from the Court's case-law that there is nothing to prevent, in principle, the grant of social benefits to Union citizens who are not economically active being made subject to the requirement that those citizens fulfil the conditions for possessing a right to reside lawfully in the host Member State*'.[67] However, those cases address special non-contributory benefits, whereas the social benefits at issue in this case are 'social security benefits', as referred to in Article 3(1)(j) of Regulation No 883/2004, read in conjunction with Article 1(z) thereof.[68] Hence, despite the fact that the Court's analysis is consistent with the recent trend in case-law (i.e. *Dano*) which has found that Member States retain the competence to refuse to grant social assistance benefits to EU migrants who are not exercising Treaty rights within a host Member State, it extends this approach to family benefits.

In both the *Brey* and the *Dano* cases, the classification of the benefits at issue in the proceedings as '*special non-contributory cash benefits*' is analysed and bears consequences for the regime applicable[69]. In *Brey*, the Court said that '*the nature of that benefit, which is the subject of the referring court's question, must be examined in the context of analysing this issue*' – which was the '*right to reside*'.[70] However, in the *UK child benefit or child tax credit* case, the Court does not concern itself with this classification – despite the fact that family benefits, as the ones at issue in the case, are social security bene-

66 O'Brien, 'The ECJ sacrifices EU citizenship in vain', 209–243; *Idem*, 'A failed Faustian pact' 824–827.

67 Case C-308/14 *Commission v United Kingdom* ECLI:EU:C:2016:436, para 68.

68 Case C-308/14 *Commission v United Kingdom* ECLI:EU:C:2016:436, para 61.

69 Case C-140/12 *Brey* ECLI:EU:C:2013:565, paras 33–45, and Case C-333/13 *Dano* ECLI:EU:C:2014:2358, paras 46–55.

70 Case C-140/12 *Brey* ECLI:EU:C:2013:565, para 30. V. 'whether a Member State may refuse to grant the compensatory supplement to nationals of other Member States on the grounds that (…) they do not, despite having been issued with a certificate of residence, meet the necessary requirements for obtaining the legal right to reside on the territory of that Member State for a period of longer than three months, since, in order to obtain that right, the person concerned must have sufficient resources not to apply for, inter alia, the compensatory supplement.'

fits and do not fall within the '*social assistance*' exclusions of Citizens' Directive, as is the case of '*special non-contributory cash benefits*'. One can also see that there is some incongruity in applying a limitation to the equal treatment provision in Regulation No 883/2004 which was developed within the context of the Citizens' Directive, which has a specific scope (the right of citizens of the Union and their family members to move and reside freely within the territory of the Member States), to a different legal act, the Regulation No 883/2004, which has a different scope. In fact, the personal scope of the Regulation is broader, including anyone who are or have been subject to the legislation of one or more Member States on matters of social security, independently of the exercise of the right to move, and including non-economically active persons[71]. The scope of the benefits included in both the Citizens' Directive and Regulation No 883/2004 is also different.[72]

The *Brey* test is apparently extended to all benefits, irrespective of their classification allowing for the application of the discriminatory '*right to reside*' condition without any specific provision in the Treaty or secondary law excluding Union citizens from equal treatment in this case.

Alternatively, the Commission contended that the introduction of the right to reside test in the national legislation inevitably results in direct, or at least indirect, discrimination, prohibited by Article 4 of Regulation No 883/2004. The CJEU admitted that the condition requiring a right to reside in the UK gave rise to unequal treatment because UK nationals could satisfy it more easily than nationals of the other Member States, which constituted indirect discrimination.[73] In order for this discrimination to be justified, according to the Court's case law, it must be appropriate for securing the attainment of a legitimate objective and cannot go beyond what is necessary to attain that objective. The Court states that the '*need to protect the finances of the host Member State justifies in principle the possibility of checking whether residence is lawful when a social benefit is granted in particular to persons from other Member States who are not economically active, as such grant could have consequences for the overall level of assistance which may be accorded by that State*'.[74] In this regard, the Court found that the UK authorities verified whether residence is lawful in accordance with the conditions laid down in the Citizens' Directive. Thus, this verification was considered to

---

71 V. Recital 42 of the Regulation No 883/2004.

72 O'Brien, 'The ECJ sacrifices EU citizenship in vain' 209–243; *Id*, 'A failed Faustian pact' 824–827.

73 Case C-308/14 *Commission v United Kingdom* ECLI:EU:C:2016:436, paras 76–78.

74 Case C-308/14 *Commission v United Kingdom* ECLI:EU:C:2016:436, para 80.

not be carried out systematically by the UK authorities for each claim, but only in the event of doubt. It followed that the condition does not go beyond what is necessary to attain the legitimate objective pursued by the UK, namely the need to protect its finances.

Furthermore, the Court considered that the Commission did not provide evidence or arguments showing that the measure does not satisfy the conditions of proportionality, that it is not appropriate for securing the attainment of the objective of protecting public finances or that it goes beyond what is necessary to attain that objective,[75] and concluded that the UK can require recipients of child benefit and child tax credit to have a right to reside in the UK.

One can say, however, that this reasoning is moot, because the condition is directly discriminatory. According to the *Grzelczyk* decision, the application of a condition to legally resident non-nationals when no such condition applies to nationals of the host Member State was recognized as being directly discriminatory and violating the provisions of EU citizenship. In the *UK child benefit or child tax credit* case the legislation at hand whilst the right to reside in the UK – which was conditional to be entitled to certain social benefits – is conferred on all UK nationals, in the circumstances prescribed in the Citizens' Directive, nationals of other Member States are not considered to have a right to reside. This means, to all effect, that only non-national EU citizens residing in the UK must provide evidence of a right to reside.[76]

Besides that, the Court accepted as legitimate the UK's Government justification of the '*need to protect the finances of the host Member State*' without requiring evidence of a threat to public finances posed by the granting of social benefits to persons from other Member States who are not economically active. The Court did not question if the condition imposed was in itself appropriate or proportional, only the verification procedures.

Finally, in cases where discrimination was found to result from a legal regime, the burden to demonstrate that their actions were justified lied usually with the potential infringer. It was up to the Member State, not the Commission, to prove that they are pursuing a legitimate aim, that the means are proportionate and appropriate, and do not go beyond what is necessary.[77]

---

75 Case C-308/14 *Commission v United Kingdom* ECLI:EU:C:2016:436, para 85.

76 O'Brien, 'The ECJ sacrifices EU citizenship in vain' 209–243; *Id*, 'A failed Faustian pact' 824–827.

77 V., *v.g.*, Case C-237/94 *O'Flynn*ECLI:EU:C:1996:206, paras 15 and 26, and Case C-379/87 *Groener* ECLI:EU:C:1989:599, paras 15–18.

The *UK child benefit or child tax credit* case will probably never be considered one of the greatest decisions of the CJEU.[78] The Court does not give full weight, in its reasoning, to Article 18 TFEU or Article 4 of Regulation 883/2004, the appropriateness and proportionality of the right to reside test (even in the context of *Brey*), or the consequences to EU citizenship. It was broadly criticised by legal experts[79] and, despite its timing, appears to have failed to convince a substantial number of UK voters to vote to remain in the EU. It can be seen as deeply connected with the Brexit procedure and with the discussion on the 'financial effects' of 'benefit tourism' – representing a further step in the road started with the *Dano/Alimanovic* case law which can have widespread ramifications on the social rights of EU citizens and the freedom to move.

IV. *The evolution of the case-law after the UK child benefit or child tax credit case*

In the *Gusa* case[80] the Court decided on the status of self-employed non-national EU citizens who became involuntary unemployed, namely if they maintain their status if they have worked for more than a year in their host

78 J Paju, 'On the Lack of Legal Reasoning in Case C-308/14, European Commission v United Kingdom' (2019) 48(1) *Industrial LawJournal*, 117–136.

79 O'Brien, 'The ECJ sacrifices EU citizenship in vain' 209–243; *Id*, 'A failed Faustian pact' 824–827.

80 Case C-442/16 *Gusa* ECLI:EU:C:2017:1004. The case concerned Mr Gusa, a Romanian national who moved to Ireland in October 2007. From October 2008 until October 2012, he worked as a self-employed plasterer and, on that basis, paid taxes in Ireland, as well as pay-related social insurance. In October 2012, due to an absence of work caused by the economic downturn in Ireland, he had to cease work and register as a jobseeker and applied for a jobseeker's allowance in November 2014. His application for jobseeker's allowance was refused on the basis that the provision for retaining worker status under Article 7(3)(b) of Directive 2004/38 only applied to employed persons and excludes those who have worked as self-employed persons. According to the Irish authorities, Mr Gusa no longer had a right to reside in Ireland because he had ceased his activities as a 'self-employed' person and could therefore not rely on the same protection awarded to regularly 'employed' persons on the basis of Article 7(3)(b) of the Citizens' Directive. The right to retain worker status after having worked for more than one year – granting the right to reside and equal treatment –, as interpreted by the Irish authorities was reserved exclusively for EU citizens working under an employment contract.

Member State, thereby retaining a right to reside and access to social benefits.

Article 7(3) of the Citizens Directive addresses both workers and self-employed persons when granting the right to retain their status in various circumstances. This includes the situation 'when he/she is in duly recorded involuntary unemployment after having been employed for more than one year and has registered as a job seeker with the relevant employment office' (Article 7(3)(b) of the Citizens' Directive). The question was, therefore, whether the phrase '*after having been employed*' only applied to employed persons and excludes those who have worked as self-employed persons.[81]

The Court provides a broad interpretation of '*involuntary unemployment*', stating that this should not be limited to a dismissal of an employee, but also refers to a situation in which the occupational activity – whether employed or self-employed – has ceased 'due to an absence of work for reasons beyond the control of the person concerned, such as an economic recession'.[82] The CJEU continues, stating that, although the phrase 'after having been employed' was used in the English language version of Article 7(3)(b), other language versions were formulated in more neutral terms, relating to a person who had been in an 'occupational activity'; and that the Directive drew a distinction between economically active citizens and inactive citizens and students (Article 7(1) but it did not draw a distinction between '*workers and self-employed persons*'. The structure of Article 7(3) is meant to grant both categories of persons the right to retain their status in the four listed situations.[83]A different interpretation would run counter to the Directive's objective to remedy the '*piecemeal approach*' that characterized the earlier legislation and would introduce an unjustified difference in the treatment between employed and self-employed persons.[84]

In this case, then, the Court did decide in favour of a broader interpretation of the Citizens' Directive than the Member States' in question proposed, which can be seen as opposed to the *Dano*, *Alimanovic*, and *Garcia-Nieto* cases. However, the judgment is still in line with this previous case law.[85] The Court once again emphasises the importance of economic activity, stating that the '*difference in treatment*' in this case '*would be particularly*

81 Case C-442/16 Gusa ECLI:EU:C:2017:1004, paras 26–29.
82 Case C-442/16 Gusa ECLI:EU:C:2017:1004, para 31.
83 Case C-442/16 *Gusa* ECLI:EU:C:2017:1004, paras. 32–38.
84 Case C-442/16 *Gusa*ECLI:EU:C:2017:1004, paras. 41–44.
85 AG Wathelet expressly rejected a connection between the cases stating that whereas the *Dano*, *Alimanovic*, and *Garcia-Nieto* cases "wereprimarilyconcernednotwith-

unjustified in so far as it would lead to a person who has been self-employed for more than one year in the host Member State, and who has contributed to that Member State's social security and tax system by paying taxes, rates and other charges on his income, being treated in the same way as a first time jobseeker in that Member State who has never carried on an economic activity in that State and has never contributed to that system'. [86] The question here is, once again, the economic status of the citizens and, specially, if they '*earned*' their social rights by paying their way into their host welfare system.[87] No reference to Union citizenship as a 'fundamental status' is made.

In the following year the Court decided a case on the ability of accession State nationals to access social welfare rights during the accession period established in the 2003 Act of Accession[88] – it was the *Prefeta* case.[89] The Court held that Chapter 2 of Annex XII to the referred Act had to be interpreted as permitting, during the transitional period, the United Kingdom to exclude a Polish national such as Mr Prefeta from the benefits of Article

---

theissueoftherightofresidencebutwiththespecificquestionoftheright to receive social benefits in the host State", in the *Gusa*case "the question referred to the Court relates first and foremost to the legality of residence". Case C-442/16 *Gusa* ECLI:EU:C:2017:607, Opinion of AG Wathelet, paras. 54–56.

86 Case C-442/16 *Gusa* ECLI:EU:C:2017:1004, para 44.

87 D Kramer, 'A Right to Reside for the Unemployed Self-Employed: The Case Gusa (C-442/16)' in europeanlawblog.eu/2018/01/10/a-right-to-reside-for-the-unemployed-self-employed-the-case-gusa-c-444216/. V. also J-Y Carlier / G Renaudière, 'Libre circulation des personnes dans l'Union européenne' (2018) *Journal de droit européen*141–151.

88 The Act concerning the conditions of accession of the Czech Republic, the Republic of Estonia, the Republic of Cyprus, the Republic of Latvia, the Republic of Lithuania, the Republic of Hungary, the Republic of Malta, the Republic of Poland, the Republic of Slovenia and the Slovak Republic and the adjustments to the Treaties on which the European Union is founded (OJ 2003 L 236).

89 Case C-618/16 *Prefeta* ECLI:EU:C:2018:719. Rafal Prefeta is a Polish national who was resident and employed in the United Kingdom during the transitional period, and the extension to that period, following the accession of Poland to the EU. He was legally required under domestic transitional provisions made under the Accession Treaty to register his employment. Under the 2003 Act of Accession, Member States were entitled to restrict access to rights under Articles 1–6 of Regulation (EU) No 492/2011 of the European Parliament and of the Council of 5 April 2011 on freedom of movement for workers within the Union (OJ 2011 L 141, p. 1) to Polish workers who had not been admitted to the labour market for 12 months. Mr Prefeta completed more than 12 months' employment, but only approximately two months of it were registered. After he was injured at work and became involuntarily unemployed, the question arose whether he could rely on retained rights under Article 7(3) of the Citizens Directive to access social advantages under Article 7(2) of the Regulation.

7(3) of the Citizens Directive when that person did not satisfy the requirement imposed by national law of having completed an uninterrupted 12-month period of registered work in the UK. The UK's exclusion of such individuals from the benefits of Article 7(3) of the Citizens Directive was, thus, considered lawful.[90] The Court, in this case, affirmed that the retention of the right of residence *'covers situations in which the EU citizen's re-entry on the labour market of the host Member State is foreseeable within a reasonable period'*.[91] The connexion between the right of residence and economic status of the person is once again central to the case.

Finally, the CJEU ruling in *Tarola*,[92] responding to a preliminary reference from the Irish Court of Appeal, interprets Article 7(3)(c) of the Citizens Directive. The question was, in the words of the AG Szpunar: '*Where a citizen of the Union exercises his right of free movement and residence in accordance with [the Citizens Directive] and works in a Member State other than his own for a period of two weeks, and becomes involuntarily unemployed, does that citizen retain the status of worker and, therefore, the corresponding right of residence?*'.[93]

Article 7(3)(c) of the Citizens Directive provides for the status of worker, whether employed or self-employed, to be retained, for no less than six months, in two situations: *i)* '*the worker was employed under a fixed-term employment contract of less than a year and became involuntarily unemployed at the end of that contract*'; or *ii)* '*after having become involuntarily unemployed during the first twelve months and has registered as a job seeker with the relevant employment office*'. The Court considered that this

---

90 S Cazet, 'Le retour du ‚plombier polonais': l'acte d'adhésion de 2003 permet bien au Royaume-Uni d'imposer des restrictions aux travailleurs polonais', (2018) 11 Europe 17–18.

91 Case C-618/16 *Prefeta* ECLI:EU:C:2018:719, para 39.

92 Case C-483/17*Tarola* ECLI:EU:C:2019:309. Mr. Tarola is a Romanian national who first arrived in Ireland in May 2007 where he was employed for periods of time in 2007, 2013 and 2014. He also worked as a self-employed subcontractor during a period of time in 2014. In 2013 and 2014 he applied to the Irish Minister for Social Protection for jobseeker's and supplementary welfare allowances. Both applications were refused on the ground that he had failed to produce evidence of his habitual residence in Ireland or means of support. On 6 November 2014, Mr. Tarola submitted a second application for jobseeker's allowance, which was again refused on the grounds that, since coming to Ireland, he had not worked for more than a year and the evidence produced was insufficient to establish Ireland as his habitual residence. Mr. Tarola argued that he had the right to reside in Ireland for the six months following a two-week period of employment in July 2014 under Article 7(3)(c) of the Citizens Directive.

93 Case C-483/17*Tarola* ECLI:EU:C:2018:919, Opinionof AG Szpunar, para 1.

> 'provision does not specify whether it applies to employed or self-employed persons or to both categories of worker or whether it concerns fixed-term contracts of more than a year, contracts of indefinite duration or any type of contract or activity, or, lastly, whether the 12 months to which it refers relate to the period of residence or the period of employment of the worker concerned in the host Member State'.[94]

Hence, in interpreting that provision, the CJEU resorted 'not only its wording, but also the context in which it occurs and the objectives pursued by the rules of which it is part', as well as its 'origins'.[95]

With regard to context, the Court analysed Article 7 and concluded that while the Citizens Directive '*establishes a gradation with regard to the duration of the right of all Union citizens to reside in the host Member State, by providing, between the right of residence for up to three months referred to in Article 6 thereof and the right of permanent residence referred to in Article 16 thereof, for a right of residence for more than three months, which is governed by the provisions of Article 7*' (3) of this provision also establishes a gradation with regard to the conditions for retaining their status of worker and, consequently, their right to reside in the host Member State. That gradation is made by reference to,

> 'first, the reason for the citizen's inability to work, in the case in point depending on whether he is unable to work because of illness or accident, involuntary unemployment or vocational training, and, second, the initial duration of his period of activity in the host Member State, that is, depending on whether that is longer or shorter than one year'.

An EU citizen '*who has pursued an activity in an employed or self-employed capacity in the host Member State for a period of less than one year retains his status of worker only for a period of time which that Member State may determine, provided it is no less than six months*'.[96]

The Court's conclusion was that the provision allows retention of the status for workers 'in all situations in which a worker has been obliged, for reasons beyond his control, to stop working in the host Member State be-

94 Case C-483/17*Tarola* ECLI:EU:C:2019:309, para 35.

95 Case C-483/17*Tarola* ECLI:EU:C:2019:309, para 37.

96 Case C-483/17*Tarola* ECLI:EU:C:2019:309, paras 41–43, 45, quotingCase C-483/17*Tarola* ECLI:EU:C:2018:919, Opinion of AG Szpunar, para 33.

fore one year has elapsed, regardless of the nature of the activity or the type of employment contract entered into for that purpose'.[97]

This interpretation was considered consistent with '*the principal objective pursued by*' the Citizens Directive: '*to strengthen the right of free movement and residence of all Union citizens, and with the objective specifically pursued by Article 7(3) thereof, which is to safeguard, by the retention of the status of worker, the right of residence of persons who have ceased their occupational activity because of an absence of work due to circumstances beyond their control*',[98] while, at the same time, not undermining '*the achievement of one of the other objectives pursued (…) striking a fair balance between safeguarding the free movement of workers, on the one hand, and ensuring that the social security systems of the host Member State are not placed under an unreasonable burden, on the other*'.[99]

In terms of origins, the Court examined the *travaux préparatoires* of the Citizens Directive, concluding that the '*intention of the EU legislature to extend the benefit of retention of the status of worker, limited, as the case may be, to six months, to persons in involuntary unemployment after having worked for less than a year otherwise than under a fixed-term employment contract*'.[100]

In the final part of the decision, the CJEU states that '*all Union citizens residing on the basis of that directive in the territory of the host Member State, including those retaining their status of worker or self-employed person under Article 7(3)(c) of that directive, enjoy equal treatment with the nationals of that Member State within the scope of the FEU Treaty, subject to such specific provisions as are expressly provided for in the Treaty and secondary law*'. However, following the Opinion of the AG, the Court also states that '*where national law excludes persons who have worked in an employed or self-employed capacity only for a short period of time from the entitlement to social benefits, that exclusion applies in the same way to workers from other Member States who have exercised their right of free movement*'.[101]

The Court, in its last *dictum*, draws a boundary between right to equal treatment, which is derived from the right to residence, and entitlement to social assistance. The fact that a non-national EU citizen retains the status

---

97 Case C-483/17*Tarola* ECLI:EU:C:2019:309, para 48.

98 Case C-483/17*Tarola* ECLI:EU:C:2019:309, para 49, quoting Case C-67/14 *Alimanovic* EU:C:2015:597, para 60; Case C-299/14 *García-Nieto* EU:C:2016:114, para 47; Case C-442/16 *Gusa* EU:C:2017:1004, para 42.

99 Case C-483/17*Tarola* ECLI:EU:C:2019:309, para 50.

100 Case C-483/17*Tarola* ECLI:EU:C:2019:309, para 53.

101 Case C-483/17*Tarola* ECLI:EU:C:2019:309, paras 55–56, quoting Case C-483/17 *Tarola* ECLI:EU:C:2018:919, Opinion of AG Szpunar, para 55.

of worker, and the corresponding right to reside, means that he/she should be treated by the host State as a national. Member States remain free to exclude from benefits, the workers that have worked for less time, as long as the scope of the exclusion encompasses national as well as non-national EU citizens. As in the *Gusa* case, despite the fact that the outcome appears to be favourable to the worker's access to benefits, there is an underlying concern with the objective to ensure that the Member States' social security and social assistance systems are not placed under an undue burden.[102] Once again, no reference to Union citizenship as a '*fundamental status*' is made.

V. Critical Analysis

The *Dano*, *Alimanovic*, *García-Nieto*, and *UK child benefit or child tax credit* string of decisions seems to represent a significant change in the CJEU earlier jurisprudence on non-national EU citizens' access to social benefits in host Member States. This seems not to have changed in more recent cases *Gusa*, *Prefeta*, and *Tarola*.

In the pre-*Dano* case-law, the reasoning of judgments on Union citizenship had their starting point in the Treaty, bore in mind the proportionality principle and imposed an individual assessment of the person at issue. The Citizens' Directive (and other secondary legislation) was interpreted in that light. This changed with the *Dano-Alimanovic* methodology, which is based on the assertion that '*a Union citizen may claim equal treatment with nationals of the host Member State under Article 24(1) of Directive 2004/38 only if his residence in the territory of that State complies with the conditions of that directive*'.[103] Hence, in the post-*Dano* case-law, the CJEU appears to have replaced its previous focus on the interpretation of the Treaties, with a literal (even an *ad pedem litterae*) interpretation of the Citizens' Directive.

102 F Strumia, 'Unemployment, residence rights, social benefits at three crossroads in the Tarola ruling', in *EU Law Analysis Blog*, 13 April 2019, available at eulawanalysis.blogspot.com/2019/04/unemployment-residence-rights-social.html.

103 Case C-67/14 *Alimanovic* ECLI:EU:C:2015:597, para 49. See A. Farahat, 'Solidarität und Inklusion. Umstrittene Dimensionen der Unionsbürgerschaft' (2016) 45 *Die Öffentliche Verwaltung* 45–55; C. O'Brien, 'Civis capitalist sum: Class as the new guiding principle of EU free movement rights' (2016) 53 *Common Market Law Review* 937, 943 ff, 961 ff., 973 ff.; E Spaventa, 'Earned Citizenship: Understanding Union Citizenship Through Its Scope', in D Kochenov (ed.), *EU Citizenship and Federalism: The Role of Rights* (Cambridge University Press, 2017); D Thym, 'The Elusive limits of solidarity' 25.

The previous focus on strengthening the right of free movement and residence of all EU citizens as the main objective of the Citizen Directive has been replaced by the Court with the need to strike '*a fair balance between safeguarding the free movement of workers, on the one hand, and ensuring that the social security systems of the host Member State are not placed under an unreasonable burden on the other*'.[104]

The change seems to have its roots in the discussions on the power of Member States to limit the possibility of non-national EU citizens to claim benefits in a host Member State, especially in the case of the non-economically active citizens, which has also framed the Brexit debate.[105] The discussion is posed in terms of '*benefit tourism*' and presented as a phenomenon linked to east-west migration within the EU, which is also read as the movement of poor EU citizens to the more affluent Member States.[106] It can also be seen as the vindication of the push back of Member States against the CJEU's initially generous interpretation of EU citizenship rights in the field of social benefits. The CJEU has entered was has been interpreted as a '*reactionary*' phase in its citizenship case law in the context of the European economic crisis in the late 2000s.[107] The explanation for that can be found on the responsiveness of the Judges to the political preferences of Member State governments but also on the broader EU political context, with this issue having become increasingly politicized, public opinion and political concerns are reflected in the Court's case law.[108]

---

104 Case C-483/17 *Tarola* ECLI:EU:C:2019:309, para 50.

105 V., v.g., G Davies, 'Migrant Union Citizens and Social Assistance: Trying to Be Reasonable About Self-Sufficiency' (2016) 2 *Research Paper in Law*, European Legal Studies, College of Europe; A Hofmann, 'Resistance against the Court of Justice of theEuropean Union' (2018) 14 *International Journal of Law in Context*, 258–274. On the responsiveness of the CJEU to criticism of its case-law by academics and also of media and governments as a part of a dialogic character of jurisprudence, v. I Pernice, 'CJEU Jurisprudence and the Audience: Making Law in a Public Discourse – Ten Years after CJEU Case C-144/04 Mangold v Helm', in J Czuczai and F Naert (eds) The EU as a Global Actor – Bridging Legal Theory and Practice, Liber Amicorum in honour of Ricardo Gosalbo Bono (Leiden, Brill | Nijhoff,2017), 111–144.

106 S Mantu/P Minderhoud, 'EU citizenship and social solidarity' (2017) 24(5) *Maastricht Journal of European and Comparative Law*, 703–720, 719.

107 A Hofmann, 'Resistance against the Court of Justice of the European Union' 269; E. Spaventa, 'Earned Citizenship'.

108 M Blauberger/A Heindlmaier/D Kramer/ DS Martinsen/JMS Thierry/S Angelika/B Werner, 'ECJ judges read the morning papers. Explaining the turn around of European citizenship jurisprudence', (2018) 25 (10) *Journal of European Public Policy*,1422–1441.

However, the change – and, especially, the *UK child benefit or child tax credit* case – seems to have been in vain in terms of influencing the Brexit referendum outcome.[109]

Despite the apparent change in the approach of the Court to such cases, some deny its existence. In his Opinion in the *Gusa* case, AG Wathelet states that there was no '*about-turn in the approach to understanding Directive 2004/38*' in the *Dano* case. According to him, the importance that is attached in that case '*to the secondary objective pursued by Directive 2004/38*', is due to '*the subject matter of the request for a preliminary ruling which had been submitted to it*'. After all, the cases which gave rise to the three judgments cited in the previous point in this Opinion [*Dano*, *Alimanovic*, *García-Nieto*] were primarily concerned not with the issue of the right of residence but with the specific question of the right to receive social benefits in the host State. This was therefore a question which had arisen at a point in time subsequent to the exercise of freedom of movement but was nonetheless indissociable from the legality of residence.[110] However, this approach by the AG seems somewhat contradictory because if the cases are different, there would be no need to sustain that there was any change in the case-law. At the same time, if one admits that the question of the right to receive social benefits in the host State was, in those cases, '*indissociable from the legality of residence*', one must see that there is a connection with the previous line of judicial reasoning and a new importance that is being given to '*preventing Union citizens who are nationals of other Member States from becoming an unreasonable burden on the social assistance system of the host Member State*'.[111]

Others sustain that the explanation for the change in case-law lies in the changing characteristics of the litigants themselves, that recent claims for social assistance are based on less meritorious facts.[112] However, that conclusion does not seem to hold if the same methodology is applied in similar cases before and after the perceived change in the jurisprudence of the CJEU – as is the case with the *Commission v Austria*[113] and *Commission v the*

109 O'Brien, 'The ECJ sacrifices EU citizenship in vain', 209–243.

110 Case C-442/16 *Gusa* ECLI:EU:C:2017:607, Opinion of AG Wathelet, paras. 54–56.

111 Case C-333/13 *Dano* ECLI:EU:C:2014:2358, para 74.

112 G Davies, 'Has the Court changed, or have the cases? The deservingness of litigants as an element in Court of Justice citizenship adjudication' (2018) 25 (10) Journal of European Public Policy, 1442–1460.

113 Case C-75/11 *Commission v Austria [reduced fares on public transport granted to students]* ECLI:EU:C:2012:605.

Netherlands[114] cases. Both these judgements deal with financial support for travel costs awarded to students and had different results, which means that the same benefit with a similar hypothetical user base was awarded a different legal treatment in the space of a few years. To claim that the Court has been consistent and there has been merely a change in the characteristics of the claimants does not seem to be supported by sufficient evidence.[115]

Finally, it has also been sustained that *Dano* and *Alimanovic* are not revolutionary cases but, instead, the result of a natural evolution of the case law following the introduction of the Citizens Directive and that the reasoning and outcomes of the decisions, despite some minor details are on the whole convincing.[116] This is more a criticism of the presentation of the cases as entirely surprising, than of the fact that such evolution occurred. By presenting the CJEU as merely accepting the political choices made by the EU legislature, and applying such rules as laid down in secondary legislation, it forgets the place of the Court as the '*Constitutional Court*' of the EU, in charge of checking the legality of such choices.

Despite this position, there is empirical evidence that the recent case law of the CJEU in *Brey*, *Dano*, *Alimanovic*, *Garcia-Nieto* and *UK child benefit or child tax credit* cases has drastically changed the landscape concerning access to social assistance benefits for inactive EU citizens.[117]

There is also an abandonment of the *Brey* decision in the *Dano* case law. In this decision the Court found that EU law precluded the automatic barring of economically inactive persons from entitlement to benefits without assessment of their individual circumstances, including the duration of residence, amount of income, amount and duration of benefit claimed and other relevant circumstances. A proportionality approach was adopted, which allowed for some differentiation between the possible wide range of claims of varying degrees of reasonableness. In the mentioned recent cases no proportionality test, case-by-case assessment, or individual assessment of

---

114 Case C-233/14 *Commission v the Netherlands [financial support for travel costs awarded to national students]* ECLI:EU:C:2016:396.

115 A Hoogenboom, 'CJEU case law on EU citizenship: normatively consistent? Unlikely! – A response to Davies' 'Has the Court changed, or have the cases?', in *EU Law Analysis Blog*, 13 November 2018, at eulawanalysis.blogspot.com/2018/11/cjeu-case-law-on-eu-citizenship.html.

116 D Carter / M Jesse, 'The "Dano Evolution": Assessing Legal Integration and Access to Social Benefits for EU Citizens' (2018) 3(3) European Papers, 1179–1208.

117 P Minderhoud, 'Social Assistance for Economically Inactive EU Citizens in the Member States' (2018) 3 Nijmegen Migration Law Working Papers Series, 28.

personal circumstances was made. This is especially notable in the *Alimanovic* case, where a bold contradiction of the *Brey* test can be found. The Court did not use the *Grzelczyk* characterisation of the European citizenship as '*the fundamental status of nationals*'; did not engage with the doctrine of EU citizenship; and made no reference to Article 20 TEU. The Citizens' Directive seems to be viewed by the CJEU as already creating a system of individual assessment taking into consideration various factors characterising the individual situation. The Court also made no mention to the fact that Ms. Alimanovic is the primary carer of minor children, in contradiction with previous case law.[118]

The *UK child benefit or child tax credit* case provides proof that this evolution of the CJEU case law is emerging as a general trend.[119] In this decision, the CJEU did not engage with the *Brey* test, seemingly accepting that automatic exclusion was lawful: '*As the United Kingdom submitted at the hearing, legality of the claimant's residence in its territory is a substantive condition which economically inactive persons must meet in order to be eligible for the social benefits at issue*'.[120] This is especially striking because it seems to represent a departure from the proportionality test usually associated with the 'real link' case law. *Martinez Sala*, *Grzelczyk*, *Trojani*, *Bidar* and *Förster*, all cited in the *Brey* case,[121] precluded the use of automatic exclusion rules, requiring some assessment of circumstances of the case.[122] It is impressive that the *UK child benefit or child tax credit* decision at the same time is based on and directly contradicts the *Brey* decision.

There are positive aspects to this new line of reasoning by the Court. The *Dano/Alimanovic* case law represents a noteworthy shift of emphasis, accentuating the protection of Member States' interests and a new-found respect to national legislatures.[123] Member States should be free to determine the material conditions and levels of benefit of their social security systems as part of the non-harmonisation principle[124]. It also bears in mind

118 Case C-310/08 *Ibrahim* ECLI:EU:C:2010:80, and Case C-480/08 *Teixeira* ECLI:EU:C:2010:83.

119 Paju, 'On the Lack of Legal Reasoning in Case C-308/14, European Commission v United Kingdom', 117–136; Carter / Jesse, 'The "Dano Evolution"', 1205.

120 Case C-308/14 *Commission v United Kingdom* ECLI:EU:C:2016:436, para 72.

121 Case C-140/12 *Brey* ECLI:EU:C:2013:565, para 44.

122 O'Brien, 'The ECJ sacrifices EU citizenship in vain' 209–243; *Idem*, 'A failed Faustian pact' 824–827.

123 D Thym, 'The Elusive limits of solidarity' 25.

124 F Pennings, EU citizenship: access to social benefits in other EU member states, *International Journal of Comparative Labour Law and Industrial Relations* 28 (2012), 307–334.

the financial soundness and sustainability of the Member State's social security systems, which are commonly based on principles of solidarity within national borders. The previous case-law was criticised for undermining the national social policy compromises and imposing unsustainable burdens on the welfare systems of Member States.[125]

Moreover, the Court refuses to read the Citizens' Directive extensively or creatively, respecting the will of the EU legislature. This is extremely important: it should be the democratically legitimised EU legislator rather than the CJEU to take the main responsibility in balancing the individual rights of EU citizens against the financial-political interests of the Member States to maintain social assistance systems.[126] The new line of case law also establishes clear criteria to access to benefits, providing legal certainty. The Member States and the EU citizens can now trust that the Court will follow a literal interpretation of the Directive instead of performing an individual assessment test of the case, which lead to results considered unpredictable and uncertain.[127]

Despite these positive aspects, formal and substantive criticisms can be made of this new trend in the CJEU case-law. As for the formal criticism, one can challenge the method used by the Court in overruling its previous judgments. Usually, this is done by means of evolutive interpretation. Arguably, in this case we have an instance of evolution of interpretation which lowers rather than heightens human rights protection. Although this is not unprecedented in the Court's history, one can argue that the Court needs serious reasons to depart from its own case-law not only in cases of '*progressive*' evolution but especially in opposite cases. On more than one occasion the Court itself has pointed out that evolutive interpretation should be justified by particularly strong reasons. However, the Court changed its methodology without admitting the reversal of the earli-

125 V., v.g. K Hailbronner, 'Union citizens and access to social benefits' (2005) 42 *Common Market Law Review*, p. 1245; AJ Menéndez, 'European Citizenship after Martinez Sala and Baumbast: Has European Law Become More Human but Less Social?' in M Poiares Maduro / L Azoulai (eds), *The Past and Future of EU Law. The Classics of EU Law Revisited on the 50th Anniversary of the Rome Treaty* (Oxford, Hart, 2010) p 391; M Blauberger/ SK Schmidt, 'Welfare migration? Free movement of EU citizens and access to social benefits' (2014) 1 *Research and Politics*, 1–7.

126 AP van der Mei, 'Overview of Recent Cases before the Court of Justice of the European Union (July-December 2015)' 77.

127 S.O'leary, 'Developing an Ever Closer Union Between the Peoples of Europe? A reappraisal of the case-law of the Court of Justice on the free movement of persons and EU citizenship' (2008) *Yearbook of European Law* 182.

er doctrine and once again without a specific reasoning justifying the change.

Besides, the new case law states that, in terms of access to social assistance, EU citizens can only claim equal treatment if their residence in the territory of the host State complies with the conditions to lawfully reside there, established in the Citizens Directive. This focus on the provisions of the Citizens' Directive means that the claim of equal treatment, which is established in the Treaties, is dependent on conditions set in secondary law. Restrictions to the right to reside established in Article 21 TFEU can also result from secondary legislation. In these cases, fundamental freedoms, recognised in the Treaties, are restricted by secondary legislation without the Court's reviewing the conformity of these restrictions with the Treaties – which are the parameters of the EU's rule of law – for instance, through a proportionality test. The right to equal treatment between European citizens (Article 18 TFEU) can be questioned on the basis of secondary legislation without any control.

The positive aspect of the shift of emphasis of the Court with the *Dano/ Alimanovic* case law, accentuating Member State interests, could represent also the abandonment of countervailing constitutional arguments that could have justified a different outcome[128]. The idea of solidarity between Member States and an emphatic defence of the right to move and to reside could be examples of arguments sacrificed.

Nobody denies that the Treaties and the Citizens' Directive trust the CJUE to define and control the limits of free movement. But the Court should be careful not to ignore implications for social cohesion in the internal market and the constitutional and sociological foundations of social policy and the importance of the freedom of movement of citizens (independently of being economically active or not) to the notion of EU citizenship. The Court's approach runs the risk of downplaying the risks of this reduction, in effect, of the scope of the freedom of movement to encompass merely economically active citizens.

The assessment of individual cases, burdensome as it was, served the wider objective '*to ensure that the grant of assistance* (…) [did] *not become an unreasonable burden which could have consequences for the overall level of assistance*'.[129] The '*exclusive focus on the Directive*' is problematic '*due to the lack*

128 D.Thym, 'The Elusive limits of solidarity' 25.
129 D Thym, 'The Elusive limits of solidarity' 32.

of individualised proportionality assessments, as well as an increasing range of social benefits that can be subjected to residence tests'.[130]

The change in the CJEU case-law can be especially criticised because it appears to have not been needed. The Court could have used criteria established in earlier judgments to exclude access to benefits in these cases.[131]

For example, in the *Dano* case, Advocate General Wathelet defended that the questions raised should be answered '*in the light of the principle of proportionality*' and of the case-law of the CJEU on the existence of a '*genuine link*' between Union citizens and the host Member State.[132] The Advocate General refers, more specifically, to the case law on the grant of assistance to students and social benefits for job seekers, from which he infers that the entitlement of economically inactive Union citizens to social assistance benefits '*is, in general, dependent on a certain degree of integration into the host Member State*'.[133] Also in the *Dano* case, the Court could have resorted to '*the excessive burden to the social security system of the host State*' criteria but, instead, chose as the reason to refuse access to benefits the non-fulfilment of residence requisites established in the Citizens' Directive.[134]

So, the CJEU could have made an evaluation of the national legislation in the light of the established jurisprudence, while arriving at the same conclusion (that the national legislation was compatible with the Treaties), but following a path which was coherent with its previous case law and with less erosion of the rights to move and to reside.

Additionally, the recent case law can also be criticised because of the absence of analysis of the cases in light of the EU Charter of Fundamental Rights. As was referred *supra*, the EU Charter of Fundamental Rights was deemed non-applicable in the *Dano* case. In fact, despite the clear statement, in the *Åkerberg Fransson* case, that the Charter was applicable in all

---

130 D Carter / M Jesse, 'The "Dano Evolution", 1182.

131 H Verschueren, 'Preventing "Benefit Tourism" in the EU' 363–390, p. 374.

132 Case C-333/13 *Dano* ECLI:EU:C:2014:341, Opinion AG Wathelet, para 126.

133 Case C-333/13 *Dano* ECLI:EU:C:2014:341, Opinion AG Wathelet, para 127–129. The Advocate General refers to this effect to the Case C-209/03 *Bidar* ECLI:EU:C:2005:169, para 56 and 57; Case C-158/07 *Förster* ECLI:EU:C:2008:63, paras 48 and 49; Case C-138/02 *Collins* ECLI:EU:C:2004:172, para 67; Case C-22/08 and C-23/08 *Vatsouras* ECLI:EU:C:2009:344, para 38; Case C-523/11 e C-585/11 *Prinz and Seeberger* ECLI:EU:C:2013:524, para 36; and Case C-220/12 *Thiele Meneses*, ECLI:EU:C:2013:683, para 35.

134 P Jiménez Blanco, 'Derecho de residência en la UniónEuropea y turismo social' (2015) 22 *La Ley Unión Europea* 11.

situations governed by European Union law[135], in the social rights area this clarity of purpose has eluded the Court.[136]

Also, the connection between fundamental rights and EU citizenship, established in decisions such as the *Rottmann*[137] or the *Ruiz Zambrano*[138] cases, has been read in a much more restrictive manner in the *Cholakova*[139] or *Ymeraga*[140] cases.[141] The convergence of these tendencies with the *Dano* case-law results in a deficit of protection of non-economically active Union citizens who seek access to social benefits.

The CJEU's judgments in *Dano*, *Alimanovic*, *García-Nieto* and *UK child benefit or child tax credit* introduced a level of ambiguity at the EU citizens' right to free movement and freedom to reside.

The right of an EU citizen to reside in a Member State other than its national State is made dependent on his/her ability to support themselves and their family in order to avoid becoming an unreasonable burden on the social security system of the host State. There is an implied duty to have sufficient resources and the economically inactive citizens can apparently see their right of movement restricted. In fact, the only relevant circumstance after *Alimanovic* is the duration of economic activity – not the existence of genuine link to the Member State or the family status. The *UK child benefit or child tax credit* decision extended this reasoning to all welfare benefits. EU citizenship is, therefore, once again related with worker status. That approach is maintained in the *Gusa* and *Tarola* cases. The result is

---

135 Case C-617/10 *ÅkerbergFransson* ECLI:EU:C:2013:105, para 19.

136 V., *v.g.*, Case C-265/13 *Torralbo Marcos* ECLI:EU:C:2014:187, paras 29–30, and 43; Case C-198/13 *Julian Hernández* ECLI:EU:C:2014:2055, paras 32–34, 37, and 48; Case C-117/14 *Ariza Toledano* ECLI:EU:C:2015:60, paras 28–29, and 42. In all these cases the Charter was considered not applicable. – For an analysis of the more recent decisions F Fontanelli, 'The implementation of European Union law by Member States under Article 51(1) of the Charter of Fundamental Rights' (2014) 20 (3) *The Columbia Journal of European Law*, 193–247; J Genberg, 'The scope of application of the Charter of Fundamental Rights of the European Union: quo vadimus?' (2014) 8 (1) *Helsinki Law Review* 31–60; F Wollenschläger, 'The EU Charter of Fundamental Rights and its Applicability to the Member States: A Step towards Unitarisation or Federalisation?' (2015) 13 *Ritsumeikan International Affairs* 1–12, 9–10.

137 Case C-135/08 *Rottman*, ECLI:EU:C:2010:104.

138 Case C-34/09 *Ruiz Zambrano* ECLI:EU:C:2011:124.

139 Case C-14/13 *Cholakova* ECLI:EU:C:2013:374, paras 28–29, 31.

140 Case C-87/12 *Ymeraga* ECLI:EU:C:2013:291, paras 40 and 43.

141 S Iglesias Sánchez, 'Fundamental Rights and Citizenship of the Union at a Crossroads. A Promising Alliance or a Dangerous Liaison' (2014) 20 (4) *European Law Journal*, 466–467.

that the notion of the EU citizenship as a fundamental and political status with no link with market economy is being dismantled. It also leads to the idea that EU citizenship *'virtually never protects the weak and the needy'* based on their human needs alone, merely informs the *'dogmatic ideal of a good market citizen'*.[142]

The *Dano* and *UK child benefit or child tax credit* line of cases can be seen as confirming that the CJEU now takes a back seat when it comes to protecting the legal status of economically inactive EU citizens.[143] The Court's analysis of the meaning of the Citizens Directive could be interpreted to the effect that Member States are allowed to refuse to pay any social benefits, including social security benefits, to economically inactive Union citizens who do not have the right to reside under that Directive, namely because they do not possess sufficient resources of their own.[144] It is solely up to the EU legislator, through the Citizens Directive to define the legal status of EU citizens. The CJEU no longer refers to EU citizenship as the *'fundamental status'* of citizens and seems no longer willing to use the TFEU's provisions on EU citizenship and the rights attached to it to interpret the Directive.

One may agree with the need to respect the will of the democratically legitimised legislator (national and European). However, if the EU is governed by the rule of law, it should be up to its highest Court to control the decisions of the legislatures, especially in times of socio-economic crisis. The Citizens' Directive cannot be seen as giving the Member States *carte blanche* to discriminate between EU citizens.

In this area, in fact, the EU legislator may be on the verge of intervening.

The Commission has adopted on 14 December 2016 a proposal for a Regulation amending Regulation No 883/2004[145], which is currently still under ordinary legislative procedure[146] and some of the changes proposed

142 D Kochenov, 'The Citizenship of Personal Circumstances in Europe', in D Thym (ed), *Questioning EU Citizenship* (Oxford,Hart, 2017), 37–56, 51.

143 AP van der Mei, 'Overview of Recent Cases before the Court of Justice of the European Union (July-December 2015)' 77.

144 H Verschueren, 'Preventing 'Benefit Tourism' in the EU' 378–379.

145 COM (2016) 815: Proposal for a Regulation of the European Parliament and of the Council amending Regulation (EC) No 883/2004 on the coordination of social security systems and regulation (EC) No 987/2009 laying down the procedure for implementing Regulation (EC) No 883/2004.

146 Procedure 2016/0397/COD.

are inspired by this line of case law. A new recital (5a) is to be inserted in the Regulation No 883/2004 stating that

> 'The Court of Justice has held that Member States are entitled to make the access of economically inactive citizens in the host Member State to social security benefits, which do not constitute social assistance within the meaning of Directive 2004/38/EC subject to a legal right of residence within the meaning of that Directive. The verification of the legal right of residence should be carried out in accordance with the requirement of Directive 2004/38/EC. For these purposes, an economically inactive citizen should be clearly distinguished from a jobseeker whose right of residence is conferred directly by Article 45 of the Treaty on the Functioning of the European Union. In order to improve legal clarity for citizens and institutions, a codification of this case law is necessary' (Article 1(1) of the Proposal).

According to the Proposal, '*the application of Directive 2004/38/EC to the Regulations has been elucidated by the jurisprudence of the Court of Justice in Cases C-140/12, Brey, EU:C:2013:565, C-333/13, Dano, EU:C:2014:2358 and C-308/14 Commission v United Kingdom, EU:C:2016:436*'.[147]

For this purpose, Article 4 of Regulation No 883/2004 is proposed to be amended. The current provision ('*Unless otherwise provided for by this Regulation, persons to whom this Regulation applies shall enjoy the same benefits and be subject to the same obligations under the legislation of any Member State as the nationals thereof.*') is to become Article 4 (1). Article 4 (2) will state, if the amendment is approved, that

> '2. A Member State may require that the access of an economically inactive person residing in that Member State to its social security benefits be subject to the conditions of having a right to legal residence as set out in Directive 2004/38/EC of the European Parliament and of the Council of 29 April 2004 on the right of citizens of the Union and their family members to move and reside freely within the territory of the Member States'.

Thusly, the *UK child benefit or child tax credit* decision is to become written law, a direct consequence of the UK 'Remain-Leave' referendum, effectively changing the interpretation of the principle of no discrimination to all the social benefits included in Regulation No 883/2004.

---

147 V. the Explanatory Memorandum of the Proposal, p. 9.

Several questions remain, leaving social solidarity as an element of EU citizenship at crossroads.[148]

What motivated this change? Is the CJEU being influenced by the political debates in the Member States on 'social tourism'? Is it another long-lasting effect of Brexit?[149] Or is the *Dano/Alimanovic* case law driven by the view that the previous EU citizenship case law is now seen as having been too judicially activist?[150] How far will the Court go? What is then left of the previous jurisprudence on this matter? How will the other institutions respond? Will the Citizens' Directive or Regulation No 883/2004 be amended in light of this?

If, in terms of access to social assistance, EU citizens can only claim equal treatment if their residence in the territory of the host State complies with the conditions to lawfully reside there, established in the Citizens' Directive, what happens to those EU citizens whose right to reside in the host Member State is based on other EU instruments, such as Article 45 TFEU as in the *Saint-Prix* case[151], or on national law which is more favourable than the Directive (as in the *Martínez Sala* and *Trojani* cases)? As Advocate General Wathelet pointed out, it is likely that the residence of non-national EU citizens will be jeopardised in the event of being excluded from entitlement to subsistence benefits. [152] However, the Court has drawn a clear distinction between the right to reside and the right to social benefits in the *Tarola* case. Without sufficient means of subsistence, the Union citizens could be considered "illegal", which means that a consequence of the *Dano* jurisprudence is to allow for EU citizens to be classified as "illegal migrants".[153] Can they be expelled?

Is a right to Member States to discriminate economically inactive citizens being recognised? A kind of licence to discriminate unwritten in the Treaties, but established in a Directive can be used to such an end?

One can accept that there are financial reasons shared and approved by all Member States, which justify restrictions to the principle of equal treatment regarding the granting of social assistance benefits to non-nationals residing in the territory of the host State. However, one cannot forget that,

---

148 Mantu/Minderhoud, 'EU citizenship and social solidarity' 720.

149 J Shaw, 'EU citizenship: Still a Fundamental Status?' in R Bauböck (ed) *Debating European Citizenship* (Luxembourg, Springer, 2019) 1–17.

150 AP van der Mei, 'Overview of Recent Cases before the Court of Justice of the European Union (July-December 2015)', 77.

151 Case C-507/12 *Saint Prix* ECLI:EU:C:2014:2007.

152 Case C-333/13 *Dano* ECLI:EU:C:2014:341, Opinion AG Wathelet, para125.

153 D Thym, 'The Elusive limits of solidarity', 45.

from the point of view of adversely affected citizens, this means that the free movement of citizens and workers in the European Union is still incomplete.

Immigration after Brexit: Ironies and Challenges

Daniel Thym and Mattias Wendel

This contribution argues that Brexit could facilitate legal control over the entry and stay of EU citizens, but might paradoxically render control of immigration of third country nationals, including asylum seekers, more difficult compared to the status quo. The first section examines this irony with regard to third country nationals, the second section addresses the challenging question of the British-Irish border while the third and final section relates to the migration of EU citizens and UK nationals.

I. Introduction

Immigration was a hot topic throughout the Brexit debate. The prominent slogan of 'taking back control' aimed particularly at taking back control of immigration to the United Kingdom. Many readers will remember the 'breaking point' poster used by UKIP before the referendum with a picture of migrants and asylum seekers trotting across the Western Balkans. That poster seemed to capture (and foster) a certain perception that associated the EU with chaos and open borders – both for EU citizens and third country nationals. In her Lancaster speech of January 2017, Prime Minister Theresa May was adamant that control of immigration was a central objective of the ongoing Brexit negotiations: 'The message from the public before and during the referendum campaign was clear: Brexit must mean control of the number of people who come to Britain from Europe. And that is what we will deliver.'[1]

From a legal perspective, there is a certain irony in the 'breaking point' poster. Our argument will be that while Brexit could facilitate legal control over the entry and stay of EU citizens, it need not necessarily make it easier for the UK to control the immigration of third-country nationals, including asylum seekers. It might even, paradoxically, render control of immi-

1 T May, '*A Global Britain, Speech at Lancaster House*', 17 January 2017.

gration of non-Europeans more difficult to some extent. In our first section we'll try to explain this irony, before we move on, secondly, to the challenging question of the British-Irish border and, thirdly, to the migration of EU citizens and UK nationals. The paramount importance of these aspects is also demonstrated by the fact that the British-Irish border and the protection of citizens' rights formed already part of the first of the two phases of the negotiations.

II. Immigration of Third Country Nationals: Reversed Dynamics

In the field of third country immigration, Brexit might ironically lead to reversed dynamics compared to the status quo.

A. Status Quo: Extended Opt-out

From a legal perspective, the UK has always retained widespread control of its external borders insofar as the entry and stay of third-country nationals are concerned. A major reason for this lies in the fact that the UK rejected to participate in the border-free Schengen area. It did not sign up to the Schengen Implementing Convention of 1990 and it secured an opt-out when the letter was integrated into the framework of the European Union on the occasion of the Treaty of Amsterdam.[2]

Moreover, successive British Governments decided not to participate in most legislative initiatives on immigration, visas and border controls in the so-called area of freedom, security and justice,[3] which have been adopted during the past 15 years and which have substantially reshaped the immigration law systems of countries in continental Europe.[4] The UK does not participate, for instance, in the Family Reunion Directive, the Long-Term

---

2 See today‘s Protocol (No 19) on the Schengen *acquis* integrated into the framework of the European Union ([2008] OJ C 115/290), which builds upon the original 1997 version attached to the Treaty of Amsterdam ([1997] OJ C 340/93).

3 The Schengen Protocol, ibid, is complemented by the Protocol (No 21) on the Position of the United Kingdom and Ireland in Respect of the Area of Freedom, Security and Justice ([2008] OJ C 115/295).

4 For a legal analysis of the UK's opt-out and corresponding institutional practice in recent years, see K Hailbronner and D Thym, 'Constitutional Framework and Principles for Interpretation' in ibid (eds), *EU Immigration and Asylum Law. Commentary*, 2nd edn (Munich, C.H. Beck/Hart, 2016) 1, 21–23.

Residents Directive, the Blue Card scheme for highly qualified migrants or any other instrument facilitating the entry or stay of third-country nationals. The UK can determine autonomously which third country nationals are subject to visa requirements, are allowed to take up employment or have to leave the UK. There is little primary or secondary law limiting UK sovereignty in this respect, with the notable exception of those third country nationals who are relatives of EU citizens and benefit from a derivative right of residence rooted in EU free movement law.[5]

The situation is different for the ECHR and corresponding limits to State discretion, on the basis of Articles 3 and 8 ECHR, on the expulsion of those staying illegally, including suspects of terrorism.[6] Both the human rights based principle of non-refoulement under Article 3 ECHR and the right to private and family life under Article 8 ECHR have limited the political room for manoeuvre of the national legislator considerably. That is why Theresa May apparently went as far as promoting a withdrawal from the ECHR or at least a repeal of the Human Rights Act when she was Home Secretary.[7] While leaving the ECHR or repealing the Human Rights Act might have indeed extended UK sovereignty over third-country nationals to a certain extent, it would have arguably been accompanied by a considerable constitutional price also for British citizens and a potential loss of international credibility. Such a step might even have struck a devastating blow to the already struggling system of human rights review in Strasbourg. Leaving the EU seems to appear even more costly at all levels, as the current implosion of the British political system tragically demonstrates. But it won't arguably change much regarding immigration control.

B. *Brexit: Loss of the Opt-in Option*

What is more, in a post-Brexit world the UK might even lose regulatory leverage insofar as immigration controls vis-à-vis third-country nationals are concerned. The underlying reason is simple: at the time of the Treaty of Amsterdam, the British Government of Tony Blair secured not only an

5 For two classic examples, see ECJ, judgment of 11 July 2002, Case C-60/00, *Carpenter* and ECJ, judgment of 19 October 2004, Case C-200/02, *Zhu and Chen*.

6 For two prominent examples, see ECtHR, judgment of 17 January 2012, No. 8139/09, *Othman (Abu Qatada) v. the United Kingdom*; and ECtHR, judgment of 12 Jan 2010, No 47486/06, *A.W. Khan v. the United Kingdom*.

7 *Cf* A Asthana and R Mason, 'UK must leave European convention on human rights, says Theresa May', *Guardian.com* on 25 April 2016.

opt-out from the Schengen regime. It also won an opt-in option for all immigration, visa, asylum and border control measures, which are not inseparably linked to the abolition of border controls.[8] This opt-in option was reinforced by the Treaty of Lisbon which established a hitherto unprecedented possibility of 'cherry picking' in the field of justice and home affairs legislation.[9] The UK has used this opt-in option quite extensively – and selectively – over the years,[10] including during the time when Theresa May was Home Secretary.

This selective opt-in practice focused on those measures enhancing the control powers of States, such as the Schengen Information System (SIS), in which the UK participates although it never signed up to order-free travel.[11] The UK also subscribed to many EU measures against illegal immigration, while not being bound by the rules on legal migration.[12] Most importantly, the UK participates in the Dublin system without, however, contributing to the solidarity measures, such as the relocation decisions on resettling 160,000 asylum seekers from Greece and Italy to other Member States.[13] To be sure, the Dublin system was originally based upon a convention outside the EU framework, but it has always been doctrinally linked to EU law[14] and, moreover, it ceased to exist as an instrument of public international law when it was supplanted by EU legislation in which the UK participated.[15]

---

8 See Article 4 of the Schengen Protocol No. 19 (note 2) and Article 3–4a Protocol No. 21 (note 3); and the analysis by Hailbronner and Thym (note 4), at 22–23.

9 See C Ladenburger, 'Police and Criminal Law in the Treaty of Lisbon'(2008) 4 *European Constitutional Law Review* 20, 28.

10 See House of Lords European Union Committee, The UK's opt-in Protocol: implications of the Government's approach, 9th Report of Session 2014-15, paras 31–37; and F Tekin, *Differentiated Integration at Work* (Baden-Baden, Nomos, 2012).

11 *Cf* Council Decision 2000/365/EC of 29 May 2000 concerning the request of the United Kingdom of Great Britain and Northern Ireland to take part in some of the provisions of the Schengen acquis ([2000] OJ L 131/43).

12 See D Thym, 'Legal Framework for EU Immigration Policy' in ibid/Hailbronner (note 4) 271, 273–274.

13 *Cf* Council Decision (EU) 2015/1601 of 22 September 2015 ([2015] OJ L 248/80) and Council Decision (EU) 2015/1523 of 14 September 2015 ([2015] OJ L 239/146).

14 See Recital 3 and Article 21 of the Convention determining the State responsible for examining applications for asylum lodged in one of the Member States of the European Communities of 15 June 1990 ([1997] OJ C 254/1).

15 See Recital 19 and Article 24(1) Council Regulation (EC) No 343/2003 of 18 February 2003 establishing the criteria and mechanisms for determining the

In short, as an EU Member State the UK participated in the field justice and home affairs in a highly selective and lopsided manner: it enhanced State control without promoting the rights of migrants and refugees. As a member of the EU, the UK could use the justice and home affairs Protocols to enhance control of its external borders towards other Member States through à la carte participation. The irony is that Brexit will likely reverse these dynamics.

C. *The Future: Reversed Dynamics*

In the post-Brexit legal environment, the UK will not be able any longer to decide unilaterally whether or not to participate in Dublin and the SIS by means of a simple declaration notifying the Council that it wants to exercise the opt-in option. Instead, the UK will have to negotiate with the EU post-Brexit whether it will be allowed to participate – and these negotiations will be defined, like any negotiation, by a *quid pro quo*, by reciprocal give-and-take.[16]

Thus, the UK will likely have to pay a price for being allowed to participate in the future Dublin IV Regulation or the Schengen Information System- something it got for free in the past. The EU could demand, for instance, that the UK contributes to the relocation of asylum seekers from Greece or Italy. If that happened, Brexit would entail into the opposite of what Brexiteers had promised to the British when putting up the 'breaking point' poster.

That need not happen, of course.The UK could decide, alternatively, to stay out of Dublin or it could negotiate a cross-sectoral package deal. The price the EU may wish to extract from the UK for continued Dublin participation may relate to any other policy field.

One thing, however, seems certain: the UK will not get Dublin for free any longer – like Switzerland, which was allowed to join Dublin under the condition that it subscribed to border free travel within the Schengen area

Member State responsible for examining an asylum application lodged in one of the Member States by a third-country national ([2003] OJ L 50/1).

16 It is assumed that the UK has a genuine interest in keeping Dublin, since it tends to be a beneficiary of the Dublin rules due to its geographic location; even if the numbers of those moving to the UK are relatively low at present, they might rise in the future, i.e., Dublin is a safety net in case of any future increase in the number of arrivals.

at the same time.[17] Ever since, border controls have been abolished between Germany and Switzerland. That, to us, is the irony of Brexit for immigration law sensu stricto: it might become more difficult for the UK to control the entry and stay of third-country nationals.

III. British-Irish Border: The Search For Pragmatic Solutions

To retain an open border between the Republic of Ireland and the UK is a political objective shared by the EU and the UK. Already the European Council's guidelines and the White Paper of the British Government were clear that they want to retain the Common Travel Area (CTA).[18] And in the Protocol on Ireland/Northern Ireland which forms an integral part of the not (yet, if ever) ratified withdrawal agreement,[19] the EU and the May government agreed on the goal of preventing a hard border after the transition period, i.e., the period of around two years following the UK's withdrawal from the EU.[20]

---

17 In the framework of the so-called 'bilateral II' agreements, the entry into force of the Schengen and the Dublin association agreement are linked, *cf* Article 14 Agreement between the European Community and the Swiss Confederation concerning the criteria and mechanisms for establishing the State responsible for examining a request for asylum lodged in a Member State or in Switzerland of 26 October 2004 ([2008] OJ L 53/5), which entered into force on 1 March 2008 ([2008] OJ L 53/18).

18 See European Council, 29 April 2017, Guidelines Following the United Kingdom's Notification Under Article 50 TEU, Doc. EUCO XT 20004/17, para 11 as well as the Department for Exiting the European Union: White Paper. The United Kingdom's exit from and new partnership with the European Union, February 2017, pp 21–23.

19 Draft Agreement on the withdrawal of the UK from the EU of 14 November 2018.

20 Initially the transition period should have started after the UK's withdrawal on 29 March 2019 and last until December 2020. Currently, however, it remains unclear when (if at all) a withdrawal will take place and trigger the transition period. During the transition period (see Articles 126 et seq of the draft agreement), the UK would be, in principle, treated like an EU Member State with the notable exception of participation in the institutions and governance structures of the EU.

A. *Immigration and Border Controls*

The CTA is a set of reciprocal legal rules and administrative practices which have secured the absence of border (and immigration) controls between the Republic and Northern Ireland ever since Irish home rule.[21]

In this respect, the European Council called for 'flexible and imaginative solutions'[22] regarding the British-Irish border. Such flexibility might be necessary, indeed, for a number of economic and trade issues. From a purely *legal-technical* perspective things appear to be less problematic insofar as immigration and border controls are concerned. The reason for this lies in the fact that the status quo facilitates the search for legal solutions in three inter-related ways.

Firstly, Protocol No. 20 attached to the Treaty of Lisbon states explicitly that the UK and Ireland 'may continue to make arrangements between themselves relating to the [CTA]' and that 'nothing in [the EU Treaties] or in any measures adopted under them shall affect any such arrangements.'[23] The European Council is adamant that the Protocol will continue to apply post-Brexit, and indeed, it is difficult to argue that it will lose its relevance. Thus, the CTA can be maintained as a matter of principle on the basis of Protocol No. 20, which, moreover, is quite clear that it allows for the arrangements to be modified and developed further if necessary.

Secondly, not much would have to change in terms of policy substance. Already at present, the British-Irish border is an external border of the Schengen area, although we do not have physical border controls between the Republic and Northern Ireland. There may be the need for continued practical and legislative coordination, both at present and in the future, also taking into account the legal and practical consequences of Brexit. But this coordination can be agreed upon in the framework of the CTA or, if necessary, in the Brexit agreement.

A legal side aspect is whether the UK and Ireland could agree on a bilateral mechanism on asylum jurisdiction, a sort of 'Mini-Dublin'. It seems to us that the legal answer is not crystal clear: While one can argue, on the one hand, that Protocol No. 20 allows for such bilateral mechanism to be

21 See B Ryan, 'Irish Aspects, Brexit briefing', https://www.freemovement.org.uk on 18 May 2016.
22 European Council (note 18), para 11.
23 Article 2 of Protocol (No. 20) on the Application of Certain Aspects of Article 26 of the Treaty on the Functioning of the European Union to the United Kingdom and to Ireland ([2008] OJ C 115/293).

established in the future,[24] one may maintain, on the other hand, that the EU has acquired an exclusive, ERTA-style competence for cooperation with third States on asylum jurisdiction,[25] mirroring the agreement with Switzerland.

Thirdly, we have to distinguish between border controls for immigration purposes and customs controls for economic issues. While Brexit has little impact on the former (border controls), the latter (customs control) are a different matter.

B. *Customs Controls and the so-called "Backstop"*

At present, customs controls do not exist at the British-Irish border, since both the UK and Ireland are a member of the single market and the customs union. If the UK left the single market, as advocated by May and a considerable part of the Tories, such controls might have to be introduced in the future. Under that premise, 'flexible and innovative solutions' would indeed be required, so as to minimise the negative impact on cross-border exchanges across the British-Irish border.

In the Protocol on Ireland/Northern Ireland the EU and the British Government negotiated, in essence, a three-step approach in order to prevent a hard border after the transition period. The first step or priority, enshrined in Article 2 of the Protocol, is to reach an agreement on the future relationship that would per definition eliminate the need for a hard border. The second step, laid down in Article 3 of the Protocol, would be to extend the transition period in order to reach such an agreement. The third step is a fall-back position, the so-called "back stop solution". Its core provision is Article 6 § 1 of the draft agreement, according to which a single customs territory between the EU and the UK shall be established until the future relationship becomes applicable. That this temporary solution might, in the absence of an agreement on the future relationship, become a permanent one, is one of the core arguments for a majority of MPs in the British House of Commons to refuse- three times already – to ratify "May's deal". At the moment, it is not at all clear how this problem might be

24 This argument could be maintained in particular, if there was already a bilateral asylum seekers transfer agreement between the UK and Ireland before the entry into force of the Dublin Convention; if that was not the case, it would be difficult to maintain that the introduction of such an agreement concerns the 'continu[ation]' of arrangements' on the free movement of persons on the island.

25 *Cf* Article 3(2) TFEU and corresponding case law.

solved in the future. It is not excluded, however, that a cross-party alliance between Tory and Labour MPs might reach an agreement on a future relationship that would, as a permanent solution, include a customs union between the EU and the UK.

From a personal experience it seems that it should be even possible to find a pragmatic solution in case a customs union would not be a permanent solution. The University of Konstanz is situated geographically on the Swiss border, that is an internal Schengen border (mirroring the CTA), but an external border of the customs union (as might be the case with the Irish-British border post-Brexit). One of us, Daniel Thym, crosses that border up to four times a week. On normal occasions, traffic is hardly interrupted at all – and the flow would be even smoother, if the customs formalities took place beyond the official border-crossing points that still exist between Germany and Switzerland. It should be possible, therefore, to maintain a 'green border' on the 'Emerald Isle' post-Brexit.

IV. EU Citizenship and Free Movement Of Persons

As regards the rights linked to EU citizenship and the right to free movement in particular, Brexit raised at least two core challenges.

A. Securing Citizens' Rights

The first challenge was how to secure the legal situation of EU-27 citizens residing in the UK and of UK citizens living in the EU-27 before and after Brexit. This aspect was the top priority in the first phase of the negotiation process. According to the Council's negotiation directives, "[s]afeguarding the status and rights of the EU-27 citizens and their families in the [UK] and of the citizens of the [UK] and their families in the EU-27 Member States is the first priority for the negotiations because of the number of people directly affected and of the seriousness of the consequences of the withdrawal for them".[26]

---

26 Council of the European Union, 22 May 2017, Directives for the negotiation of an agreement with the United Kingdom of Great Britain and Northern Ireland setting out the arrangements for its withdrawal from the European Union -Annex to the Council Decision authorising the Commission to open negotiations on an agreement with the United Kingdom setting out the arrangements for its withdrawal from the European Union, doc. 21009/17 BXT 16 ADD 1, para 11.

The actual number of citizens affected varies considerably, depending on the method of calculation. The most common set of numbers – often quoted in the media and reflected also by the work of the institutions – suggests that apparently 1.2 mio UK citizens live in the EU-27, while up to 3.2 mio EU-27 citizens in turn reside in the UK.[27] These numbers are essentially based on calculations by the UK (ONS)[28] and the United Nations. But, as pointed out in the literature, in particular the UN statistics do not sufficiently distinguish between country of birth and nationality[29] which is why the numbers could also be lower, with around 700.000 UK nationals living abroad in the EU-27 and 2.9 mio EU-27 nationals living in the UK. But also these numbers are quite significant and demonstrate the importance to come to terms.

In legal terms, the challenge is how to secure rights acquired and derived from EU citizenship before the end of the transition period. This starts with the definition of the personal scope of application. In this respect, the EU wanted to follow as closely as possible the existing acquis. According to the Council's negotiation directives, the personal scope should be equated with that of the directive 2004/38 on free movement, covering both economically active persons and economically inactive citizens, i.e., workers and self-employed, as well as students or pensioners.[30] Furthermore, the EU aimed at including family members who accompany or join mobile EU citizens as well as individuals covered by the Regulation 883/2004 on the coordination of social security systems irrespective of their place of residence.[31] In this respect, the EU was successful in the negotiations, as demonstrated by Article 10 and Article 30 of the draft agreement which widely correspond to the EU's negotiating goals.

The EU was also quite successful regarding the scope of rights that shall be guaranteed to UK nationals who live in the EU-27 or EU-27 nationals who reside in the UK before the end of the transition period and keep doing so afterwards. Also in this respect, the EU managed to achieve a close

27 See, amongst others, European Commission, document TF50 (2019) 59, p 14.
28 UK Office for national statistics.
29 S Carrera, E Guild and N C Luk, 'What does Brexit mean for the EU's Area of Freedom, Security and Justice', *CEPS Commentary* 2016, at https://www.ceps.eu/system/files/What%20does%20BREXIT%20mean%20for%20the%20EU.pdf (accessed 30 March 2019) 4 et seq.
30 Council of the European Union, negotiation directives (note 26), para 21 lit. a).
31 Ibid.

approximation to the existing *acquis*.[32] The same applies for frontier workers and family members.

Technically such an approximation is far from being trivial, however. Part II of the draft agreement – related to citizens' rights -bears witness as to the complexity of the issue. A core provision is Article 13 § 1, according to which EU citizens and UK nationals who lived in the host State before the end of the transition period and keep living there afterwards shall have the right to reside in the host State under the limitations and conditions as set out in Articles 21, 45 or 49 TFEU and in the relevant provisions of Directive 2004/38. Article 13 § 2 and 3 grants rights of residence to family members (EU citizens, UK or third country nationals), while Article 13 § 4 bars the host State to impose any limitations or conditions for obtaining, retaining or losing residence rights of these groups of persons, other than those provided for in the agreement. The provision also stipulates that there "shall be no discretion in applying the limitations and conditions" other than in favour of the person concerned. Such specifications were considered to be necessary, given that EU law ceases to apply in the UK once the withdrawal takes effect.

Even more important, Article 39 of the draft agreement makes clear that the individuals concerned shall enjoy the rights provided for in Part II "for their lifetime, unless they cease to meet the conditions set out" there. Hence, the draft agreement would provide for continuity and legal certainty far beyond the transition period as long as the respective legal status would have been gained before the end of that period and the conditions would still be met.

The migration regime which is intended to substitute the current acquis for rights and legal status acquired until the end of the transition period is spelled out in detail in Articles 14 to 29 of the draft agreement. These stipulations pay attention to specific transitional problems, like the calculation of periods, relevant i.a. for the right to permanent residence, or status changes, for example between student, worker, self-employed person and economically inactive person.

The status quo is not only widely perpetuated with regard to residence rights, but also with regard to equal treatment and access to social security. § 23 of the draft agreement replicates Article 24 of Directive 2004/38, including the exceptions according to which Member States can refuse to grant social assistance. Finally, Articles 30 et seq. contains a specific regime

32 Ibid, para 21 lit. b).

on the coordination of social security systems, essentially substituting regulation 883/2004.

To conclude, the EU has managed to widely perpetuate the current acquis on the free movement of persons for EU citizens, UK nationals and their relatives who reside in the host State before the end of the transition period and keep doing so after its expiry. However, this achievement depends on entering into force of the agreement – an instance which may never happen when taking into consideration that ratification has been rejected three times already in the House of Commons.

B. Intra-European Mobility and Immigration After Brexit

How could the design of the future relationship between the EU-27 and the UK with respect to intra-European mobility and immigration look like? Will there be a future regime of free movement between the EU and the UK? Unfortunately, things have not become clearer in this respect, although almost three years have passed since the memorable referendum of 23 June 2016.

The uncertainty starts with the question whether or not Brexit will happen at all, given that a unilateral withdrawal of the declaration under Article 50 TEU is, in principle, possible at any time.[33] The European Court of Justice has, in the context of the Dublin-III-regulation, also implicitly denied a preventive or pre-effect of Brexit before the withdrawal is actually put into effect.[34] As of today, the status quo still applies and the UK even participates in the European elections in May 2019.

The uncertainty is particularly apparent when it comes to concrete plans on the future regime of mobility and immigration between the EU-27 and the UK. The House of Commons, for instance, has made much more articulate what it does not want than what it actually favours. Against the backdrop of the political Brexit chaos in early 2019 it is almost impossible to give any meaningful estimation as to what is going to happen. In the light of the fruitless votes in the House of Commons and the political battles be-

---

33 See ECJ, judgment of 10 December, case C-621/18 – *Wightman*.

34 ECJ, judgment of 13 January 2019, case C-661/17 – *M.A. et al*, para 54 with reference to Wightman and with regard to the discretionary clause under the Dublin-III-regulation. On the discretionary clause in the context of the migration crisis see in more detail M Wendel, 'The Refugee Crisis and the Executive: On the Limits of Administrative Discretion in the Common European Asylum System' (2016) 17 *German Law Journal* 1005.

tween and within the major political parties in the UK, it appears to be rather unlikely that the UK will, in the future, opt for a full participation in the internal market, because this would – as the EU negotiators have repeatedly stressed – necessarily include the free movement of persons.

Against this background, it also seems unlikely that the future relationship between the EU and the UK could be aligned to the model of the European Economic Area which would lead to a *de facto* full integration in the internal market without major exceptions – and without participation. It could very well be that the future relationship will, in the end be based at least on a customs union with some additional elements. For the free movement of persons between the UK and the EU-27 this would certainly mean a major step backwards.

V. Conclusion

The analysis of the law of immigration after Brexit is situated in a volatile context which makes it difficult to give any substantial assessment at the moment. As far as immigration of third country nationals is concerned, there lies a certain irony in the fact that Brexit will likely produce results that openly run counter to the Brexiteers' promise of taking back control. When it comes to the delicate question of the British/Irish Border, much will depend on the reasonableness of political actors, given that the legal dimension does not pose a major challenge. Finally, in the field of intra-European migration, it currently seems unlikely that the future relationship between the EU and the UK will be based on the continuity of the internal market and the free movement of persons once the transition period is over. It is here that Brexit could lead to a major rupture with the status quo in the future.

Part III
EU Policies –
Perspectives of Cooperation with the UK

The Future of Monetary and Financial Policy after Brexit

Jean-Victor Louis

Abstract

This chapter starts with recording the essential features of the Brexit negotiations up to recent developments, and stresses in particular the importance for the subject treated in this chapter of the so-called non-binding 'Political declaration setting out the framework for the future relationship between the EU and the UK'. The first section of the chapter relates to the more straightforward institutional consequences of the Brexit in monetary and financial affairs, the UK loosing in particular the possibility to interfere from within the Union in the preparation of legislation on economic and financial affairs. The second section bears on the remaining participation of the UK to international fora from which it keeps the ambition of influencing the drafting of norms and the adoption of policy orientations by the EU. Section 3 describes the economic and social consequences for the UK of leaving the EU, especially for the finance industry. This is an important challenge for the City of London and other financial places in the UK. Section four analyses the impact of Brexit on the continental financial markets. The respective standpoints on this matter from UK and EU authorities are analysed. The section evokes in particular the question of the localisation and surveillance of Central Counterparties (CCP).

The chapter closes by some considerations about the attitude of Britain towards European integration. It expresses the hope of a cooperation between the UK and an EU remaining faithful to its objective to build 'an ever closer Union'.

I. Introduction

This report will sketch, from a legal standpoint the presumed effects of Brexit on Monetary Policy as well as on financial regulation and supervision. Competences of the EU legislator and of the ECB are at stake. The relationship between monetary stability and the smooth functioning of financial markets (both banks and non-banks) and the specific role played by the ECB and National Central Banks in supervision are well-known.

The Delors report of 1989 described a complete single market as a basic element of EMU.[1] This relation is evident if we contemplate the role of an effective free movement of capitals for the smooth transmission of monetary policy.

But before entering into our subject we think necessary to recall some essential features of the context of Brexit negotiations up to the present no-deal and the new delay which was conceded at her request to the British Prime Minister, after the triple rejection by the House of Commons (on 15 January, 12 March and 29 March 2019) of the draft Agreement on the withdrawal of the United Kingdom from the European Union.

The latest date for the ratification of the Agreement was on 29 March 2019, two years after the notification of the UK decision to withdraw from the EU. A first request for extension was introduced by the UK Government on 20 March 2019 until 30 June. With the agreement of the UK, the European Council decided to extend the period until 22 May in the event the House of Commons approved the Withdrawal Agreement by 29 March 2019. 'If that were not the case, the European Council agreed to an extension until 12 April 2019.' A new prolongation was asked for until 30 June 2019, which was denied. On 10 April, the European Council agreed to a further extension which 'should last as long as necessary and, in any event, no longer than 31 October 2019'. So, the withdrawal should take place 'on the first day of the month following the completion of the ratification procedures or on 1 November 2019, whichever is the earliest.' The conceded extensions were indeed conditional to the prior ratification of the Withdrawal Agreement.

At the moment of revising this text, it was far from certain that the UK will, at the end, ratify the Withdrawal Agreement. It seems useful to recall some important points of the negotiations, without entering in a description of the successive, negative and sometimes incoherent votes of the House of Commons.

Six days after the vote of the UK to leave the EU and Euratom, the Heads of State and Government at 27, as well as the Presidents of the European Council and the European Commission, adopted on 29 June 2016 a 'Statement' including a number of principles which would guide the attitude that will be adopted by the EU in the negotiation. The first points

---

1 Committee for the Study of Economic and Monetary Union, Report on economic and monetary union in the European Community, 1989: '*Economic and Monetary Union* in Europe would imply complete freedom of movement for persons, goods, services and capital, as well as irrevocably fixed exchange rates between national currencies and, finally, a single currency.' p 13.

raised were on the procedure to be followed under Article 50 TEU which is applicable if a Member State decides to leave the Union. Other elements refer to the substance of the future agreement, which would have to be built 'on a balance of rights and obligations'. And the statement recalls one of the crucial points for the EU that 'Access to the Single Market requires acceptance of all four freedoms.' It so opposed the intention expressed by the UK Government to seriously limit the persons' freedom of movement. It was at this early stage an advertisement that the EU would not accept a 'cherry-picking' among the very bases of the Single Market.

After the UK notification under Article 50 TEU, on 29 March 2017, the European Council adopted on a draft prepared by the Commission, the first guidelines[2] for the negotiations that it was from then possible to open. Considering the 'significant uncertainties' created for people and business by the UK's decision to leave the Union, the European Council proposed a 'phased approach giving priority to an orderly withdrawal. National authorities, businesses and other stakeholders should take all necessary steps to prepare for the consequences of the United Kingdom's withdrawal.'

For the EU, the first phase of the negotiations which was thereafter familiarly called 'the conditions of the divorce' would aim to 'provide as much clarity and legal certainty as possible to citizens, businesses, stakeholders and international partners on the immediate effects of the UK's withdrawal from the Union' and 'settle the disentanglement of the UK from the Union and from all the rights and obligations the UK derives from commitments undertaken as Member State'.

It would only be in a second phase, when the UK has become a third country, that an 'agreement on a future relationship between the Union and the UK as such could be 'finalised and concluded'. This phasing which prevented the UK to start negotiations with third States, for example on future trade relations, was a surprise for the British negotiators. Nevertheless, the future relations could be in some measure considered as Article 50 TEU requires to take into account the framework for the future relationship with the Union of the exiting Member State. That inevitably would determine the kind of relations that the UK would be able to develop in the future, on trade and tariffs for example, with the outside World. The Union declares itself ready to identify 'an overall understanding on the framework for the future relationship…during a second phase of the negotiations under Article 50 TEU.' The Union stands also ready 'to engage in preliminary and preparatory discussions to this end …if the European

2 Council of the European Union, 22 May 2017, XT 210116/17, Add 1 Rev 2.

Council decides that sufficient progress has been made in the first phase towards reaching a satisfactory agreement on the arrangements for an orderly withdrawal'.

The UK directives of negotiation made evident the two different conceptions of the object of the negotiations which were conceived by the British negotiators essentially as the building of a new partnership.[3] Michel Barnier, a former Commission member and French minister, head of the EU delegation, received the mandate from the European Council to negotiate in a first period, with his counterpart, Brexit secretary David Davis, about three politically sensitive questions: the respective rights of the citizens of both the EU and the UK, the conditions of the so-called 'divorce' in budgetary figures and the regime for Ireland. If the two first points were not easy to solve, the last one still remains today a serious point of contention.

This latest question is surely one of the most delicate to settle in order to avoid any risk to compromise the ever fragile implementation of the so called Good Friday agreement between the two parts of the island.[4] The most rational solution would be to consider the unification of the island. This idea appears however to be unacceptable for the UK and its realisation could endanger the peace in the Northern part of the island. Furthermore, the Irish Prime Minister has repeatedly affirmed that to build a hard frontier between the North and the South of the island would be vetoed by Ireland, a position of which the other EU members have taken note. The Brexiters were opposed to the possibility under the Protocol on Ireland, for the EU to require the temporary recourse to a so-called backstop.

3 See www.gov.uk/government/publications/the/united/kingdoms-exit-from-and-new-partnership-with-the-european-union-white-paper 2 February 2017. See also the Lancaster speech of the Prime Minister of 17 January 2017, 'The government's negotiating objectives for exiting the EU: Prime Minister speech', in an updated version of 3 February 2017, https://www.gov.uk/government/speeches/the-governments-negotiating-objectives-for-exiting-the-eu-pm-speech on the theme: 'we are leaving the European Union but we are not leaving Europe', and the Florence speech of Mrs. May of 22 September 2017 https://www.gov.uk/government/speeches/pms-florence-speech-a-new-era-of-cooperation-and-partnership-between-the-uk-and-the-eu.de

4 Ireland is opposed to the building of a rigid frontier with Norther Ireland (which now is a very theoretical one) and the UK refuses to consider the option of the building of a frontier at the border of the island, which would mean a physical separation with the rest of the UK, i.e. a loss of sovereignty on the island. This question has received a very enigmatic solution in the 8th December joint report mentioned in n 7.

This would result in 'keeping the UK in a customs union which would torpedo their dream of a 'global Britain' able to strike trade deals around the World, and set its own regulatory path, free from Europe.'[5] The acting government of the Northern Republic, and Mrs May, UK Prime Minister who led a minority government supported by the Belfast Government could not accept either the division of the United Kingdom through the creation of customs barriers in the Ocean. Some opponents to the backstop would be satisfied by a 'ready exit mechanism, or time-limit'. It was the object of the so-called Strasbourg agreement, signed by the Union and the United Kingdom, on 11 March 2019.[6] It was said and repeated in this agreement that the backstop was à provisional solution but it remained to be decided what would be the definitive regime.

After various rounds of negotiations, a joint report was adopted on 8 December 2017 on progress during phase 1 of difficult negotiations under Article 50 TEU "on the United Kingdom's orderly withdrawal from the European Union".[7] On this basis and on a report from the Commission on the state of the negotiations[8], the European Council which met on 15 December 2017,[9] without the UK Prime Minister, decided that 'it is sufficient to move to the second phase related to transition and the framework for the future relationship'. So it called

---

5 See *The Guardian*, 13 December 2018.

6 Instrument relating to the Agreement on the withdrawal of the United Kingdom of Great-Britain and Northern Ireland from the European Union and the European Atomic Energy Community, published on the TF50 website on 11 March 2019. On the legal force of this agreement, see among others, Michel Dougan, Brexit: legal analysis of May's Strasbourg deal, https://news.liverpool.ac.uk/2019/03/12. See also HM Government, UK Government Commitments to Northern Ireland and its integral place in the UK, 9 January 2019, referring to and complementing the Protocol on Ireland and Northern Ireland guaranteeing that 'there will not be a hard border between Northern Ireland and Ireland or a splitting of the UK customs territory.' All these efforts by the British Government were not sufficient in order to rally opponents who supported the rejection of the deal by the acting Northern Irish Government.

7 TF50 (2017) 19 – Commission to EU 27, 8 December 2017. We will not comment on the content of this report which has been analysed by a good specialist of European Affairs, Jacob Funk Kirkegaard, in a short paper under the title: 'Britain Opts for 'Brexit in Name Only'', (2017) Peterson Institute for International Economics (PIIE), Washington, December 11, referring specifically to the Irish border sketched solution which many consider as ambiguous. We will see later on that the December 2017 'Guidelines' of the European Council are very clear on the fact that the UK will not be bound anymore with the rules on the single market.

8 COM (2017) 784 final.

9 EUCO XT 2011/17.

> 'on the Union negotiator and the United Kingdom to complete the work on all withdrawal issues, including those not yet addressed in the first phase, in conformity with the European guidelines of 29 April 2017, to consolidate the results obtained, and to start drafting the relevant parts of the Withdrawal Agreement. It underlines that negotiations in the second phase can only progress as all commitments undertaken during the first phase are respected in full and translated faithfully into legal terms as quickly as possible'.

Time was indeed pressing. In principle, and if no prolongation of the negotiations were agreed within two years after the Brexit decision,[10] the UK would have had to leave the EU without an agreement with the EU on the conditions of exit. Such a solution would have been damaging for both the UK and the EU. For trade relations, it would have meant that the regime between the two parts would be determined by the WTO rules and (lengthy) discussions in this framework should take place of the UK with all the membership of the Geneva institution.

The risk of a *cliff-edge*, i.e. no agreement between the two partners and a rough breakdown so often mentioned in the UK would have materialised. In order to avoid, temporarily, a situation of vacuum, also if negotiations were in the end successful, the UK had repeatedly asked for a transitory period allowing UK the necessary time for organising the new regime in the relationship of the UK, as a third country and the EU at 27. In its report on Brexit and financial services, the House of Lords EU Committee recommends, 'both for the business environment and for financial stability, a considered and orderly transition to any new relationship.'[11] The UK Prime Minister 'has made a clear commitment to avoid a disruptive cliff-edge and associated risks to UK and EU financial stability and business cer-

10 The notification of the demand to exit the EU under article 50 TEU was made on 29 March 2017. If a prolongation of the deadline is not decided by a unanimous vote of the European Council, under Art 50, para 3, the treaties will cease to be applicable to the UK on 29 March 2019.

11 9th Report of session 2016-2017, 15 December 2016, Conclusions, n°4, p 39. See also in favour of transitional arrangements in proportion of the time required between agreement on any new rules and their required implementation by market participants within a financial services regulation context, the letter of the Chief Executive of the Financial Conduct Authority (FCA) to the Chairman of the Treasury Committee of the House of Commons, of 13 January 2017: "…transitional arrangements should facilitate, rather than hinder, the eventual establishment of the future framework."

tainty.'[12] Although this appeared as a reasonable request, the organisation of such transition raised a number of questions. One of the difficulties consisted in the judicial control during the transition between the application of common EU rules and the new regime as agreed during the negotiations. The refusal of continued jurisdiction of the Court of justice appeared as one of the problems of the transition.
In its guidelines adopted on 15 December 2017,

> 'the European Council noted the proposal put forward by the UK for a transition period of around two years, and agreed to negotiate a transition covering the whole of the EU acquis, while the UK, as a third country, will no longer participate in or nominate or elect members of the EU institutions, nor participate in the decision making of the Union bodies, offices and agencies.'

The European Council specifies (point 4) that in order to ensure a level playing field in the single market, 'changes in the acquis adopted by institutions, bodies, offices and agencies 'will have to apply both in the UK and the EU' and 'all existing Union regulatory, budgetary, supervisory, judiciary and enforcement instruments and structures will also apply, including the competence of the Court of Justice of the EU'.

It is in the same guidelines (point 6) that the European Council envisaged 'identifying an overall understanding of the framework for the future relationship' which 'should be elaborated in a political declaration accompanying and referring to in the Withdrawal Agreement.' A full paragraph of the Guidelines was devoted to the consequences of the UK's intention to no longer participate in the Customs Union and the Single Market after the transition period. The European Council announced that it will

> 'calibrate its approach as regard to trade and economic cooperation in light of this position so as to ensure a balance of rights and obligations, preserve a level playing field, avoid upsetting relations with other third countries, and to respect ...in particular the need to preserve the integrity and proper functioning of the Single Market.'

A 'Political declaration setting out the framework for the future relationship between the European Union and the United Kingdom', was officially adopted by the European Council and the United Kingdom on 25 November 2018 in parallel with the Withdrawal Agreement. This non-

---

12 See Government response to the House of Lords European Union Committee Report, of 15 December 2016, (2017) 'Brexit: financial services' 21 March, p 2.

binding instrument should serve as a basis for hypothetical further negotiations on the basis of Article 50(2) TEU.

The declaration mentions in its introduction the determination of the Union and the United Kingdom

> 'to work together to safeguard the rules-based international order, the rule of law and promotion of democracy, and high standards of free and fair trade and workers' rights, consumer and environment protection, and cooperation against internal and external threats to their values and interests.' (Point 2).

Without the list of subjects covered by the Declaration being exhaustive (other areas of cooperation are possible), it mentions the establishment of the parameters of an ambitious, broad, deep and flexible partnership across trade and economic cooperation, law enforcement and criminal justice, foreign policy, security and defence and wider areas of collaboration. Reference is made on the shared values of the Union and the UK and on their shared heritage… (Point 3). In point 4, is mentioned the need for the relationship to be 'based on balance of rights and obligations taking into account the principles of each Party'. That means for the EU, to ensure the autonomy of decision making and the consistency with Union's principles, 'in particular with respect of the integrity of the single market and the indivisibility of the four freedoms'. For the UK, it means 'to ensure its sovereignty and the protection of its internal market, while respecting the result of the 2016 referendum including the development of its independent trade policy and the ending of free movement of people between the Union and the UK'.

Point 5 mentions, on the basis of the large period of membership of the UK to the Union, a 'unique context' that will inevitably needs to be taken into account. This means that the future relationship 'should be approached with high ambition'.

We cannot analyse here the 147 points of the Political Declaration. We should only limit the developments to what concerns the *Services* and more specially, the *Financial services* in Part II, Economic Partnership, I. Objectives and Principles, III. Services and Investment, and IV. Financial Services.

Section I, on *Objectives and Principles*, point 16 – valid for the whole *economic partnership* – starts with an obvious but important observation: the recognition by the Parties of the 'particularly important trading and investment relationship, reflecting more than 45 years of economic integration', 'the size of their two economies and their geographic proximity'. All that 'has led to complex and integrated supply chains'.

Points 17 and 18 develop the principles enounced in the introduction. The objective of the parties is to develop 'an ambitious, wide-ranging and balanced economic partnership'. This partnership 'will be comprehensive, encompassing a free trade area as well as wider sectoral cooperation where it is in the mutual interest of both Parties'. This is particularly important in financial services where the authorities are well used to such bilateral and multilateral cooperation. Provisions ensuring a level playing field for open and fair competition are also mentioned as well as the objective of facilitating trade and investment 'between the Parties to the extent possible' within the limits already mentioned in point 4 of the Introduction (quoted above) to which is added the recognition of 'the development of an independent trade policy by the United Kingdom beyond this economic partnership.' Point 18 is related to the 'autonomy and the ability' of the Parties to 'regulate economy activity' pursuing objectives deemed appropriate of which a non-exhaustive list is produced. Sustainable development is mentioned as 'an overarching objective' of the economic partnership. The text also mentions 'appropriate general exceptions' with, as an example, security. Point 19 recalls the determination of the Parties to replace the backstop solution on Northern Ireland by a subsequent agreement.

Section III. *Services and Investment* under A. Objectives and principles refers first (in Point 29) to the intention of the parties ('should') of concluding 'ambitious, comprehensive and balanced arrangements on trade and services and investment in services and non-services sectors, respecting each Party's right to regulate.' Furthermore, 'the Parties should aim to deliver a level of liberalisation in trade and services well beyond the Parties' WTO commitments and building on recent EU Free Trade Agreements (FTAs), an evident allusion to CETA concluded with Canada.

Point 30, referring to Article V of the GATT, requests to the Parties to aim (should) at 'substantial sectoral coverage, covering all modes of supply and providing for the absence of substantially all discrimination in the covered sectors, with exceptions and limitations as appropriate.' A non-exhaustive list of sectors follows with among them: financial services.[13]

Under B. Market access and non-discrimination, are included provisions related to market access, national treatment in order to facilitate non-discrimination 'including with regard to establishment' (Point 31), 'tempora-

13 This doesn't exclude any kind of services. Cp with the content of a declaration made one year before by Michel Barnier to *The Guardian* (and other newspapers): 'UK cannot have a special deal for the City', 18 December 2017: 'There is no place [for financial services]. There is no single trade agreement that is open to financial services.'

ry entry and stay of natural persons for business purposes in defined areas (Point 32). Under C, Regulatory aspects, point 33, 'while preserving regulatory autonomy', arrangements should include 'horizontal provisions such as on licensing procedures, and specific regulatory procedures in the sectors of mutual interest such as telecommunication services, financial services, delivery services, and international maritime transport services' as well as 'provisions on the development and adoption of domestic regulation that reflect good regulatory practices.' Point 35 adds in this text that Parties should establish a framework for voluntary regulatory cooperation in areas of mutual interest, including exchange of information and sharing of best practice. Point 36 encourages the development of arrangements on those professional qualifications which are necessary to the pursuit of regulated professions, where in the Parties' mutual interest.

What strikes in the formulation of the Political Declaration is the open-ended way in which its provisions are drafted. Perhaps this has been made possible by the non-binding feature of it. This remark could also apply to Section IV exclusively dedicated to *Financial Services*. Point 37 relates to the objectives of their financial policy: 'preserving financial stability, market integrity, investor and consumer protection and fair competition' with the traditional caveat: 'while respecting the Parties' regulatory and decision-making autonomy' with the addition of 'their ability to take equivalence decisions in their own interest'. Point 38 is entirely on equivalence. As we will see later on in the text, equivalence seems to sometimes appear as a second best to the establishment of a subsidiary in the positions defended by ECB supervision authorities. Point 39 includes an agreement on the need of 'close and structured cooperation on regulatory and supervisory matters which is in their mutual interest.' A cooperation grounded in the economic partnership and based 'on the principles of regulatory autonomy, transparency and stability.' The declaration also lists the fields where the cooperation should apply.

After this sketch of the content of the Political Declaration, that we hope will be useful in an indeterminate time in the future, let us come back to the presumed effects of Brexit in monetary and financial matters.

II. The more straightforward institutional consequences of the Brexit in monetary and financial matters

Protocol No 15 to the Lisbon Treaty on the so-called British opt out under which "the United Kingdom shall not be obliged or committed to adopt the euro without a separate decision to do so by its government and Parliament" would be abrogated. The UK could not anymore candidate for adopting the euro, after the Brexit, without having first applied for re-accession to the EU and after the end of the negotiations under Article 49 TEU.

The Bank of England's governor would not any more participate in the European System of Central Banks General Council,[14] an organ grouping all the governors of Central Banks in the EU and which has very limited competences under the ESCB statutes. The Bank of England would recuperate the modest part of its participation in the capital of the European Central Bank[15], to which it had to subscribe on the same basis as Central Banks of countries with a derogation, in order to participate to the functioning costs of the institution.

The EU rules in the field of banking and payment services would no longer apply to the United Kingdom.

The UK would cease to participate to the authorities constitutive of the ESFS (European System of Financial Supervision): EBA (European Banking Authority), ESMA (European Securities and Markets Authority), EIOPA (European Insurance and Occupational Pensions Authority) and the European Systemic Risk Board (ESRB) and of the Single Resolution Mechanism (SRM) and the Single Resolution Fund (SRF).

As a consequence, the UK would lose the benefit of the double majority arrangement that it obtained in the voting rules for important decisions in the EBA,[16] which provides that some of these decisions adopted with a simple majority should require the positive votes of a majority of representatives of competent authorities of countries having adopted the euro and of a majority of the representatives of such authorities of non-euro countries.

---

14 We recall that all the EU National Central Banks form, with the ECB, the European System of Central Banks. Only those having adopted the euro are members of the Eurosystem with the ECB, see art 282, para 1, TFEU and Art 1, Protocol No 4.

15 ESCB and ECB Statutes, Protocol n°4, art 47. See also Protocol No 15, art 8, c.

16 See Regulation (EU) No 1022/2013 of the European Parliament and of the Council of 22 October 2013 amending Regulation (EU) No1091/2010 establishing a European Supervisory Authority (European Banking Authority) as regard of specific tasks on the European Central Bank pursuant to Council Regulation (EU) No 1024/2013, Article 1 (24) amending article 44 of Regulation No 1091/2010.

The UK will also lose the possibility, opened for all EU Member States "wishing to participate",[17] to enter into a 'close cooperation' with the Single Supervisory Mechanism (SSM), through a decision adopted by the ECB under article 7 of the Regulation (EU) No 1024/2013. A close cooperation which would also include the automatic participation to the Single Resolution Mechanism (SRM), and .to the intergovernmental agreement about financing the Single Resolution Fund.

The UK would also have to leave the European Investment Bank (EIB).[18]

In any regard, it would become a third country in these fields.

In a Notice to stakeholders of 8 February 2018, the Commission has produced a document listing the legal provisions, 'subject to any transitional arrangement that may be contained in a possible withdrawal agreement, as of the withdrawal date', that will not apply to the UK.[19] The Notice includes provisions related to authorisations, arrangements and exposures and contracts.

III. The unchanged situation of both the UK, EU and national authorities in the international financial institutions and a future cooperation

The Bank of England and other financial authorities participate at the international standards-setting bodies, like the Basle Committees (parts of the Bank for International Settlements – BIS structure), or the Financial Stability Board (FSB), an organism under the guidance of the G20, which will continue after Brexit to inspire national and EU legislative action, and so to act as an instrument of convergence. One should also allude in this respect to the International Organisation of Securities Commissions (IOSCO), a private institution which has an important coordinating role. We have mentioned that the Political Declaration provides for an obligation of cooperation of the UK and the EU Member States in the international financial 'institutions'. For the UK, the participation to these stan-

---

17 See at this regard, Christos V. Gortsos, The Single Supervisory Mechanism (SSM). Legal aspects of the first pillar of the European Banking Union (NomikiBibliothiki SA, Athens 2015), p 183 ff.

18 See article 308 TFEU and Protocol No. 5, art 3.

19 European Commission, Notice to stakeholders. Withdrawal of the United Kingdom and EU rules in the field of Banking and Payment Services, 8 February 2018, at https://ec.europa.eu/info/sites/info/files/180208-notice-withdrawal-uk-banking-services_en.pdf.

dards setting bodies offers an indirect possibility to influence EU legislation from the outside, and especially the Euro area Member States. The Report of the House of Lords of 15 December 2016, already quoted, mentions in its paragraph 59: 'The UK's influence on international standard-setting bodies, such as the Basel Committee and the Financial Stability Board, will be crucial to ensuring that changes in regulation are consistent internationally'. It added that '...it is in the UK's and EU's mutual interest that the UK should maintain direct influence within the EU, especially in areas where there are less well-developed international standards." And the report continues with a suggestion to the Government which 'should encourage direct regulatory cooperation between UK and EU authorities and, as part of its negotiation, should seek UK input to EU regulation-setting upstream'.[20] This suggestion is on the same line of thinking than the Political Declaration.

The answer given by the Government to this request of the House of Lords also deserves a full quotation:

> 'While we are leaving the EU, we will remain close partners with our neighbours in Europe and will continue taking a leadership role in international regulatory forums...The report is correct in noting the close relationship between UK and EU markets and regulators. The government is looking for a sensible discussion in negotiations about how the UK and EU financial markets can continue to serve one another, and what is needed to support that. This is very much in the interests of both parties.'

If an 'upstream' influence on EU legislation as wished by the House of Lords, appears as difficult to conceive, a cooperation in some fields could be explored. It could be the case, as we will see *infra*, in some limited although sensitive fields.

The continued participation of some Euro area Member States in international standards setting bodies in fields on which they have lost their competence in favour of the EU and the ECB is not compatible with EU law. One may suspect that the presence of the UK in these organs will en-

---

20 See in the same line of thinking, the third report of the International Regulatory Strategy Group (IRSG), an emanation of the City, a report produced in cooperation with Hogan Lovells, London, September 2017, which suggests 'the establishment of a joint committee called "Forum for Regulatory Co-operation" for the purpose of ensuring a strong relationship, promoting regulatory alignment and addressing questions of divergence', Section 6, Summary, p 61.

courage these countries to resist to a possible substitution of their national authorities by a European institution.

The same is true for the G20, especially for its financial branch (where Finance ministers meet) and the IMF. How to persuade countries like France or Germany to progressively renounce to some aspects of their representation in the IMF[21], if the UK remains a full member in all the organs of this institution? How, in the same context, to progress towards a European Monetary Fund that is the object of a proposal of the EU Commission[22] if the UK preserves, with some EU Countries, its individual seat in the Washington's organisations?

IV. The economic and social consequences for the UK

A 'hard Brexit' for the City of London and the other financial places in the UK – meaning the loss for banks located in the UK of the famous passport allowing for doing business in the EU – would (will) have important negative consequences for the UK as in all other sectors.[23] We should refer to some data in order to illustrate the present weight of the UK in the financial industry: from figures given by the British Government on 21 March 2017,[24] the sector employs approximately 1.1 million people and generates approximately £60-67 billion. In a recent article, *The Economist* mentions that 'The sector and its ecosystem of lawyers, consultants, lobbyists and the

21 See *infra*.

22 See the Proposal for a Council Regulation on the establishment of the European Monetary Fund, COM(2017) 827 final, 6 December 2017 (which implied a transformation in a EU body of the present Financial Stability Mechanism (FSM) which was based on an international treaty; this proposal was not accepted by a number of Member States which marked a preference for keeping the European Stability Mechanism as an intergovernmental organisation) and the earlier proposal for a Council Decision laying down measures in view of progressively laying down measures in view of progressively establishing a unified representation of the Euro area in the International Monetary Fund, COM(2015) 603 final, 21 October 2015, a proposal that seems also to have no chance to be adopted.

23 See Adam S. Posen, (2017) 'Drawbridge Economics: The Brexit Reality Check Is Coming', Peterson Institute for International Economics, Washington, November 13, p 8.

24 See Government response to the House of Lords European Union Committee Report, (2016) 'Brexit: financial services', 15 December, on file with the author. See also the figures mentioned by Governor Mark Carney, in his speech on (2014) 'The high road to a responsible, open financial system', Thomas Reuters, Canary Wharf, London, 7 April, p 4.

like employ 2.2 m people, not only in the wealthy centres of the Square Mile, Canary Wharf and Edinburgh but also in places like Cardiff and Bournemouth'.[25] The UK is a global leader in complex insurance, wholesale/investment banking, market infrastructure, portfolio management – associated with asset management – and other areas of financial activities. Other data given by the British Government confirm the importance of the volume of activities involved: over 75 per cent of the EU 27 capital market business is conducted through the UK, and the financial industry in the UK manages £1.2 trillion of pension and other assets on behalf of EU clients. In December 2017, the IMF gave the following figures: 'the financial sector in the UK represents about 7 per cent of GDP but accounts for around 10 per cent of tax revenues and 14 per cent of exports'.[26] In the already quoted article, *The Economist*, referring to a paper written by economists of the Bank for International Settlements, mentions 'the City's centrality to EU financial operations. About half of all the €2.6trn of euro area bonds bought by the ECB's asset-purchase programme came from institutions outside the Eurozone. Banks in Britain were the main facilitators of bond sales.' Moreover, 'the City of London is the leading global player in trading and clearing of derivatives: more than US dollars 450trn of swaps and derivatives are processed through London. Meanwhile, London dominates the processing of euro-denominated interest rate swaps, with 75 per cent of the cleared in the UK. The Bank of England has estimated that about GBP 41trn of these contracts will be affected by Brexit.[27] The Conservative Manifesto for the June 2017 elections observed: 'Our global businesses and London's position as the global centre of finance make us more interconnected with the global economy than any comparable nation.' [28] This explains why the British Government 'believes that an agreement that secures deep market access, on a reciprocal basis, is in both the EU and the UK's interests.' If not, one can expect a transfer to the Continent of systemic international banks.[29]

25 'City under siege. Brexit and political turmoil have broken London' spell as the 'capital of capital', *The Economist* June 29th –July 5th 2019, p 67-70 ad 68.

26 See IMF. Mission concluding statement. United Kingdom: Staff Concluding Statement of the 2017 Article IV Mission, December 20, 2017.

27 Anthony Morton, 'Clearing the Euro: temporary solution only on offer in a no-deal Brexit', March 2019, https://nortonrosefullbright.com/en-de/knowledge/publications/9e4b5910/

28 *The Conservative and Unionist Party Manifesto 2017*, https://www.conservatives.com/manifesto

29 See Marie-Claude Esposito, 'La City de Londres en attendant le Brexit', (2017) Michel Korinman (dir.), *BREXIT !*, L' esprit du temps, Paris, 77-83.

The transfer to the Continent of Global Systemic banks (which will have lost their European passport) and a great part (most?) of the activities of Central Counterparties (CCP) or compensation rooms could mean the loss of more than 100.000 jobs in favour of the EU and the US.[30]

There are predictable consequences for the employment market and the exchange rate of the Pound, which has already lost value in comparison with its more important competitors.

The diminution of fiscal revenue from financial institutions is also to be predicted.

The removal from London of the European Banking Authority (EBA) (and the European Medicines Agency (EMA) is both a symbolic and a material loss.[31]

V. *The impact on the continental financial markets*[32]

Is there a risk of disordered competition of financial places on the basis of attractive regulation for British institutions: a race to the bottom? National authorities involved in the admission of delocalised bank entities are up to resist but they are confronted with uncertainty, time constraint and new problems. The ECB and the national supervisory authorities it coordinates, as well as the banking industry, were already preparing for the hypothesis which appeared to be the more plausible considering the rhythm of the negotiations: the hard Brexit. Would this be the outcome, in spite of the negative vote of the Parliament of 14 March 2019, or could no appropriate solution be found in an agreement on the future relationship of the UK with

30 See *ibid*, p. 80, the declaration of the president of the London Stock Exchange, in September 2016. Paris mobilises at this regard for attracting banks leaving the UK. See also, Laure Baquero, (2019) 'Brexit: déclinaison financière, les grandes lignes', Eco. Conjoncture, March, economic-research.bnpparibas.com.

31 The European Council has adopted on May 24, 2017 a document presented by President Tusk and President Juncker, on the criteria for relocating agencies established in the UK, EMA and EBA for a decision to be taken by the Council, in October 2017, after an assessment by the Commission, see "EU sets out criteria for relocating UK agencies" by Eszter Zalan, *EU Observer*, 24 May 2017. The deadline for a decision was postponed. On 20 November 2017, the decisions were finally taken by drawing lots after votes were tied: Amsterdam got the EMA (against Milan) and Paris, the EBA (against Dublin).

32 See in this respect: (2017) André Sapir, Dirk Schoenmaker and Nicolas Véron, 'Making the Best of Brexit for the EU-27 Financial System', Peterson Institute for International Economics, *Policy Brief*, Washington, February,17-8.

the EU, a number of problems remain: It was generally admitted that only a small number of countries are really attractive to British banks and this feeling was confirmed. The criterion is said to be the quality of the local supervisory authorities and the infrastructure as well as the effectiveness of the resolution process. Many questions are new. For example, how much local management could be integrated in the global management chain? Which interference should be allowed from the group in the management of subsidiaries in the Euro area?[33] Would the localisation of EBA in Paris be positive for the French capital? This was believed by the Government but what has been the real benefit?

The ECB appears decided to 'stick to [their] standards'[34]. As a matter of fact, there is no place for a smooth Brexit either, especially as far as supervision of significant banks is concerned; it means that there can be no doubt about who is in charge. The ECB, as a supervisor, will have many different interviews with banks intending to establish themselves in the EU area, getting the business plans for several years to come. How banks want to structure their activities, how they want to grow, what kind of booking they want to do, what kind of risk management. There are already experienced methods, like the Supervisory Review and Evaluation Process (SREP), and there is a new instrument: the 'Targeted Review of Internal Models' (TRIM) which can be used in order to control the internal model adopted by the banks. Mrs Lautenschläger has a definitive view on this question: 'The ECB has a great quality, which distinguishes it from national authorities: it is neutral in its judgment; it does not fight for one location in lieu of another.'

What is firmly stated is that there will be no 'grandfathering' of British models. We quote again Sabine Lautenschläger, vice chair of the Single Supervisory Board, on this specific point:

> 'We are aware that banks would like us to simply grandfather existing model approvals that were given by the British supervisor. We will not do that. It is not feasible from a legal point of view, and it would not be the most prudent thing to do. Internal models need to be approved by the relevant supervisor, also to meet the obligation of equal treatment: therefore, banks that relocate to the euro area would have to seek a new permission from us'.[35]

33 Questions raised at a Bruegel think-tank meeting in Brussels, 2 June 2017.
34 S. Lautenschläger, vice president of the Single Supervisory Board, 4 May 2017.
35 Speech of May 4, 2017, p 2.

The message of S. Lautenschläger, speaking in Dublin recently, was the same:

> 'From the start, we identified areas of concern for individual banks – particularly those that plan to relocate from the United Kingdom to the EU. We made it clear that we would not accept "empty shells". And we made it clear that we would not accept comprehensive back-branching practices, where banks would provide services to EU clients from branches in the United Kingdom'.[36]

This standpoint doesn't exactly seem to concord with the one expressed two years ago by Mark Carney, the Governor of the Bank of England[37] who proclaimed in 2017:

> 'Brexit will be a litmus test of the future of international cooperation. The UK and the rest of the EU have exactly the same rules and the most highly developed frameworks of supervisory cooperation. Their capital and banking markets are already highly integrated. They have the potential to create the template for trade in financial services'.[38]

This extraordinarily open statement – but which could seem near to the perspectives opened in 2018 by the 'Political Declaration' – contrasts with views expressed by the Governor in a recent past on the specificities of the UK financial system, and the need to preserve them, considering in particular the importance of its financial sector in a widely open economy. Hence the accent put by the Bank of England and its Governor on specific rules, especially on the control of variable compensation (bank bonuses) for banks senior employees in order to fight misconduct with international

36 'A supervisory perspective on 2019 and beyond', 17 January 17 2019, p 1. The whole speech should be quoted where the speaker marks her clear preference for subsidiaries in lieu of branches, because it gives to the European banking supervision 'a whole picture'. But she observes that 'it is not us supervisors who make the rules.

37 We do not pretend by this quotation and the followings to give a complete picture of the position of Governor Carney and the BoE before and after the referendum of June 2016. For a description, see Sylviane de Saint-Seine, 'La Banque d'Angleterre face au Brexit: une campagne houleuse', in Michel Korinman, *Brexit !*, (Bègles, L'esprit du Temps, 2017) Collection Outre-Terre, 68-76. It is, indeed, well-known that some positions adopted by the Governor were criticised by the Brexiters, the Governor being accused to be 'defeatist' on the effects of Brexit for British economy.

38 Mark Carney, 'What a Difference a Decade made', Remarks at the Institute of Finance' s Washington Policy Summit, 20 April 2017, p10.

repercussions (LIBOR, EURIBOR ...)[39] and on ensuring really fit and proper managers.

We must add that the coincidence of rules at a given moment (underscored by Mr Carney[40]), doesn't include any guarantee for the future, after the materialisation of Brexit. The Governor nevertheless observes that the EU and UK are...ideally positioned to create an effective system of deference to each other's comparable regulatory outcomes, supported by commitments to common minimum standards and open supervisory cooperation' (ibid) and he adds that 'Such an outcome would be entirely consistent with the UK Government's stated aim of a new *comprehensive, bold and ambitious free trade*[41] relationship with the EU that embraces goods, services and network industries.' He nevertheless recognised that financial services are only part of the negotiation and 'Given our responsibilities to promote financial stability, the Bank – like its counterparts on the continent – must plan for all eventualities.'

What precedes demonstrates that in the reaction of the Euro area supervisors we are far from kind of automatic mechanisms of recognition as the principle of equivalence, traditionally applied with banks of third countries. One has to take into account that both the application of a (two years) transitory period provided in the Leaving agreement and the negotiation under the terms of the Political Declaration depends on the entry into force of the agreement itself. Hence, the initiatives of the European Commission, the advertisements of the European and supervisory authorities as well as of professional associations addressed to national authorities, stakeholders and private parties. The Commission published a Contingency Action Plan on 13 November 2018.[42] In the 'Questions and Answers' document quoted in note 39, the Commission mentions that 'after exam-

39 The Bank of England observes that limitation by EU law of variable compensation (banker bonus) in relation with fixed salaries results in an uncontrollable inflation of the fixed salaries, on which the authorities have no power.

40 'The High Road to a responsible, Open Financial System', 7 April 2017, p 9.

41 The words are borrowed to the letter of Mrs May to the President of the European Council, Donald Tusk, 29 March 2017.

42 See, for example, European Commission, Notice to stakeholders. Withdrawal of the United Kingdom and EU rules in the field of Banking and Payment Services, Brussels, 8 February 2018; European Commission, Preparing for the withdrawal of the United Kingdom from the EU on 30 March 2019: Implementing the Commission's Contingency Action Plan, 19 December 2018, Com(2018) 890 final https://eur-lex.europa.eu/legal-content/EN/TXT/PDF/?uri=CELEX%3A52018DC0890; European Commission, MEMO, Questions and Answers: the consequences of the United Kingdom leaving the European Union without a ratified Withdraw-

ining the risks linked to a no deal scenario in the financial sector, and taking into account the views of the European Central Bank and the European Supervisors Authorities, the Commission has concluded that only a limited number of contingency measures are necessary to safeguard financial stability in the EU27.' The two temporary and conditional measures are necessary 'because preparedness actions from market operators alone are clearly insufficient to address these risks by the withdrawal date'. They concern the regulatory framework applicable to central counterparties and to central securities depositories. In these two cases, the UK regulation would temporarily be judged equivalent to the EU regulation in these fields.

The ECB will not accept 'empty shells' companies. 'Any bank that operates in the euro area must be a "bank". And any "real" bank has adequate risk management, sufficient local staff and operational independence.'[43] The ECB will be cautious of regulatory and supervisory arbitrage. Some banks requiring entrance in the EU would be significant; in that case, they will be subject to direct supervision by the ECB. If they are not, they will be supervised by national authorities 'under the common European supervisory approach by the ECB'. The third-country branches of banking groups (and investment firms) may pose a problem for their integration in the Euro area because there are different rules applying to branches in third countries. That 'will run counter to the idea of a level playing field in the euro area'. What Ms. Lautenschläger holds for a fragmented approach could be treated in the present revision of the Capital Requirement Regulation (CRR) and Directive (CRD) (*ibid.*). So there could be a possibility to get 'a holistic view of all the activities within a banking group'.

Anyway, as said by Mrs. Nouy, chair of the Supervisory Board of the ECB:

> 'What is sure for us is that the UK will always be important. We will always have very important and intense relationships with our colleagues on the other side of the Channel.'[44]

The correct reaction would consist in more integration in lieu of fragmentation of the Euro area banking industry. There is now a revision in

---

al Agreement (no deal Brexit). 19 December 2018, https://ec.europa.eu/info/sites/info/files/contingency_qanda_on_pdf.

43 S. Lautenschläger, 'Some supervisory expectations for banks relocating in the euro area', speech, Frankfurt, 4 May 2017, p 16.

44 D. Nouy, Introductory statement to the press conference on the ECB Annual Report on supervisory activities 2016, 27 March 2017, p 1.

progress of the legislation that has made possible the transfer of competences from the Member States Authorities to the ECB and the SRM. Progressing is an answer to Brexit: the strengthening of the regulatory and supervisory powers of ESMA and EIOPA is necessary along the model of the European Supervisory Board of the ECB. The relocation of Central Counterparties (CCP), which was stopped by the General Court for the reason of the absence of a legal basis in the EU primary law,[45] was also a possibility if article 22 of the Statutes of the ESCB and the ECB would have been revised, but other ways are open. It is precisely this sector which was mentioned by Governor Carney as an example for cooperation in the framework of a renewed cooperation. In a speech of 20 June 2017 the Governor of the Bank of England specifically mentioned the case of CCP's, centralised compensation organs in the field of derivatives, as a specific example of such a process[46] but his remarks could have a broader meaning. They could apply to any critical cross-border infrastructures for financial markets. So LCH in London which works in eighteen currencies for the undertakings in 55 jurisdictions, handling more than 90 per cent of compensated swaps of interest rate and 98 per cent of compensated swaps in euro.

From another speech, we will extract a sentence which sums up the thinking of Governor Carney: 'The combination of robust international standards and greater trust as a consequence of transparent implementation and intensive supervisory cooperation can create a system of equivalence and mutual deference'.[47]

In this context, the question of the localisation and surveillance of CCP's is particularly striking. The Commission has proposed in 2017 to strengthen the rules applicable to the supervision of these mechanisms in the perspective of the departure of the EU from the more important European financial centre. Two regulations have been adopted at this regard. The first one, called EMIR Review1, is Regulation (EU) 2019/834 of the European Parliament and the Council of 20 May 2019 amending Regulation (EU) No 648/2012 as regards the clearing obligation, the suspension of the clearing obligation, the reporting requirements, the risk-mitigation techniques for OTC derivatives contracts not cleared by a central counterparty, the registration and supervision of trade depositories and the re-

---

45 See *infra*, p xx: GC 4 March 2015, T-496/13, *United Kingdom v ECB*, ECLI: T:2015:133.

46 'A Fine Balance' speech at the Mansion House, London, 20 June 2017, p 11.

47 'What a Difference a Decade Makes' Remarks at the Institute of Finance's Washington Policy Summit, The Reagan Centre, Washington DC, 20 April 2017, p 8.

quirements for trade repositories.[48] The other regulation, EMIR Review2, is more specifically relied to the Brexit. The proposal COM(2017) 331 has been agreed by both the EP and the Council but it will be at the agenda of the European Parliament after the Summer 2019 due to the need for the Plenary to adopt a corrigendum. It will amend Regulation (EU) No 1095/10 establishing a European Supervisory Authority (ESMA) and Regulation (EU) No 648/12 as regards the process and authorities involved for the authorisation of the procedures and authorities involved for the authorization of CCPs and requirements for the recognition of third-country CCPs.

At the same time the European Central Bank had adopted a draft for a decision of the European Parliament and the Council, taken under the simplified revision procedure foreseen in Article 129, par. 3 TFEU for the modification of article 22 for the ESCB and ECB Statutes. This proposal aimed at adding a competence for the ECB to set up rules on compensation systems in the field of financial instruments.

It is well-known that the General Court, in a case opposing the UK to the ECB (Case T-496/11 4 March 2015 ECLI.EU.T.215.113) denied that article 22 of the Statutes of the ESCB and the ECB which allows it to regulate clearing and payments systems in euro could extend to the regulation of all clearing systems, including those related to transactions in securities. Using for the first time the procedure, provided by articles 129, par.3 TFEU and 40 of the statutes of the ESCB and ECB which allows to the ECB to propose by an unanimous recommendation the revision of some articles of its statutes, which could then be adopted by the ordinary legislative procedure, the ECB made a recommendation for a decision amending article 22 of the statutes.[49] In its opinion of 3 October 2017, on this recommendation, the Commission which positively welcomes the initiative of the ECB complementing its proposal on clearing systems for financial instruments denominated in euro, suggests amendments in order to, on the one hand, refer to the 'objectives of the ECB' and to the carrying of its tasks and on the other hand, to the imperative of the future ECB regulations to be 'consistent with acts adopted by the European Parliament and the Council and with measures adopted under such acts'.[50]On 20 March 2019 the ECB withdrew its recommendation amending Article 22 of the

48 OJ L141, 28 May 2019, p 42-63.

49 See the ECB recommendation (ECB/2017/18), OJ C212, 1-7.2017, p 14.

50 OJ C340, 11.10.2017, p 1; see European Parliament. Legislative train schedule. Updated rules on Central Counterparty (CCP) Supervision/EMIR Review 2, 20 June 2019.

Statute of the European System of Central Banks and the European Central Bank because it considered that the changes introduced by the legislator during the trilogue would have drastically limited the powers of the ECB on this matter, have seriously distorted its proposal and interfered 'with some fundamental principles of the Treaty, with the institutional balance and with the independent exercise by the ECB of its monetary policy competence', as mentioned in the Press communiqué of 20 March 2019, including a letter from which we draw the quotation from President Draghi to Mr Tajani, President of the European Parliament.[51]

The second regulation (EMIR review 2) includes a modification of the regulation on markets infrastructures (EMIR) as well as procedures and authorities related to the authorisation of CCP's of third countries.[52] It aims to equip the Capital Markets Union with a more effective and coherent system of surveillance of the CCP's in the interest of pursuing the integration of capital markets, financial stability and a level playing field. Third countries CCP's would be classified as not important (tier 1) and systematically important ones or susceptible to become so (tier 2) which could compromise the financial stability of the Union. The first ones would be submitted for their recognition to the same rules as the organisms active within the Union, the others would be submitted to supplementary measures. An executive specific section of ESMA would be in charge of establishing whether or not rules applicable in third countries to the CCP's under tier 2 are comparable to the rules imposed to CCP's established under EU legislation. If ESMA, with the agreement of the central bank issuing the related currency, recommends to the Commission to not recognise a tier 2 mechanism, the Commission could adopt an execution act requiring the organism in question to be established within the EU and authorizing it to exercise there its functions.

In a Communication prior to its regulation proposal[53] the Commission affirms its remaining engagement in favour of the integration of financial

---

51 See https://www.ecb.europa.eu/press/pr/date/2019/html/ecb.pr190320~df3e12da5a.en.html. A letter was also addressed to the Bulgarian Presidency.

52 Proposal of the Commission, 13 June 2017, COM (2017) 331 final.

53 Communication from the Commission to the European Parliament, the Council and the European Central Bank, Responding to the challenges for critical financial market infrastructures and further developing the Capital Markets Union, COM(2017) 225 final, May 4 2017. See also Proposal for a regulation of the European Parliament and of the Council, amending Regulation (EU) No 648/2012 as regards the clearing obligation…, 4 May 2017 COM (2017) 208 final. This proposal was approved on plenary by the European Parliament, on 18 April 2019.

markets, of its international obligations and the possibility of [recognising] the equivalence for the CCP's, and states that it is conscious of the necessity to avoid an undue fragmentation of the global system. It nevertheless insists that specific arrangements based on objective criteria are necessary for ensuring that, where CCP's play a systemic key role for financial markets and have a direct impact on the responsibilities, including financial stability and monetary policy of institutions and authorities of the EU and its Member States, that they are submitted to safeguards provided by the legal framework of the EU. And the Commission concluded with these words: 'This includes, where necessary, enhanced supervision and/or location requirements.' We may see in these considerations a kind of answer to the speeches of the Bank of England Governor: cooperation among authorities is needed but responsibilities in future will be separated. A common interest to be preserved.

The remaining links between the UK and the Continent in financial matters will be important. Let us briefly quote as examples:

1. The participation to international organisations: IMF, BIS and Basel committees, FSB, G7, G20, with a more central role for EU institutions. As already mentioned, the continued presence of the UK in these organisms could make the substitution of the EU to its Member States and institutions not easier. We particularly refer to 'the progressively establishing unified representation of the euro area in the IMF', as included in a proposal of the Commission for a Council decision in line with the so-called Five Presidents report of June 2015 on Completing Europe's Economic and Monetary Union.[54] This proposal opts for a 'gradual approach' involving "intermediate transitional steps for representation in the International Monetary and Financial Committee (IMFC) and the IMF Executive Board. This cautious approach derives from the fact that if the ECOFIN Council has agreed in the past (2006) on the necessity of a representation of the EU in the IMF, it considered this move as a longer-term goal, the move to a single euro area as does, it should be noticed, the Commission in the Explanatory Memorandum of its proposal: 'the external representation of the euro area will also depend on the future status of the euro area in the IMF that member countries of the IMF would be willing to grant.'[55]

54 COM (2015) 603 final, 21 October 2015.

55 The European Central Bank, on 6 April 2016, has issued an opinion on this proposal, CON/2016/22, OJ C216, 16 June 2016, which includes some reservations.

2. Swap agreements and other kinds of bilateral agreements, more or less formal, between respective central banks, will be ready to be activated in consideration of the remaining role of the City in financing continental banks and the general practice among global currencies in time of crises.

VI. Some short conclusive remarks

The continuity in British official attitude since the beginning of European integration is remarkable: from the initial refusal of the UK Government to participate to the building of the Communities and its intend to dilute the young EEC in a free trade area, the five so-called economic tests of Gordon Brown to be met for the adoption of the euro by the UK, the addition of opt-outs from crucial realisations of the Union, to the David Cameron's Bloomberg speech of 23 January 2013, the short-lived Arrangement of 18 and 19 February 2016 concluded within the Council between Cameron and his counterparts, but which didn't prevent the negative result of the referendum in June 2016, the extraordinary favourable referendum of 1975 and the more than 40 years of membership of the EU both appear as almost incredible exceptions in the history of the relations between the UK and the Continent after the second World War during which we ought so much to its resistance.

Perhaps an opportunity exists to manage a reasonable cooperation on common vital interests between the two entities should Brexit really happen: a UK having become a third country and the EU progressing towards a sui generis federal construction.

While outlining the objectives of the negotiation in her Lancaster speech of January 2017,[56] she mentioned first 'Certainty and clarity', commenting that this 'first objective is crucial'. This remains true now.

The Brexit is bad for the British financial sector as it is in general a disaster for Britain. It should encourage us, anyway, despite of all odds to reform the process of continental integration and cultivate a sound relation with our difficult neighbour.

---

56 See the reference in note 3.

Comments on Jean-Victor Louis

Stefan Griller

Abstract

Should the UK indeed leave the EU, there is a fair chance that the dynamics of EMU-deepening could change, including the Banking Union. Of course, there is no guarantee for that. But a heavyweight with the tendency of decelerating progress will disappear.

After a 'No-Deal-Brexit' any directly enforceable right to establishment for British financial institutions under EU law would be dependent on secondary EU legislation. This should not be too high a hurdle given that secondary legislation allows for the establishment of financial institutions owned by third country nationals of third country enterprises.

A specific issue concerns Clearing Houses. It would be preferable if at least those of them providing services of systemic relevance would be established within the Euro area. However, there is need for a transitory arrangement. An ESMA-decision would be advisable in order to guarantee the smooth transition of clearing services into the post Brexit era.

Introductory Remarks

These comments are brief, for the simple reason that I fully concur with Jean-Victor Louis' analysis, be it the identification of the most salient issues or be it his respective observations. Some complementary aspects shall nevertheless be added.

Given that, at the time of writing, still no agreement under Article 50 TEU could be reached, my working hypothesis is that there will be no such agreement and that the UK would on 31 October 2019, find itself as a third country without specific treaty arrangement with the EU ('no deal Brexit');[1] but that it would, with some adjustments of its WTO-commitments, *remain* a WTO-member, and that, consequently, its trade relations

1 COM (2018) 556 final/2, Communication from the Commission, Preparing for the withdrawal of the United Kingdom from the European Union 30 March 2019, p 4.

with the EU and its members would thus be regulated by WTO law.[2] Governing the business of financial service providers and thus closely EMU-related is the General Agreement on Trade in Services (GATS), including the Understanding on commitments in financial services, together with country specific schedules.[3] The latter would have to be adjusted at the occasion of the UK leaving the EU, which might equally take some time.

The envisaged alternative scenario:[4] that there would be a transition period until 1 January 2021 for negotiating the future relations between the EU and the UK, would make a smooth transition into such relations much more likely.

As always, the legislator, in this case, the EU and the UK could by concluding an agreement under Article 50 TEU render most (but not all) of the following irrelevant from one day to another.

I. On the Dynamics of EMU-participation and EMU-reform

At a very general level we may ask: Will the dynamics of EMU-participation change once the UK would have left? Legally, there is not much to say. Protocol 15 will be abrogated. That Protocol provides, side by side with Protocol 17 on Denmark, for an exemption from the general obligation to participate in the 3rd stage of the EMU. It is well known that the Council's decision to end derogation could, once the convergence criteria are met, be taken by qualified majority, theoretically even against the will of the Member State in question. This obligation is now to be found in Article 140 TFEU. Nevertheless, some of the younger Member States like Poland used to point at the UK when it comes to debates on the obligation to join the EMU. Once the UK will have gone, Denmark remains the only Member State without such an obligation. This might result in an in-

2 Compare more in detail, stressing the numerous complicated problems which are, also under WTO law, being caused by Brexit: Christoph Herrmann, 'Brexit and the WTO: challenges and solutions for the United Kingdom (and the European Union)', in ECB Legal Conference 2017. Shaping a new legal order for Europe: a tale of crises and opportunities (2017), 165–179.

3 Compare the Understanding on commitments in financial services: https://www.wto.org/english/tratop_e/serv_e/21-fin_e.htm and the current EU schedule on specific commitments: https://docs.wto.org/dol2fe/Pages/FE_Search/FE_S_S009-itsDP.aspx?language=E&CatalogueIdList=31391 or http://i-tip.wto.org/services/GATS_Detail.aspx/?id=23178&sector_path=0000700044 (accessed September 2018).

4 COM(2018) 556 final/2, at p 4.

creased pressure on the others to respect their obligation including Sweden. However, in times of differentiation and disintegration, also the contrary might be true. For we have to realise that exerting pressure on a Member State might in the near future even more easily result in initiatives to trigger Article 50 TEU. Therefore, the resulting perspective is ambiguous.

The second point is closely related: will the dynamics of EMU-deepening change, including the Banking Union? We might remember that the UK has a reputation of watering down draft initiatives sometimes to a point where the original idea had almost been lost, only to in the end block the remains anyway. The most famous example in recent years was the Treaty on Stability, Coordination and Governance in the Economic and Monetary Union, including the so-called Fiscal Compact. Earlier, both a treaty amendment and secondary legislation had been envisaged. It had been mainly the UK blocking these solutions, which led to the famous escape from EU law to international law.[5] After Brexit we could expect that the fiscal compact could be integrated into the Treaties, possibly even by secondary legislation,[6] considering that it's watered-down final version comes very close to the respective obligation under the six pack. However, it remains to be seen whether this incorporation will happen. Brexit could thus turn out as revitalising the Community method also in the field of EMU. However, we cannot rule out that the poison of intergovernmentalism has already done its work and that nothing would happen. What I would, at any event, not expect is that the remaining Member States would, at the occasion of integrating the matter into EU law, revitalise the more ambitious first drafts of the fiscal compact rules.

Similar, but, as far as details are concerned, different examples can be found in pieces of secondary legislation, namely banking union legislation, where the UK had strongly influenced the outcome, not the least by arguing that it would otherwise face disadvantages as a nonparticipating member, and sometimes by even pointing to possible later EMU accession, which would be more likely if the UK's ideas would be reflected. Also here, the remaining Member States could take or accept fresh initiatives,

5 Compare Paul Craig, The Stability, Coordination and GovernanceTreaty: Principle, Politics and Pragmatism, ELRev (2012) 231, 232 f.

6 In fact, this is the core of the Commission proposal COM(2017) 824 final from 6 December 2017, to enact, mainly on the basis of Article 126 (14) TFEU, a Council directive laying down provisions for strengthening fiscal responsibility and the medium-term budgetary orientation in the Member States.

once the heavy stumbling block is no longer there.[7] However, we can only speculate whether that will happen.

II. On the Importance of Commercial Presence on 31 October 2019

My third point is related to the freedom of establishment and the strategic options of British financial service providers, mainly credit institutions during the transitory period to Brexit. A first assumption is that the single licence to do business by way of providing services (in the sense of Articles 56 et seqq. TFEU) would disappear in the case of a no deal Brexit.[8] Another assumption is that the EU commitments under the GATS would in principle remain unchanged, and thus also be applicable to the UK as a third country.[9]

Would it, under such circumstances, be better for British banks to move or to establish subsidiaries before or after the lapse of the (prolonged) two year period? Again, all of that may be irrelevant from one day to the other once an arrangement between the EU and the UK is reached.

WTO-commitments of the EU regarding financial services would, under the assumption that they will, without any substantive change, be applied to UK financial service providers after the leave of the EU, not include the right to "actively" provide services within the EU without any establishment – the so-called "presence of natural persons" in WTO-terminology.[10] Thus, UK service providers would need to obtain a licence in one of the 27

7 Compare, in this regard, COM (2017)291 final, Reflection paper on the deepening of the economic and monetary union, p 19; COM(2017) 592 final, Communication on completing the Banking Union, both with further references.

8 Generally, compare COM(2018) 556 final/2, at p 14 et seq.; as well as the 'Notice to stakeholders' issued by the European Commission, 8 February 2018: 'Withdrawal of the United Kingdom and EU Rules in the Field of Banking and Payment Services'.

9 This assumption is not self-evident, but, it is argued, likely. To a certain extent this would probably also depend on reciprocity: that the UK in turn would, in the absence of a specific trade agreement with the EU, treat EU Member States' financial institutions as third countries' institutions, and to apply the standards it used to apply as an EU vis-à-vis third countries.

10 Compare the Understanding on commitments in financial services: https://www.wto.org/english/tratop_e/serv_e/21-fin_e.htm and the current EU schedule on specific commitments: https://docs.wto.org/dol2fe/Pages/FE_Search/FE_S_S009-its DP.aspx?language=E&CatalogueIdList=31391 or http://i-tip.wto.org/services/GATS_Detail.aspx/?id=23178&sector_path=0000700044 (accessed September 2018).

EU Member States. Regarding such authorisation, there will be no automatism in accepting the prudential supervision arrangements that British financial service providers established with their home authorities.[11] By contrast, e.g. in the field of banking, the ECB would, in the case of "significant" banks, have to fully scrutinise all relevant conditions before an eventual authorisation to take up the business of a credit institution under regulation 1024/2013. However, such decisions should be taken without any discrimination, flowing from the right to national treatment under the General Agreement on Trade in Services (GATS), including the Understanding on commitments in financial services.[12]

Such non-discriminatory scrutiny applies already today for UK financial service providers who seek getting established in another EU Member State, i.e. through commercial presence especially by creating a new service provider or a subsidiary. As long as the UK is an EU member, however, there is a right to establishment flowing from the treaties. There doesn't seem to be a point for restricting that right resulting solely from triggering the exit procedure.[13] Once established, the financial service provider would later benefit from fundamental rights protection when it comes to a possible withdrawal of the existing authorisation, even after Brexit. Paradoxically, the freedom to conduct a business and the right to property[14] would provide firm protection for established banks even after a no deal Brexit, probably even better if compared to the rights of natural persons.

However, after the materialisation of Brexit, and in the absence of any agreement, any directly enforceable right to establishment under EU law would be dependent on secondary EU legislation.[15] UK banks would then be third country banks. This should not be too high a hurdle, though, given that secondary legislation allows for the establishment of financial institutions owned by third country nationals of third country enterprises.

11 Compare also Louis' contribution.

12 Compare supra n 3.

13 Compare in this regard, even if in a totally different field, the judgment of the ECJ on the validity of a European arrest warrant: Case C-327/18 *PPU, RO*, ECLI:EU:C:2018:733.

14 Articles 16 and 17 EU Charter of Fundamental Rights.

15 This applies also to the right to establishment flowing from WTO law, given the reluctance of the ECJ to directly enforce WTO obligations according to its standing jurisprudence, starting with Case C-149/96, *Portugal vs. Council*, ECLI:EU:C:1999:574.

However, Regulation 1024/2013[16] establishes that the ECB, when deciding on authorisation requests, has to apply also national legislation. Should a Member State restrict the establishment of third country banks -even if this should happen mainly to reduce competition for its own banks – that could be disadvantageous for British banks. Such restriction appears rather unlikely given that Member States might feel tempted to draw advantage from offering investment opportunities, and the established bank would then benefit again from its right to establishment in any other EU Member State. Consequently, economically speaking this should not be a big issue.

There is an alternative solution to this scenario: equivalence decisions to be issued by the European Commission.[17] This might be done on the basis of individual scrutiny of the third country, here: the UK after a no deal Brexit. Such a decision is to be drafted for specific services and requirements and includes broad discretion for the European Commission.[18] Therefore, this can also be seen as a bargaining chip in the ongoing negotiations.

Even if we might assume that, given the common standards which have been developed during the last decades, the UK system should in many instances qualify as equivalent, there is no guarantee of such respective decision, nor that it would be swiftly taken by the Commission. At any event, compared to a financial service provider established within the EU, there is surely a disadvantage in legal certainty and enforceability. Hence, if British financial service providers want to be on the safe side it would be advisable to move or to create subsidiaries before the materialisation of a no deal Brexit.

---

16 Article 4 Council Regulation 1024/2013 conferring specific tasks on the European Central Bank concerning policies relating to the prudential supervision of credit institutions, OJ 2013/L 287/63.

17 It should be added that doing business for third country financial institutions can be simplified by a number of so-called equivalence decisions to be issued by the European Commission; compare the overview at https://ec.europa.eu/info/business-economy-euro/banking-and-finance/international-relations/recognition-non-eu-financial-frameworks-equivalence-decisions_en#documents; https://ec.europa.eu/info/sites/info/files/overview-table-equivalence-decisions_en.pdf (last visited October 2018); compare also *European Parliament, Directorate General for Internal Policies*, Implications of Brexit on EU Financial Services (2017).

18 For more details compare *European Parliament* (above n 17) at pp 53 ff.

III. On the Systemic Importance of Clearing Houses

While, generally speaking, creating establishments for financial service providers within the EU-27 is mainly a question of (continuity for) business opportunities, this might be different when it comes to the specific issue of authorising central counterparties' (CCPs) businesses;[19] a CCP is a 'legal person that interposes itself between the counterparties to the contracts traded on one or more financial markets, becoming the buyer to every seller and the seller to every buyer'.[20] Today, around 99% of the Euro denominated Union Market is being cleared by UK based CCPs – with estimated daily values of repos and open positions in interest-rate swaps of respectively € 101 billion and € 33 trillion.[21]

Consequently, in respect of CCPs, smooth transition might be of systemic importance for the EMU in general.[22]

To start with, disturbances in clearing systems might impact on the primary objective set for the ECB's monetary policy: price stability. Effects might weaken the liquidity position of credit institutions which in turn might harm the payment system. Moreover, such disturbances might impair the transmission system of the ECB's monetary policy.

Against this background there is, as the ECB has pointed out,[23] even a case for requiring CCPs to be located within a Euro area Member State. Already today, specific supervisory arrangements between the ECB and the Bank of England are in place, the smooth functioning of which is not be-

---

19 Compare also Louis, in this volume, at p. 221 ff.

20 Article 2(1) of Regulation 648/2012 on OTC derivatives, central counterparties and trade repositories, OJ 2012/L 201/1, last amended by Commission Delegated Regulation 2017/979, OJ 2017/L 148/1.

21 ECB/2017/18), Recommendation for a Decision of the European Parliament and of the Council amending Article 22 of the Statute of the European System of Central Banks and of the European Central Bank, OJ 2017/C 212/14, p. 15.

22 Compare, on the risk reducing purpose of regulating such business Commission Staff Working Document, Impact Assessment, Accompanying the documentProposal for a Regulation of the European Parliament and of the Councilamending Regulation (EU) No 1095/2010 establishing a European Supervisory Authority (European Securities and Markets Authority) and amending Regulation (EU)No 648/2012 as regards the procedures and authorities involved for the authorisation ofCCPs and the requirements for the recognition of third-country CCPs, SWD(2017) 246 final, 13 June 2017.

23 ECB/2017/18), Recommendation for a Decision of the European Parliament and of the Council amending Article 22 of the Statute of the European System of Central Banks and of the European Central Bank, OJ 2017/C 212/14. Compare also the respective Commission Opinion of 3 October 2017, 2017/C 340/1.

yond doubt. Consequently, even with the UK as an EU member, it would be preferable if CCPs – at least those providing services of systemic relevance – would be established within the Euro area and thus being subject to the regulatory power of the ECB. This is even more so once the UK would be a third country. For any authorisation of a CCP under Article 14 of Regulation 648/2012 would lapse after Brexit. Consequently, any such CCP would, in order to smoothly continue with its clearing activities, need an authorisation as a legal person established in the EU. Otherwise, the smooth continuation not only of the CCP's business, but moreover of the European clearing system as such would be endangered with the UK becoming a third country.

This might be somehow mitigated by the possibility for third country CCPs to get recognised for providing clearing services in the EU.[24] However, this is only possible on the basis of a respective decision by ESMA, interacting with the Commission, and including a certain margin of appreciation. Consequently, action is paramount in order to guarantee the smooth transition of clearing services into the post Brexit era.

The background for this initiative is a judgment handed down by the General Court, Case T-496/11, *UK vs ECB*, ECLI:EU:T:2015:133, denying the competence of the ECB to set such a requirement.

24 Article 25 of Regulation 648/2012.
See also COM(2017) 331 final of 13.6.2017, with a proposal to amend that regulation (not yet passed).

Common Foreign and Security Policy After Brexit

Maria José Rangel de Mesquita

Abstract

Within the wider context and scope of CFSP the EU Global Strategy and some subsequent developments on CSDP may be relevant to the shaping of the future EU-UK relationship after Brexit raising the question of what could be the status of the UK regarding participation in CFSP: a mere third State or ex-EU third State. Different forms of future cooperation have been envisaged in several initiatives, both from the EU and the UK side, addressing the issue of CFSP and CSDP after Brexit. The contents of both the texts of the Withdrawal Agreement and of the Political Declaration of 25 November 2018 regarding the area of CFSP/CSDP may indicate that the future EU-UK relationship in this area, on one hand is rather programmatic and modest and that the concrete terms of the participation are rather narrow and still need to be detailed (in future agreements) and that no specific ex-EU Member State statute is envisaged; and, on the other hand, that some of the concrete areas in which closer cooperation is envisaged (in particular PESCO and defence capabilities development) relate to the sub-area of CSDP. However, the guidelines laid down in both texts appear to still leave room to shape a differentiated third State status in the field of CFSP/CSDP. Even in areas where the status of third State is clearly mentioned – PESCO and EU missions and operations – neither the rules of third States participation are definitively defined nor is the envisaged Framework Participation Agreement necessarily bound to follow a single model. The next step – negotiating and agreeing on more detailed rules – appears to be an opportunity to envisage the features of a possible differentiated third State status in the field of CFSP/CSDP.

I. Introductory remarks: External Action, Global Strategy and beyond

A. The wider context: EU External Action and CFSP and CSDP within the CFSP

Addressing the issue of the future of European Union (EU) Common Foreign and Security Policy (CFSP) after Brexit requires two previous remarks regarding its *context* – the EU External Action as the wider (area of competences) context of CFSP – and its *scope* – the CFSP itself including the subarea of competences regarding specifically the Common Security and Defence Policy (CSDP). And this is so for two main reasons: firstly, whatever the model of the future relations between the EU and the United Kingdom (UK) within and beyond the framework of the withdrawal agreement may be in the specific area of CFSP, it cannot exclude the overall framework and approach in the field of EU External Action, including CFSP, laid down in the *Global Strategy for the EU's Foreign and Security Policy* (EU Global Strategy) and the subsequent developments; secondly, within the (largest) CFSP the CSDP raises particular issues regarding the future possible cooperation between the EU and UK, especially regarding participation in EU CFSP instruments and international (either regional or universal) organizations in the field of international security and defence involving military capacities, in particular NATO.[1]

Within the wider context and scope of CFSP the EU Global Strategy and some subsequent developments may be particularly relevant to the shaping of the future EU-UK relationship (see B. below), raising the question of what could be the status of the UK regarding participation in CFSP: a mere third State or ex-EU third State. The text will further address initiatives regarding CFSP and CSDP after Brexit, both in the EU and UK perspective (see II. below), as well as the final text of the Withdrawal Agreement and the Political Declaration of 25 November 2018 (see III. below) and the way they envisage the future EU-UK relationship in the field of CFSP and CSDP – and whether they admit or, at least, do not exclude the participation of the UK in CFSP and CSDP and respective initiatives with a status that may differ from the status of the third States that have already been allowed to cooperate with the EU in that field of CFSP and CSDP. Finally, the text will focus on the issue of shaping a possible differentiated third State status in the field of CFSP and CSDP (see IV. below).

---

1 The text corresponds essentially to the intervention in the European Constitutional Law Network, Lisbon Workshop 23–24 June 2017, *Brexit – Challenge or end of EU constitutional law? The future of EU policies after Brexit* although some subsequent developments have been further considered in the text. In order to avoid overlapping with other External Action-related topics addressed in the Conference, the text focuses mainly on CFSP (as a significant part of External Action), including the CSDP and does not address as well the issue of the consequences of a UK break out on the possible design of the relationship with the EU (see T Oliver, 'What if the UK were to break up? A closer look at an English Foreign policy', available at www.blogs.lse.ac.uk/brexit/2017/06/09/english-foreign-policy-what-if-the-uk-were-to-break-up/).

B. *The Global Strategy for the EU's Foreign and Security Policy and follow-up: trends on the EU side*

The presentation of the *Global Strategy for the EU's Foreign and Security Policy* (EU Global Strategy)[2] by the High Representative of the Union for Foreign Affairs and Security Policy intends to establish a new (although ambitious) overall framework and approach – a political vision – in the field of EU External Action, including CFSP and establish the EU priorities in this respect.

The EU Global Strategy assumed that present times are times of «existential crisis, within and beyond the EU» and that the European project is being questioned in many ways, thus proposing a «stronger Europe» – that EU citizens deserve and the wider world expects – based on shared interests (and values) and oriented by clear principles (and principled pragmatism) and focused to pursue *five* clear priorities – the security of the Union; promoting State and Societal Resilience to EU East and South; developing an integrated approach to conflicts and crisis; promoting and supporting cooperative regional orders; and, finally, reinforcing global governance for the 21st Century, based on International law, including the principles of the UN and the Helsinki Final Act[3] – which are related to the macro-area of competences of the EU External Action as such, as foreseen by the Treaty of Lisbon.[4] The intention to assume the responsibility of the EU as a global stakeholder, as the Treaty of Lisbon announced, is envisaged by the EU Global Strategy as a shared responsibility meaning being engaged with other players and partnerships in a connected (networked) world. Moreover, and concerning the priorities established in the EU Global Strategy, three features must be underlined: first, regarding promoting security of the Union (in the fields of defence, cyber, counter terrorism, energy and strategic communications) the idea of an «appropriate level of ambition and strategic autonomy» is announced – possibly (also) meaning a shift of strategy to the further development of an own EU defence policy; second, the idea of promoting resilience (of States and societies), both at east and south, within and beyond European neighbourhood policy, as a

2 Shared Vision, Common Action: a Stronger Europe. A Global Strategy for the European Union's Foreign and Security Policy (June 2016) – consulted as well as the other EU documents further mentioned in www.eeas.europa.eu.

3 See EU Global Strategy (2016), 3.1 to 3.5.

4 See also *Conclusions on the Global Strategy for the External and Security Policy of the Union* approved by the EU Foreign Affairs Council (FA Council), 17 October / 2016, CFSP/PESC 814, CSDP/PSDC 572.

way to achieve transformation and attraction towards the EU- namely through the establishment of closer relations within the European Neighbourhood Policy (ENP) in order to spur transformation in neighbour (and also other) third countries and the targeting of the most acute cases of governmental, economic, societal and climate/energy fragility and the development of more effective migration policies for Europe and its partners; third, the clear aspiration, as a global player, to aim at transformation (rather than preservation) of the existing international order – mainly through striving for a strong UN as the bedrock of the multilateral rules-based order and the development of global coordinated responses and also its commitment to global governance by the determination to reform the UN, including the Security Council.[5]

Two connections may be established between the EU Global Strategy and the future EU-UK relationship in the field of CFSP/CSDP: on one hand the timing of its presentation can be read (also) as a 'reaction' to the Brexit referendum (since the EU announces its political will to reinforce its role as a global player); on the other hand the translation of the EU «political vision» (as presented in the EU Global Strategy) into action has led to a significant development in the field of CFSP, mainly CSDP, through the adoption of three main categories of initiatives – political, institutional and financial – in some of which the UK may participate during and after the transition period.

In fact, the subsequent translation of the ‚political vision' and the five broad priorities expressed in the EU Global Strategy into concrete initiatives and actions has led to the significant development of the CSDP, leading to the EU Security and Defence package» based on three pillars:[6]

i) a '*new level of ambition in security and defence*' agreed within the Council[7] as new political goals and ambitions for Europeans to take more responsibility for their own security and defence;
ii) the *European Defence Action Plan,*[8] aimed at facilitating and incentivising defence cooperation between Member States through the establish-

5 See EU Global Strategy (2016), 3.2 and 3.5.

6 See European Defence Action Plan, Introduction, 3.

7 Council Conclusions on implementing the EU Global Strategy in the Area of Security and Defence – (Foreign Affairs) Council Conclusions of 14 November 2016, especially Level of Ambition, 7, a., b. and c., and Actions, 11–18.

8 Communication from the Commission to the European Parliament, the European Council, the Council, the European Economic and Social Committee and the Committee of Regions – European Defence Action Plan (COM(2016)950 final of 30 November 2016).

ment of a research and of a capability window and foreseeing new financial tools to help Member States and the European defence industry to develop defence capabilities, including the *European Defence Fund* (EDF);

iii) a set of concrete actions (as a follow up to the Warsaw *EU-NATO Joint Declaration of 8 July 2016*[9] which identified seven key areas of cooperation[10]) adopted in parallel by the Council of the EU and Foreign Ministers of NATO on 6 December 2016[11] which foresees forty-two concrete proposals for implementing in the seven areas of cooperation.

Therefore, in the specific field of CFSP/CSDP and in the period 2016–2019, the three main categories of initiatives above mentioned were adopted by either sources of binding secondary law or soft law instruments: (i) *political and strategic*; (ii) *institutional and operational*; and (iii) *financial initiatives*.

Within the *first category* – political and strategic – several instruments were adopted by the EU. The above-mentioned Commission's European Defence Action Plan, contributes to ensuring that the European defence industrial base is able to meet Europe's current and future security needs and, in that respect, enhances the Union's strategic autonomy, strengthening its ability to act with partners. It focuses on capability needs and supports the European defence industry and is based on three main pillars – launching a European Defence Fund, fostering investments in defence supply chains and reinforcement of the single market for defence – and aims also at maximising civil/military synergies across EU policies.

Afterwards, the *Implementation Plan on Security and Defence*[12] sets out proposals to implement the EU Global Strategy in the area of security and defence and mainly it sets up the aims of the proposed «new Level of ambi-

---

9 Joint Declaration by the President of the European Council, the President of the European Commission and the Secretary General of the North Atlantic Treaty Organization of 8 July 2016 (see www.natolibguides.info).

10 Ibid. The seven key areas of cooperation identified are: countering hybrid threats; operational cooperation including maritime issues; cyber security and defence; defence capabilities; defence industry and research; parallel and coordinated exercises; defence and security capacity-building.

11 Statement on the implementation of the Joint Declaration signed by the President of the European Council, the President of the European Commission, and the Secretary General of the North Atlantic Treaty Organization of 6 December 2016 and Annex (Common set of proposals for the implementation of the Joint Declaration).

12 *Implementation Plan on Security and Defence* presented to the Council of 14 November 2016 (14392/16).

tion» – developing a stronger Union in security and defence, which is able to tackle today's threats and challenges more effectively, with the right capabilities, tools and structures to deliver more security for its citizens. Moreover, it outlines the goals that the EU and its Member States set out to achieve within the three priorities which are mutually reinforcing – responding to external conflicts and crisis, capacity building of partners and protecting the Union and its citizens – and puts forward concrete actions (actionable proposals) to implement the level of ambition in respect of setting capability development priorities, deepening defence cooperation, adjusting structures, tools and (financial) instruments, drawing on the full potential of the Treaty regarding PESCO and actively taking forward CS-DP Partnerships[13].

Subsequently the Commission's *Reflection Paper on the future of the European defence,*[14] the Reports on the implementation of the EU Global Strategy (Years 1 and 2),[15] the Civilian Capability Development Plan, the Civilian CSDP Compact[16] (which aims to strengthen EU's capacity to deploy civilian crisis management missions whose objectives are to reinforce the

13 See *Implementation Plan on Security and Defence,* Level of Ambition, 5 and ff., especially 5 and 6, and Implementing the Level of Ambition, 19 and ff.

14 Reflection Paper on the Future of European Defence (COM(2017)315 of 7 June 2017) – which followed the Reflection Paper on the Social Dimension of Europe (COM(2017) 206 of 26 April 2017), the Reflection Paper on Harnessing Globalisation (COM(2017)240 of 10 May 2017) and the Reflection Paper on the Deepening of the Economic and Monetary Union (COM(2017) 291 of 31 May 2017). It was published to launch a debate on how the EU (now) 27 might develop by 2025 in the area of defence. – This 4th Reflection Paper followed the White Paper on the Future of Europe. Reflections and scenarios for the EU27 by 2025 (COM(2017)2025 of 1 March 2017.

15 *From Shared Vision to Common Action: Implementing the EU Global Strategy Year 1*, June 2017; *From Shared Vision to Common Action: Global Strategy for the European Union's Foreign and Security Policy – Implementation Report Year 2,* June 2018.

16 Council Conclusions on strengthening civilian CSDP (document 9288/18 of 28 May 2018, COPS 171, CIVCOM 89, CFSP/PESC 475, CSDP/PSDC 475, RELEX 451, JAI 493), namely Next Steps, n.ºs 8 e 9. – On 22 May 2018 a provisional agreement was reached on a regulation establishing the *European Defence Industrial Development Programme* (EDIDP) that will be submitted to the EP for a vote and subsequently to the Council for final adoption and which is expected to finance the first capability projects in 2019. See also Conclusions of the Council and of the representatives of the Governments of the Member States, meeting within the Council, on the establishment of a Civilian CSDP compact, as adopted by the FA Council in its meeting held on 19 November 2017 (14305/18, COPS 432, CIVCOM 231, POLMIL 207, CFSP/PESC 1046, CSDP/PSDC 656, JAI 1135 of 19 November 2018) – see I (Strategic Guidelines) and II (Commitments).

police, the rule of law and the civil administration in fragile and conflict setting) and the EU Action Plan on Military Mobility (aiming at improving mobility of military personnel, material and assets within and beyond the EU, both in PESCO and in the context of EU-NATO cooperation, by addressing the existing legal, infrastructural and procedural barriers between the EU Member States)[17] were adopted.[18]

Within the *second category* – institutional and operational initiatives – in March 2017 the Council of the EU approved *Conclusions on progress in implementing the EU Global Strategy in the Area of Security and Defence*[19] that address four main issues: i) improving CSDP crisis management structures, including a Military Planning and Conduct Capability (MPCC) for its non-military missions within the EU Military Staff (EUMS) to be reviewed by the end of 2018; ii) Permanent Structured Cooperation (PESCO); iii) Coordinated Annual Review on Defence (CARD), to be implemented on a voluntary basis; and iv) developing civilian capabilities.

Two of these issues and respective initiatives may be particularly relevant to the EU-UK relationship after Brexit: PESCO and CARD.

According to Articles 42(6) and 46 of the TEU, as well as Protocol 10, the PESCO provides a framework to deepen defence cooperation among the Member States participants – in which the participation of the UK will be admitted. After presenting in September 2017, a list of common commitments in the main areas foreseen in Protocol 10, notably defence investment, capability development and operational readiness, 23 Member States signed a joint notification on the PESCO on 13 November 2017, setting out the principles, a list of 20 binding common commitments they have agreed to undertake as well as proposals on the governance of

17 See Joint Communication to the European Parliament and the Council of 28.2.2018 (JOIN(2018) 5 final of 28 March 2018) and European Commission Factsheet on Military Mobility (available in www.eeas.europa.eu). See previously Joint Communication to the European Parliament and the Council, Improving Military Mobility in the European Union (Join(2017) 41 final, of 10 October 2017) according to which by March 2018 the High Representative and the Commission would submit an Action Plan on Military Mobility for Member States' endorsement.

18 The various initiatives have been supported at highest political level – see in particular Conclusions of the European Council of 28 June 2018, II. Security and Defence, 13. See also Conclusions of the European Council of 18 October 2018, III. External Relations (10–14).

19 Council Conclusions on progress in implementing the EU Global Strategy in the area of Security and Defence of 6 March 2017 (see Press Release 110/17 of 06/03/2017).

PESCO.[20] Afterwards, the Council adopted a decision establishing PESCO and its list of (25 Member States) participants[21][22], leading to the adoption by the Council (in formation of the PESCO) of a first set of 17 projects (which cover areas such as training, capability development and operational readiness in the field of defence) and their participants.[23]

PESCO represents therefore a step further within the CSDP, through the implementation of 17 collaborative projects in three different areas (common training and exercises (2) operational domains (land, air, maritime and cyber (6)) and joint and enabling capacities ((9) bridging operational gaps)). The *Roadmap for the implementation of PESCO* (12/2017–12/2019) namely provides strategic direction and guidance on how to structure further work on processes and governance, sets out a calendar for the review and assessment process of the national implementation plans, provides a timeline for agreements on possible future projects and the main tenets of a common set of governance rules for projects. Finally, the FA Council[24] adopted a Council Decision establishing a common set of governance rules for PESCO projects,[25] in order to provide a framework able to ensure coherent implementation compatible with PESCO projects.

---

20 Notification on Permanent Structured Cooperation (PESCO) to the Council and to the High Representative of the Union for Foreign Affairs and Security Policy.

21 Council Decision establishing Permanent Structured Cooperation (PESCO) and determining the list of the Participating Member States (all except Denmark, UK and Malta – 14866/17, CORLC 548, CFSP/PESC 1063, CSDP/PSDC 667, FIN 752, 8.11.2017) – Council Decision (CFSP) 2017/2315 of 11 December 2017 establishing permanent structured cooperation (PESCO) and determining the list of participating Member States, OJ L 331, 14/12/2017, p. 57.

22 See also Declaration on PESCO projects by member states participating in PESCO.

23 Council Decision establishing the list of projects to be developed under PESCO (6393/18, CORLX 98, CFSP/PESC 169, CSDP/PSDC 83, FIN 145, 1.3.2018) and Council Decision (CFSP) 2018/340 of 6 March 2018 establishing the list of projects to be developed under PESCO (OJEU L65 of 8/3/2018, p. 24). – See also Council Recommendation concerning a roadmap for the implementation of PESCO (6588/1/18 VER 1, CORLX 123, CFSP/PESC 196, CSDP/PSDC 93, FIN 174, 6.3.2018).

24 Conclusions on Security and Defence in the context of the EU Global Strategy, document 10246/18 of 25 June 2018, Annex (CFSP/PESC 589, CSDP/PSDC 351, COPS 227, POLMIL 91, CIVCOM 122). The informal meeting of the EU Ministers of Defence of 4–5 May 2018 decided to adopt more projects later in the end of 2018, including military mobility, most relevant within EU-NATO cooperation

25 Ibid, Annex, Permanent Structured Cooperation, 1. and Council decision establishing a common set of governance rules for PESCO projects.

In the perspective of the future EU-UK relationship after Brexit PESCO is rather relevant since it is one of the new instruments in the field of CS-DP in which the participation of the UK would be expressly envisaged during the transition period and after its end (see below III.) – although the conditions for third State participation in PESCO projects have not been yet established by the Council.

Moreover, since the EU Global Strategy called for a gradual synchronisation and mutual adaptation of national defence planning cycles and capability development practices to enhance strategic convergence between Member States and facilitate and promote defence cooperation among them, CARD is envisaged as an instrument to help foster capability development addressing shortfalls, deepen defence cooperation and ensure more optimal use, including coherence, of defence spending plans. Its objective is to develop on a voluntary basis a more structured way to deliver identified capabilities based on greater transparency, political visibility and commitment of Member States.[26]

Although UK participation in CARD is not expressly foreseen after the end of the transition period it may not be completely out of question that the UK may have some participation in CARD within one of the guidelines regarding the EU-UK future relationship in the field of CFSP (coordination).

Finally, within the *third category*, three financial initiatives were adopted and/or proposed: the launching of the *European Defence Fund* in 2017;[27] the new European Peace Facility (EPF) proposed by the High Representa-

---

26 The EDA in cooperation with the European External Action Service (EEAS) subsequently produced a concept paper detailing the various CARD elements. The elements and procedural steps are the following: initial information (analysis of all CARD relevant information available in EDA databases or being made available by Member States), bilateral dialogues (between EDA and each member State), CARD analysis (produced by EDA that will present aggregate data and identify trends regarding defence spending plans, implementation of priorities resulting from the Capability Development Plan and relevant to defence research programmes, as well as opportunities for cooperation) to be further discussed with Member States and will form the basis of the final report to be submitted to Ministers that will present the main results of the review as well as associated recommendations (see CARD Factsheet, available at www.eeas.europa.eu). The Council agreed to initiate a CARD which a 'trail run' involving all Member States as of autumn 2017, in view of a first CARD report within 2018 and the first full CARD cycle occurs in 2019.

27 Communication from the Commission to the European Parliament, the Council, the European Economic and Social Committee and the Committee of Regions – Launching the European Defence Fund (COM(2017)295 final, 7/6/2017).

tive, as a new financial tool outside the EU multi-annual budget; and the proposal to reinforce the EU budget allocated to CFSP/CSDP in the framework of the Multiannual Financial Framework (MFF) 2021–27, meaning a reinforcement of € 27, 5 billion.

The EDF presents two main strands – Research and Development and acquisition – and is able to generate a total investment of €5 billion per year after 2020. Moreover, the Commission's proposal regarding the future MFF 2021–27 confirms the EDF as a key initiative within CFSP since it proposes, besides other initiatives (such as the dedicated budget for the Connecting Europe facility connected to military mobility), an envelope of €13 billion (over the 7 year period) to be dedicated to the EDF in order for the EU to step up its contribution to Europe's collective security and defence, working with its partners, especially NATO.[28] In addition, the EPF is an EU off-budget fund (i.e., outside of the EU's multi-annual budget) worth of € 10.5 billion (and financed through contributions by EU Member States based on a Gross Nacional income distribution key) over a period coinciding with the next MFF, to build peace and strengthen international security since it is intended to enable the financing of operational actions under the CFSP that have military or defence implications (not funded under the EU budget according to Article 41 (2) TEU) on a permanent basis, thus facilitating rapid deployment and enhancing flexibility[29] to the extent that the framework of the future EU-UK relationship does not exclude the participation of the UK in EU military missions and operations, the terms of participation of the UK in its financing, (namely through the EPF), will have to be further considered.

Finally, besides the outlined developments and adoption of new initiatives, by the EU in the framework of EU Global Strategy, a last development must be mentioned concerning EU-NATO's closer cooperation. In this respect, both the above mentioned Warsaw *EU-NATO Joint Declaration of 8 July 2016* in order to strengthen and deepen the cooperation and the

---

28 This increase, including in respect of EU-NATO projects, probably takes into consideration the weight of the UK in defence spending within NATO (see the document Defence Expenditure of NATO Countries (2010–2017), 29 June 2017 (Communique PR/CP(2017) 111, available at nato.int). – See also European Commission Press Release EU budget for 2021–2027: Commission welcomes provisional agreement for the future European Defence Fund (IP/19/1296 of 20 February 2019).

29 The EPF will also draw together existing off-budget mechanisms, namely the Athena and the African Peace Facility, increasing the common financing of the cost of military operations.

endorsement of a common set of (42) proposals for its implementation demonstrates that despite the evolution on the field of EU defence the partnership with NATO remains essential to its future in a complementary (by the time not competing) perspective on key areas of mutual interest. Furthermore, in order to consolidate progress and ensure further advances in all areas, both the EU and NATO Councils endorsed in 2017 a common set of new proposals,[30] including a total of further 32 concrete actions for the implementation of the Joint Declaration and addressing new topics, namely counter-terrorism, military mobility and promoting the role of women in peace and security.[31] Finally, a new Joint declaration of EU-NATO cooperation was signed on 8 July 2018 according to which the progress will continue to be reviewed on a yearly basis.

The issue of EU-NATO cooperation is also relevant to the shaping of the EU-UK relationship, since the UK seems to envisage NATO as a cornerstone of European defence – and therefore it is possible that it will not fully participate in EU CSDP initiatives that may jeopardize the prominence of NATO's role in such respect.

The above mentioned developments show that after a long period since the approval of the *European Security Strategy* (2003)[32] and almost a decade after the signature of the Treaty of Lisbon, the EU is trying hard to push forward further developments in the field CFSP and CSDP within EU's External Action – although not yet at the stage of taking a (unanimous) European Council decision on the establishment of a 'common defence' (as foreseen in Art. 42 (2) TEU).

30 Common set of new proposals on the implementation of the Joint Declaration signed by the President of the European Council, the President of the European Commission and the Secretary General of the North Atlantic Treaty Organization of 5 December 2017.

31 See also Council Conclusions on the implementation of the Joint Declaration by the President of the European Council, the President of the European Commission and the Secretary General of NATO (14801/17, CFSP/PESC 1057, CSDP/PSDC 661, COPS 372, POLMIL 153, EUMC 147 of 5 December 2017). The next report on progress on implementation was expected to be presented in June 2018 (see Conclusions, no 7) and was presented in 31 May 2018.

32 European Security Strategy – A Secure Europe in a Better World» of 12/12/2003. See also, afterwards, the 2008 Report on the implementation of the ESS – Providing Security in a Changing World.

It may be concluded from the 2016–18 CFSP, especially CSDP,[33] developments and the whole of the concrete initiatives and instruments adopted by the EU within the framework of the EU Global Strategy and its ambitious goals, that a new path seems to arise in this field of competences: i) the reinforcement of the EU autonomous strategy regarding CFSP/CSDP (and at the same time of the cooperation with the EU partners in the framework of a multilateralism approach); ii) strong efforts to strengthen effective cooperation between Member States in the area of CSDP through a wide range of initiatives, including PESCO, to improve Member States defence capabilities; iii) clear reinforcement of the (EU and Member States) financing of CFSP/CSDP either through the increase of EU budget, or through specific financial instruments within the EU budget (EDF) or outside (EPF); iv) despite the aim of reinforcement of the EU autonomous strategy regarding CFSP/CSDP and the strengthen of CSDP cooperation between EU Member States, the simultaneous reinforcement of the participation of the EU in collective defence in the framework of NATO with a complementary approach.

That is therefore the overall context and framework which the design of the future relationship between the EU and the UK regarding CFSP and CSDP will have to consider and on which the terms of the future cooperation (during and after the transition period) may depend regarding its scope, nature and instruments.

Regarding the concrete participation of the UK in the CFSP and CSDP, four main periods can therefore be identified in the light of Brexit: (i) pre-EU Global Strategy, (ii) post-EU Global Strategy, (iii) transitional period (from the entering into force of the Withdrawal Agreement until the end of the transitional period) and finally (iv) post-transitional period.

Until the endorsement of the EU Global Strategy at political level, the UK participated in the CFSP/CFSP as a full Member State, namely in the CFSP decision making process, in the financing of the CFSP through the EU budget, in the CSDP initiatives and in some of the EU missions and operations (on a voluntary basis). After the post-EU Global Strategy, the UK can also fully participate in the CFSP/CSDP decision making process and initiatives as an EU Member State, even though it has chosen not to participate fully in all new CFSP initiatives since it has not signed the joint declaration on PESCO as a participant Member State and therefore will

33 For an overall view see Jochen Rehrl (ed.), *Handbook on CSDP, The Common Security and Defence Policy on the European Union*, 3rd edition, 2017 (available at eeas.europa.eu).

only participate as a third State (according to the requirements that will be adopted by the EU in this respect). The participation of the UK in the CFSP/CSDP during the transition period and after the end of the transition period ending 30 May 2020 are foreseen, respectively, in the Withdrawal Agreement and in the Political Declaration setting out the framework for the future relationship between the EU and the UK of 25 November 2018 – and the terms of the UK participation in the CFSP and PCSD during those two periods (and further explained in III., A. and B. below) are progressively limited and will probably evolve mainly on the basis of a third State status.

Before the analysis of the final versions of the Withdrawal Agreement and in the Political Declaration some indicators concerning the future EU-UK relationship in the field of CFSP/CSDP may be found in some initiatives and documents addressing this subject, both in the EU and the UK perspectives (II, A. and B. below).

Moreover, as addressed above (see III. and IV), the future EU-UK relationship in the field of foreign policy, security and defence will take into consideration the values on which the post-EU Global Strategy, including in the field of CFSP/CSDP, is based – as a common ground for cooperation – and will also consider the participation of the UK in EU instruments and structures aimed at achieving some of the objectives laid down in the EU Global Strategy, such as the EU integrated approach to conflicts and crisis in which EU missions and operations play an important role (and the participation of the UK is also envisaged), or the European Defence Agency.

II. Initiatives addressing CFSP and CSDP after Brexit: the EU and the UK perspectives

A. The EU Perspective

After the 23rd June referendum and following the United Kingdom's notification under Article 50 TEU on 29 March 2017 of its intention to withdraw from the EU and Euratom, several documents have been adopted since then by different EU institutions: the European Council, the Council, the European Parliament (EP) and the Commission, under the form of either *guidelines*, *negotiation directives*, *resolutions* and finally the *Withdrawal Agreement*.

From the EU perspective – and in the sequence of the principles set out in the statement of Heads of State or Government and of the Presidents of the European Council and the European Commission on 29 June 2016 – the most relevant political documents to the shaping of the EU-UK relationship in the field of CFSP/CSDP, during and after the transition period (to be addressed either in the Withdrawal Treaty and in a Political Declaration) are those adopted by the European Council and the European Parliament.

The EP Resolution of 14 March 2018[34] addresses, besides other issues, the Framework of the future relationship of the EU and the UK, under the form of a *political declaration* associated with the Withdrawal Agreement, the (nine) *principles* that are a condition of the endorsement of such Framework by the EP, the future negotiation of an association agreement as an appropriate framework for the future relationship and the *four* pillars on which the future relationship should be based according to the EP[35]. In those four pillars, the EP includes, besides trade and economic relations, internal security and thematic cooperation, also *foreign policy, security cooperation* and development cooperation. Specifically regarding foreign policy and security cooperation (and development cooperation), the EP namely admits that, although the UK as a third country will not be able to participate in the EU's decision-making process, consultation mechanisms are not excluded in order to allow the UK to align with EU foreign policy positions, joint actions or multilateral cooperation, especially in the framework of the UN, OSCE and Council of Europe, and supports coordination on sanction policy and implementation; that such partnership (under the Framework Participation Agreement) would make it possible for UK participation (with no lead role) in civilian and military missions and EU operations, programmes and projects in different areas, including projects developed under PESCO; that any cooperation in such areas that involves shared EU classified information including on intelligence is conditional on a security information agreement; that the UK could participate, based on other similar third country arrangements, in EU programs in support of defence and external security and the EU is open to the possibility of the

34 Guidelines on the Framework of the future EU-UK Relations – European Parliament Resolution of 14 March 2018 on the Framework of the future EU-UK relationship (2018/2573(RSP) – P8_TA-PROV(2018)0069), following its previous resolutions of 5 April 2017 on negotiations with the United Kingdom following its notification that it intends to withdraw from the European Union and of 3 October 2017 and of 13 December 2017 on the state of play of negotiations with the United Kingdom (respectively Texts adopted, PA_TA(2017)0102, PA_TA(2017)0361 and PA_TA(2017)0490).

35 Ibid, especially 2, 4, 5 and 6.

UK continuing to contribute to EU's external financing instruments in pursuit of common objectives, especially in the common neighbourhood policy; and finally that EU-UK cooperation in development, cooperation and humanitarian aid would be mutually beneficial.[36]

The Guidelines approved by the European Council that are relevant to the future EU-UK relationship are those adopted, successively, on 29 April 2017, 15 December 2017 and 23 March 2018.

Firstly, in the *Guidelines* approved on 29 April 2017 that define the framework for negotiations under Article 50 TEU and set out the overall positions and principles that the Union will pursue throughout the negotiation[37] have not set aside the issue of CFSP and CSDP. In fact, besides some other references to the international relations field and international (EU or mixed) agreements,[38] a specific mention is made to *security, defence and foreign policy* stating that the EU 'stands ready to establish partnerships in areas unrelated to trade, in particular the fight against terrorism and international crime, as well as security, defence and foreign policy'.[39] Although relevant, the CFSP and CSDP seemed not to be, from the EU perspective, a top priority to be addressed within the first phase of the negotiation of the withdrawal agreement.[40]

---

36 Ibid, (ii) Foreign policy, security cooperation and development cooperation, no 21–25.

37 Special meeting of the European Council (Art. 50) of 29 April 2017, Guidelines following the United Kingdom's notification under Article 50 TEU. See also the resolution of the European Parliament of 5 April 2017 (EUCO XT 20004/17, BXT 10, CO EUR 5, CONCL 2 of 29 April 2017).

38 Ibid, *II.A phased approach to negotiations*, especially 4 and 13 (this regarding the issues of (international) agreements concluded by the EU or by the Member States on its behalf or by the Union and its Member States acting jointly).

39 Ibid, IV. Preliminary and preparatory discussions on a framework for the Union – United Kingdom future relationship, 22.

40 In the subsequent Guidelines adopted at the Special meeting of the European Council (under art. 50 TEU) following the United Kingdom's notification under Article 50 TEU on 29 March 2017 of its intention to withdraw from the EU and Euratom the abovementioned trend was a constant. – The Directives for the negotiation of an agreement with the United Kingdom of Great Britain and Northern Ireland setting out the arrangements for its withdrawal from the European Union (Annex to the Council Decision authorising the opening of negotiations with the United Kingdom of Great Britain and Northern Ireland for an agreement setting out the arrangements for its withdrawal from the European Union (XT 21016/17, ADD 1 REV 2, BXT 24 of 22 May 2017)) does not expressly address CFSP and CSDP but includes a reference to a constructive dialogue on a common possible approach towards third country partners, international organisations and conventions in relation to the international commitments contracted before the with-

Afterwards, in the Guidelines adopted on 15 December 2017, the European Council reconfirms its readiness to establish the above-mentioned partnerships, including security, defence and foreign policy – although no specific guidelines are set in this respect.[41]

Finally, in the Guidelines adopted on 23 March 2018, the European Council reiterates the determination of the EU to have as close as possible a partnership with the UK in the future that should cover other areas than trade and economic cooperation, in particular the fight against terrorism and international crime, as well as *security, defence and foreign policy.*[42] In this document the European Council also took into account the stated positions of the UK, which limit the depth of future partnership, thus setting out further guidelines with a view to the opening of negotiations on the overall understanding of the *framework for the future relationship*, that will be elaborated in a *Political Declaration* accompanying and referred to in the Withdrawal Agreement.[43] The European Council considers that in view of the shared values between EU and UK 'there should be a strong EU-UK cooperation in the fields of foreign, security and defence policy' while 'a future partnership should respect the autonomy of the Union's decision-making, taking into account that the UK will be a third country, and foresee appropriate dialogue, consultation, coordination, exchange of information, and cooperation mechanisms. As a pre-requisite for the exchange of information in the framework of such cooperation a Security of Information Agreement would to have to be put in place'.[44] No further indication regarding such strong EU-UK cooperation is given by the 2018 guidelines.

---

drawal date, by which the UK remains bound (and therefore to mixed agreements) – *cf* no18.

41 European Council (Art. 50) meeting (15 December 2017) – Guidelines (EUCO XT 20011/17, BXT 69, CO EUR 27, CONCL 8, 15 December 2017), no 8. These Guidelines were preceded by the Communication from the Commission to the European Council (Article 50) on the state of the progress of the negotiations with the United Kingdom under Article 50 of the Treaty on European Union (COM(2017)784 final of 8 December 2017) and the Joint report from the negotiators of the European Union and the United Kingdom Government on progress during phase 1 of negotiations under Article 50 TEU on the United Kingdom's orderly withdrawal from the European Union of 8 December 2017.

42 European Council (Art. 50) meeting (23 March 2018) – Guidelines on the framework for the future EU-UK relationship (EUCO XT 20001/18, BXT 25, CO EUR 5, CONCL 2, 23 March 2018), no 3.

43 Ibid, no 5.

44 Ibid, no 13, ii). The European Council will follow the negotiations closely, in all their aspects, and will return to the remaining withdrawal issues and to the Framework for the future relationship at its June meeting (no 16).

Afterwards,[45] the Chief negotiator M. Barnier stated that the UK's commitment to Europe's security as restated in the UK paper *Framework for the UK-EU Security Partnership* of 9 May 2018 was welcome and that the future EU-UK relationship could be underpinned by a set of the (above mentioned 5) mechanisms set up in the 23 March 2018 European Council's Guidelines – *dialogue, consultation, coordination, cooperation and exchange of information*. Elaborating further on these mechanisms, the Chief negotiator indicates that future partnership could include five dimensions: i) close and regular consultations with the UK on foreign policy; ii) when projecting the EU's support worldwide, EU will be open to the UK's contribution; iii) in defence matters the UK should have the possibility (where it adds value) to actively take part in a number of the European Defence Agency's Research and Technology projects; iv) exchanging information in incidents that makes the partners more effective in fighting cyber-attacks; v) a EU-UK Security of Information Agreement.

From the point of view of the EU-UK post-Brexit relationship, it can be concluded that the above-mentioned documents contributed to shape the draft of the Withdrawal Agreement and the subsequent Political Declaration setting out the framework for the future EU-UK relationship specifically in the field of CFSP/CSDP. Some main ideas arise from these documents. First, that both parties, despite their respective autonomy, agree to a partnership in the *foreign, security and defence policy*, based on a set of five instruments (dialogue, consultation, coordination, cooperation and exchange of information) and where concrete thematic areas of mutual interest exist (and therefore allowing UK alignment or participation – at least – as a third State) are already identified: policy of international sanctions; EU civilian and military missions and operations; EU defence projects through the EDA; and, more generally, cooperation within International Organisations (UN, Council of Europe, OSCE) and exchange of information. Second, the UK participation can take place either through existing instruments (used with third States, such as a Framework Participation Agreement for EU missions and operations or an Administrative Agreement regarding the EDA) or new models of closer cooperation. Therefore, al-

45 See Speech/18/3785, delivered on the 14th May High Level panel discussion on 'The future of EU foreign, security and defence policy post Brexit' at EU Institute for Security Studies, Brussels (available at TF50, www.ec.europa.eu.) – where he stated that the security of the EU and the UK is bound together, although there is still a lot of uncertainty, and there should be no uncertainty about the EU commitment to a future security partnership since the challenges are by their nature cross border.

though the participation of the UK as a (mere) third State can be admitted, the envisaged EU-UK 'strong cooperation' in the fields of foreign policy, security and defence neither explicitly admits nor excludes a different third State status.

All the topics addressed by the EP Resolution and the European Council Guidelines still would have to be more detailed in the text of Withdrawal Agreement and in the Political Declaration which the first refers to (as well as in subsequent future EU-UK agreements that will apply after the transition period).

Within the framework of the Guidelines adopted by the European Council (29 April 2017 and 15 December 2017), the Commission adopted on the 28 February 2018 a *Draft Withdrawal Agreement*[46] which contains articles with references to CFSP and Security and Defence both in Part Four (Transition) and Part Five (Financial provisions). The main steps of the subsequent path that led to the approval of the (final) text of the Agreement on the Withdrawal of the UK from the EU can be summarized as follows.

At the informal meeting of the heads of State or government held on 19–20 September 2018 in Salzburg, EU's 27 leaders agreed to have a *joint political declaration setting out the framework of the future relations between the EU and the UK* in different areas, including in the area of security and defence, thus providing as much clarity as possible in the future relations.[47]

46 Draft Withdrawal Agreement on the withdrawal of the United Kingdom of Great Britain and Northern Ireland from the European Union and the European Atomic Energy Community,TF50 (2018) 33 – Commission to EU 27 (to be presented to the Chief negotiator to the CRP Art. 50 and to the Brexit Steering Group on 28 February 2018 and to be further discussed with the Council (Art. 50) and the Brexit Steering Group before transmission to the UK authorities for negotiation (see the TF50 at www.ec.europa.eu). The subsequent document TF50(2018) 35 – Commission to EU27, of 19 March 2018 contains the Draft Agreement highlighting the progress made (coloured version) in the negotiation round with the UK of 16–19 March 2018. The text of the Draft Withdrawal Agreement was published at the website of the UK Government (www.gov.uk/policies/brexit).

47 In this informal meeting the EU leaders also agreed that there will be no Withdrawal Agreement without a solid, operational and legally binding Irish backstop. – See also *Preparing for the withdrawal of the United Kingdom from the European Union on 30 March 2019* – Communication from the Commission to the European Parliament, the European Council, the Council, the European Central Bank, the European Economic and Social Committee, the Committee of the Regions and the European Investment Bank – COM(2018) 556 final of 19/7/2018, as corrected by COM(2018) 556 final/2, of 27/8/2018.

An understanding on pending issues was achieved and a *final version* of text of the Draft Agreement on the Withdrawal of the UK from the EU, as agreed at the negotiator's level on 14 November 2018 was presented[48] together with an outline of a Political Declaration setting out the framework for the future relationship between the EU and the UK, as agreed at negotiator's level on the same date.[49]

Subsequently, the special meeting of the European Council (Art. 50) of 25 November 2018 endorsed the draft Brexit withdrawal agreement and approved the draft Political Declaration on the future EU-UK relations.[50]

Subsequently, on 11 January 2019 the Council (Art. 50) adopted a decision on the signing of the withdrawal agreement as well as one draft decision on the conclusion of the withdrawal agreement which was forward to the EP for its consent.[51] Both the text of the *Instrument relating to the withdrawal agreement* (which constitutes a document of reference that will have to be made use of if any issue arises in the implementation of the Withdrawal Agreement having legal force and binding character to this effect) and of the *Joint Statement supplementing the Political Declaration* setting out the framework for the future relationship between the European Union

48 TF50 (2018) 55 – Commission to EU27 of 14 November 2018.

49 TF50 (2018) 56 – Commission to EU27 of 14 November 2018.

50 Conclusions, EUCO XT 20015/18, BXT 110, CO EUR 27, CONCL 8 of 25 November 2018. These Conclusions were reconfirmed in the special meeting of the European Council (Art. 50) of 13 December 2018 (Conclusions, EUCO XT 20022/18, BXT 131, CO EUR 32, CONCL 9 of 13 December 2018). In the 25 November Conclusions the European Council also invited the EP and the Commission to take the necessary steps to ensure that the agreement can enter into force on 30 March 2019, so as provide for an orderly withdrawal. See previous Document BXT 111 CO EUR-PREP 54 of 22 November 2018 and Annex.

51 Council Decision (EU) 2019/274 of 11 January 2019 on the signing, on behalf of the EU and of the European Atomic Energy Community, of the Agreement on the withdrawal of the United Kingdom of Great Britain and Northern Ireland from the European Union and the European Atomic Energy Community, [2019] OJ L 47 I/1, and attached text of the Withdrawal Agreement (published in [2019] OJ C 66 I/01). The text of the Political Declaration was published in [2019] OJ C 66 I/02. – See also previous documents COM(2018) 833 final and COM(2018) 834 final of 5 December 2018; Council Decision on the signing, on behalf of the EU and of the European Atomic Energy Community, of the Agreement on the withdrawal of the United Kingdom of Great Britain and Northern Ireland from the European Union and the European Atomic Energy Community – XT 21106/18, BXT 125 of 7 January 2019; Council Decision on the conclusion of the Agreement on the withdrawal of the United Kingdom of Great Britain and Northern Ireland from the European Union and the European Atomic Energy Community – XT 21105/18, BXT 124 of 9 January 2019.

and the United Kingdom of Great Britain and Northern Ireland[52] were approved in the special meeting of the European Council (Art. 50) of 21 March 2019.[53]

Following the position of the House of Commons declining to approve the Withdrawal Agreement and the subsequent request of the UK on 5 April 2019 for a further extension[54] to the Article 50 period until 30 June 2019, the special summit of the EU leaders on 11 April finally agreed to a further extension of Article 50 in any event no longer than 31 October 2019 and the EU decision taken in agreement with the UK extending the period of Article 50 was approved.[55] During the extension period, the UK will remain a Member State with full rights and obligations in accordance with the same Article 50; the UK has a right to revoke its notification at any time; and the Withdrawal Agreement may enter into force on an earlier date, should the parties complete their respective ratification procedures before 31 October 2019[56].

Finally, Council Decision (EU) 2019/642 on the signing of the Withdrawal Agreement was adopted[57] – an adapted draft decision on the con-

52 Annex to the document XT 21014/19, BXT 15, CO EUR-PREP 10 of 20 March 2019 (Instrument relating to the Agreement on the Withdrawal of the United Kingdom of Great Britain and Northern Ireland from the European Union and the European Atomic Energy Community); annex to the document XT 21018/19, BXT 24, CO EUR-PREP 11 of 20 March 2019. Both these texts have been agreed at the negotiator's level, agreed between UK Prime Minister and the President of the European Commission on 11 March 2019 in Strasbourg and have been endorsed by the Commission on the same day.

53 Conclusions, 2 (EUCO XT 20004/19, BXT 20, CO EUR 7, CONCL 2 of 21 March 2019).

54 See European Council Decision (EU) 2019/476 taken in agreement with the United Kingdom of 22 March 2019 extending the period under Article 50(3)TEU [2019] 80I/1); see also previous document European Council Decision taken in agreement with the United Kingdom, extending the period under Article 50(3) TEU (EUCO XT 20006/19, BXT 26 of 22 March 2019).

55 Conclusions of the special meeting of the European Council, 2 (Art. 50), EUCO XT 20015/19, BXT 40, CO EUR 9, CONCL 4 of 10 April 2019; European Council Decision (EU) 2019/584 taken in agreement with the United Kingdom of 11 April 2019 extending the period under Article 50(3)TEU ([2019] OJ L101/1); see also previous document European Council Decision taken in agreement with the UK extending the period under Article 50(3) TEU (EUCO XT 20013/19, BXT 38 of 11 April 2019).

56 Ibid, 6.

57 Council Decision (EU) 2019/642 of 13 April 2019 amending Decision (EU) 2019/274 on the signing, on behalf of the EU and of the European Atomic Energy

clusion of such agreement[58] was also adapted and attached to that Decision.[59]

From the point of the CFSP/CSDP post Brexit, three aspects of the 2019 developments and in particular of the European Council decision of 11 April 2019 must be underlined: i) since the further extension of the period of Article 50(3) TEU must not undermine the regular functioning of the Union and its institutions, the UK fully participates on the decision making procedures regarding CFSP/CSDP in this period; ii) since the extension excludes any re-opening of the Withdrawal Agreement and cannot be used to start negotiations on the future relationship, it does not affect the terms laid down in the Withdrawal Agreement regarding CFSP/CSDP which would apply during the transition period; iii) the Joint Statement supplementing the Political Declaration setting out the framework for the future relationship between the EU and the UK agreed in March 2019 does not affect the framework already set in the Political Declaration (of 22 November 2018) concerning the future relationship in the field of CFSP/CSDP (see III, A. and B. below).

B. *The UK perspective*

On the UK official side, the consequences of the Brexit regarding the future relationship with the Union regarding the CFSP and CSDP were worth attention, both at the government and at the Parliament level. In

---

Community, of the Agreement on the withdrawal of the United Kingdom of Great Britain and Northern Ireland from the European Union and the European Atomic Energy Community ([2019] OJ L 110 I/1) and previous document Council Decision on the signing, on behalf of the EU and of the European Atomic Energy Community, of the Agreement on the withdrawal of the United Kingdom of Great Britain and Northern Ireland from the European Union and the European Atomic Energy Community – XT 21027/19, BXT 44 of 11 April 2019.

58 Council Decision on the conclusion of the Agreement on the withdrawal of the United Kingdom of Great Britain and Northern Ireland from the European Union and the European Atomic Energy Community (adapted text) – XT 21105/18, REV 2, BXT 124 of 11 April 2019.

59 Agreement on the Withdrawal of the United Kingdom of Great Britain and Northern Ireland from the European Union and the European Atomic Energy Community, XT 21028/19 BXT 45 of 11 April 2019 – the adapted text was published in [2019] OJ C144 I/1 and attached to Council Decision (EU) 2019/642. The subsequent references to articles of the Withdrawal Agreement will refer to this final (adapted) text.

this respect are, among others, worth mentioning: the so called 'Brexit White Paper' – *The United Kingdom's exit from and new partnership with the European Union*[60] – since it details out the (12) principles which would guide the Brexit, including regarding European security; short afterwards the Evidence session held by the *EU External Affairs Sub-Committee on Common Foreign Security Policy (CFSP) post Brexit;*[61] as well as the previous House of Lords Library Note *Leaving the European Union: Foreign and Security Policy Cooperation*[62] – the last two because they address a wide range of issues in respect of the EU-UK relationship in the field of CFSP/CSDP and possible models for the future cooperation.

Afterwards, more recent documents are also relevant in respect of the EU-UK relationship after Brexit in the area of CFSP and CSDP, namely the *Framework for the UK-EU Security Partnership* of 9 May 2018[63] or the *Technical note on consultation and cooperation on external security* of 24 May 2018 (DExEU Policy paper)[64] which in particular contains a more detailed list of proposals of what the future UK-EU consultation and cooperation in that

60 17 January 2017 (text available at www.gov.uk/government/uploads/system/uploads/attachment_data/file/589191/The_United_Kingdoms_exit_from_and_partnership_with_the_EU_Web.pdf).

61 One-off Evidence session with Professor Richard Whitman and Professor Karen Smith held on 6 April 2017 by the EU External Affairs Sub-Committee on Common Foreign Security Policy (CFSP) post-Brexit (www.parliament.uk/business/committees/committees-a-z/lords-select/eu-external-affairs-subcommittee/news-parliament-2015/academics-common-foreign-security-policy/ and video and audio at www.parliamentlive.tv/Event/Index/e6a38ead-7c7e-4a97-9d72-ec93b0d3dd62). The reference of the transcript of the evidence taken in public in this paper is made considering the contents of numbers 1 and 2 on the 'Use of the transcript'.

62 House of Lords Library Note *Leaving the European Union: Foreign and Security Policy Cooperation* of 13 October 2016 (LLN 2016/051). See also House of Commons Library, Briefing Paper Number CBP7798, 31 March 2017, *Brexit: implications for national security* (by Joanna Dawson, text available in www.researchbriefings.files.parliament.uk) and House of Commons Library, Briefing paper Number CBP 7742 12 June 2017, *Brexit reading list: defence and security*, in particular *5. Future cooperation* (text available in https://www.researchbriefings.files.parliament.uk).

63 Policy paper, *Framework for the UK-EU Security Partnership*, published on 9 May 2018, Department for Exiting the European Union (available at www.gov.uk/ Department for Exiting the European Union).

64 Available at www.gov.uk/ Department for Exiting the European Union – see also www.parliament.uk/brexit (see Committees/Exiting the European Union Committee). See more recently House of Lords, European Union Committee, 16th Report of Session 2017–19, *Brexit: Common Security and Defence Policy missions and operations* and Government response (available at www.publications.parliament.uk).

area may be – both subsequent to the Draft Withdrawal Agreement of February 2018.

An overview of the contents of such documents (as detailed below) allows a preliminary conclusion that a partial convergence may exist with the EU position in respect of the EU-UK relationship after Brexit in the field of the CFSP/CSDP. Firstly to an extent that dialogue, cooperation, coordination and consultation in general are envisaged by both parties. Secondly, because the alignment of the EU-UK positions in foreign policy is also a possibility for the EU and the UK, namely in respect of sanctions and participation in international organisations and fora. Thirdly because close participation of the UK in EU civilian and military missions and operations and some EU agencies, such as the European Defence Agency, is also admitted by both.

However, two main issues seem to drive the EU and the UK apart. Firstly, the status of the UK, since the EU seems to admit UK's cooperation and participation as a third State – and expressly neither admits nor exclude a differentiated third State status – while the UK in the mentioned documents does not put aside a model of cooperation and participation that may go beyond the current model of participation of third States in EU CFSP/CSDP. Secondly, the relationship with NATO as a corner stone of European defence – that may be jeopardised by the development of a more integrated CSDP within the EU which seems to be one of the more evident consequences of the implementation of the EU Global Strategy.

The (chronologically first) document – House of Lords Library Note *Leaving the European Union: Foreign and Security Policy Cooperation* – expressly addresses current cooperation of the UK within the EU *vs* future prospects regarding CFSP and CSDP[65]. The Note addresses a wide range of issues, namely those regarding: the (direct) *institutional consequences* of Brexit (the end of the participation of the UK in several EU organs such as the FA Council or the EEAS); the consequences of Brexit in respect of *international agreements* binding the UK, especially the issue of replacement of international agreements in which the UK is part because of its membership of the EU (mixed agreements or EU agreements, depending on the category of competences), Association agreements or Partnership Cooperation agreements within ENP (renegotiation, changing the title of its binding nature (UK itself instead of UK as an EU Member State)); the future

65 See 2. Common Foreign and Security Policy, 2.3 Future Prospects, 3. Common Security and Defence Policy, 3.3 Future Prospects (and 4. Security and Policy Cooperation, 4.3 Future Prospects).

possibility of alignment with EU foreign policy positions, including implementing sanctions, as a third country, since the EU already allows non-Member States to align themselves with EU common positions despite no involvement in its formulation (vg cases of Norway and Switzerland); the future possibilities regarding cooperation with the EU in the (sub-area of CFSP) CSDP, bearing in mind naturally the terms of the current UK involvement as a Member State within CSDP and its implementation – participation in military CSDP missions/operations and CSDP civilian missions, participation in initiatives within the CSDP to improve the military assets and capacities of EU Member States (European Defence Agency, EU Battlegroups and UK as Lead Nation). In this regard, the main topics for the future path seemed to envisage the UK as a 'Key player in European defence' through NATO (and therefore US) and cooperation between NATO and the EU (in the line of the Warsaw Declaration); the possibility of future cooperation with the EU in missions that are in the UK interest, or in theory even of participation in the EDA or EU Battlegroups. In fact, non-EU members have already participated in EU CSCP (military and civilian) missions and operations (though with different levels of involvement) and can also participate in the EDA through Administrative Agreements approved at the level of the EU Council (that is the case of Norway (2006), Switzerland (2012), Republic of Serbia (2013), Ukraine (2015)). Non-EU Member States can also be invited by Member State and therefore participate in the EU Battlegroups (e.g. Norway and Nordic Battlegroup).

One of the issues worth attention in the Note was of course the impact of Brexit on the prospects of further European defence integration and a future European army because of the alleged risks to undermine NATO as a cornerstone of European defence (to which the UK as EU Member State has opposed). To sum up, three different models are envisaged, depending upon the preferences both of the UK and the EU partners: commitment on European security through NATO, continuing the participation in EU structures and operations as a third country (nevertheless the fact that its design may change after the Brexit towards a more integrated EU CSDP) and bilateral relations with EU partners (such as France).

In January 2017 *Brexit White Paper*, the reference to the CFSP and CSDP is rather short and generic.[66] In this respect, it is intended in general that the UK 'will continue to be one of the most important actors in interna-

66 See 11. Cooperation in the fight against crime and terrorism, pp 61–64 (where the topics *The UK in the World and European Security* are addressed), especially 11.8 and 11.9 and 11.11 – 11.14.

tional affairs' considering its specific features (vg the permanent seat on the UN Security Council and the percentage of the GDP spent on defence). Besides, it is intended to use national tools and the UK privileged position in international affairs 'to continue to work with the EU on foreign policy security and defence', to continue to play a leading role alongside EU partners in buttressing and promoting European security and influence around the world and to enhance the strong bilateral relationship with the EU partners and beyond. Moreover, and remembering the UK participation and role in several CSDP military missions/operations and CSDP civilian missions the objective enounced is to 'ensure that the EU's role in defence and security is complementary to, and respects the central role of, NATO' and to 'remain committed to European Security and add value to EU foreign and security policy'. The document also underlines the intention that the UK will continue to play a leading role as a global foreign and security policy actor within NATO.

Finally in the second initiative above mentioned – Evidence session held by the *EU External Affairs Sub-Committee on Common Foreign Security Policy (CFSP) post Brexit* – the issue of the CFSP and CSDP post-Brexit is addressed in more detailed way, the contribution of the two Professor witnesses allowing to identify the main questions and problems involved and possible ways of shaping further relationship EU/UK in the area of EU competences in question. In this respect, three of the topics seems to be particularly relevant.

First, the one regarding the three possible models for future relationship between the UK and the EU foreign, security and defence policy as proposed by Professor Richard Whitman:[67] integrated, associated and detached. It is so because it raises the issue of the will of both parties to shape a new model to address the future EU-UK relationship that goes beyond the current model and instruments of participation of third States in the present (especially in the EU sanctions policy which is more effective due to its collective nature and in the EU missions, operations and bodies such as the EDA, namely through a framework agreement or an administrative agreement), raising therefore the issue of the (in)adequacy of existing models for participation of third States in CFSP and CSDP (e.g. Norway). If such a path surely depends on both Parties political will, Brexit has put forward the possibility of a different status, i.e., ex-third State – which in-

67 RG Whitman 'The UK and EU foreign, security and defence policy after Brexit: integrated, associated or detached?' (2016), National Institute for Economic Review, 238 (1), pp 43–50.

evitably has a common past linked to the EU integration, including in the field of CFSP/CSDP.

Second, if a new – or at least a different model – of participation of a third State is envisaged, the issue of UK participation in decision making process, or at least decision shaping process, is particularly sensitive, especially at the political level, since at present no regular participation (of third States) appears to be envisaged. In this respect one could consider the existing status of State participation in international organisations, such as (formal or informal) observers. The example of the draft agreement on the accession of the EU to the ECHR may be of interest since it foresees the participation of the EU (without being a member) in the organs of the Council of Europe that have competence regarding the ECHR.

Third, the issue of the relationship between the EU, the UK and NATO. Despite the fact that the scope of NATO is defence and EU CSDP has a wider scope, the closer EU-NATO relationship in the framework of the EU Global Strategy is parallel to the increasing reinforcement of the EU CSDP since 2017. In this respect, the approach of the EU to CSDP has changed into more autonomous EU27 capabilities and even if no unanimous decision to proceed to a common defence is (ever) reached, the reinforcement of the CSDP and of the EU Member States capabilities may have in the future, despite different political views within the NATO, repercussion in its leadership and the role of the UK in the organisation.

Therefore, it must be seen whether the (final) version of the Withdrawal Agreement as well as the Political Declaration setting out the framework for the future EU-UK relationship allows any space for new methods or instruments adapted to the UK capacity of ex-EU Member State; admit any concrete form of participation of the UK in decision shaping and making and under which terms; and foresee any particular rule regarding EU-UK cooperation within the NATO.

Besides the documents above mentioned, the *Framework for the UK-EU Security Partnership* on 9 May 2018, focuses on how the UK will look to achieve a new partnership with the EU which builds on the shared interests and values and goes beyond any existing third country arrangements, covering both internal and external security,and will form on the UK perspective the basis of ongoing negotiations with the EU. Furthermore, the *Technical note on consultation and cooperation on external security* of 24 May 2018 (DExEU Policy paper) sets out a non-exhaustive list of proposals describing what a future framework of UK-EU consultation and cooperation on external security might be, stressing that it should be flexible and scalable to enable both EU and UK to cooperate more closely when it is of their mutual interest respecting both EU autonomy and UK sovereignty.

The proposed framework in respect of foreign policy mainly envisages consultation and cooperation: in Brussels (mainly UK/EEAS strategic talks and consultations at various levels and where appropriate with the Commission); with the EU27 that may include ad-hoc meetings with the FA Council as well as with the Political and Security Committee in informal sessions; in multilateral fora and third countries (vg EU head of Delegation and UK Embassy); on sanctions by exchange of information on listing and their justification, an EU-UK sanctions dialogue and adoption of mutually supportive sanctions – as well as the possibility of joint outcomes namely joint statements, positions and demarches. Specifically in respect of CSDP the proposed framework also foresees consultation and cooperation through the various EU institutions and relevant organs (FA Council, EUMC, EUMS); cooperation on diplomatic support for crisis management; whenever the UK participates to a EU mission or operation, the participation in the respective operational headquarters; administrative agreements with the EDA and a coordinated approach to European capability development and planning and UK participation in specific projects and initiatives and in the EDF. In particular, the last document seem to take into consideration the general rules on consultation and cooperation on foreign policy, security and defence already laid down in the Draft Withdrawal Agreement.

Despite the wide range of issues and models for cooperation considered in the documents detailed above and the convergence in some main topics allowing to shape the grounds for the future EU-UK relationship in respect of CFSP/CSDP, it cannot be ignored that the so-called (flexible and scalable) consultation and cooperation between the EU and the UK does not exclude an autonomous foreign and security policy – meaning autonomous (although convergent in some areas) internal decision making process.

Despite the mentioned convergence, the exact terms of the future relationship in the field of CFSP/CSDP – either during or after the transition period – would be definitively established both in the Withdrawal Agreement (transitional period) and in the Political Declaration of 25 November 2018 applicable after the transition period (both analysed in III. below), thus confirming some of the ways of cooperation already envisaged by both parties but also stressing out the divergences between them.

III. The Agreement on the Withdrawal of the UK from the European Union and the Common Foreign and Security Policy and the Political Declaration and 'Foreign Policy, security and defence'

Both the texts of the Withdrawal Agreement and the Political Declaration setting out the framework for the future relationship between the EU and the UK[68] (as mentioned in Article 184 of the Agreement and which terms will be foreseen in future agreements to be negotiated and concluded by the EU and the EU), include rules addressing issues and possible forms of cooperation in the field of CFSP and CSDP.

On one hand, the Withdrawal Agreement addresses CFSP and CSDP issues in three articles: both Article 127 ('Scope of transition'), 2 and 7(a) and 129 ('Specific arrangements relating to the Union's external action'), mainly 2, 6 and 7, of Part Four on *Transition*; and Article 156 ('The United Kingdom's obligations from the date of entry into force of this Agreement') in Part Five on *Financial provisions.* On the other hand, the Political Declaration addresses CFSP and CSDP issues in its Part III (Security Partnership, III. Foreign policy, security and defence, A. to G. (92–109).

The main differences regarding the scope of application and the contents of both texts, specifically in respect of CFSP/CSDP, can be identified as follows:

First of all, the Agreement foresees rules defining the UK legal status (rights and obligations) regarding CFSP/CSDP *during* the transition period (starting on the date of entry into force of the Agreement and ending on 31 December 2020[69]); and the Political Declaration, mainly foresee objectives and principles (III, 92–94) and guidelines (III, 95 and A. to G, 96 and following) regarding the future relationship in the field of 'Foreign policy,

---

68 All the references mentioned in the text refer to their respective versions as adapted and supplemented by 11 April 2019 – Agreement on the withdrawal of the United Kingdom of Great Britain and Northern Ireland from the European Union and the European Atomic Energy Community ([2019] OJ C144 I/1); and Political Declaration setting out the Framework for the future relationship between the European Union and the United Kingdom (XT 21095/18, BXT 111, CO EUR-PREP 54 of 22 November 2018) endorsed by the European Council of 25 November 2018 ([2019] JO C 66I/02), as supplemented by the Joint Statement supplementing the Political Declaration setting out the Framework for the future relationship between the European Union and the United Kingdom of Great Britain and Northern Ireland (XT 21018/19, BXT 24, CO EUR-PREP 11 of 20 March 2019) as endorsed by the European Council (Art. 50) of 25 November 2018 and of 21 March 2019.

69 See Arts 2(e) and 126 of the Withdrawal Agreement.

security and defence' (as a part of a broader 'Security partnership') *after* the end of the transition period.

Secondly, the specific articles included in the Agreement regarding CFSP and CSDP defining the UK legal status during the transition period mainly address two forms of derogation of the general rule of Article 127 (1) of the Agreement according to which (unless otherwise provided in the Agreement) EU law, including in the field of CFSP/CSDP (Chapter 2 of Title V of the TEU i.e. 'Specific provisions on the CFSP'[70]) shall apply to and in the UK during the transition period: (i) a full derogation of EU rules before the end of the transition period depending on an EU-UK agreement governing their relationship in the area of CFSP which becomes applicable during the transition period (Art. 127, 2)[71] as well as (ii) specific thematic derogations and an 'opt-out' clause which apply during the transition period.The specific paragraphs of the Political Declaration regarding the issue of 'Foreign policy, security and defence' mainly address guidelines identifying the mechanisms to be used in the future relationship between the EU and the UK in this field which is based, despite some common objectives, in parallel EU and UK foreign policies according to their respective strategic and security interests and in close cooperation when those interests are shared – through dialogue, consultation, coordination, exchange of information and cooperation mechanisms (Part III, III, 94–95).

Thirdly, the articles of the Agreement regarding CFSP and CSDP that foresee thematic derogations refer specifically to the application of CSDP rules – permanent structured cooperation (PESCO) and EU missions and operations (Art. 127, 7(a) and 129, 7) – while the 'opt-out' clause (based on 'vital and stated reasons of national policy' – Article 129, 6[72]) regards the non-application of a decision of the Council falling under CFSP including

70 Chapter 2 (Specific provisions on the Common Foreign and Security Policy) of Title V (General provisions on the Union's External Action and Specific provisions on the Common Foreign and Security Policy) of the TEU – including both *Section 1 Common provisions* (Arts 23 to 41) and *Section 2 Provisions on the Common Security and Defence Policy* (Arts 42 to 46).

71 In which case the rules of the TEU and respective secondary law will simply cease to apply to the UK from the date of application of that agreement. – Without prejudice to Art 127 (2), Art 129 (5) of the Withdrawal Agreement foresees that whenever there is a need for coordination, the UK may be consulted, on a case-by-case basis

72 Art 129, 6 of the Withdrawal Agreement foresees that Following a decision of the Council falling under Chapter 2 of Title V TEU, the UK may make a formal declaration to the High Representative of the Union for Foreign Affairs and Security

CSDP (Chapter 2 of Title V of the TEU). The specific paragraphs of the Political Declaration regarding the issue of 'Foreign policy, security and defence' foresee guidelines identifying firstly the establishment of general structured consultation and regular thematic (general and sectorial) dialogues identifying areas and activities for close cooperation (III, A, 96–98) and also some specific areas of future consultation and cooperation (sanctions, crisis management missions and operations both civilian and military, defence capabilities developments, intelligence exchanges and development cooperation – III, B. to G., 99–109).

Some relevant details of both texts should still be underlined in the perspective of the CFSP and CSDP post-Brexit.

A. *The Agreement on the Withdrawal and the Common Foreign and Security Policy*

Four aspects of the rules laid down in the Withdrawal Agreement must be underlined.

The text of the Agreement envisages the possibility of an EU-UK agreement governing their relationship in the area of CFSP, which becomes applicable during the transition period (Art. 127 (2)) ending on 31 December 2020. Such a thematic agreement on one hand may indicate that CFSP is a sensitive political area in which the UK would like not be bound by EU rules as soon as possible – that both the opt-out clause (CFSP) and the derogations on CSDP (PESCO and EU missions and operations) may already confirm; and, on the other hand, cannot be understood and designed outside of the framework and guidelines set out in the Political Declaration regarding foreign policy, security and defence – namely the specific areas of future consultation and cooperation and the mechanisms already identified, which have to constitute a common basis for the future relationship between the EU and the UK in this respect.

Moreover, the two derogations regarding CSDP – PESCO and EU missions and operations – may indicate the will of the UK not to be involved in principle neither in the deepening and the development of the EU security and defence policy nor in assuming leading responsibilities within EU

Policy, indicating that for vital and stated reasons of national policy, in those exceptional cases, it will not apply the decision (and that in a spirit of mutual solidarity, the UK shall refrain from any action likely to conflict with or impede Union action based on that decision and the Member States shall respect the position of the UK).

missions and operations conducted under Articles 42, 43 and 44 TEU (or operational actions under Article 28 TEU).[73] In special, considering that PESCO is a form of enhanced cooperation that is at the core of the recent defence policy developments post EU Global Strategy, the derogation regarding PESCO is in line with the fact that the UK did not sign the Joint Notification on PESCO in November 2017. However, this derogation does not preclude the possibility for the UK to be invited to participate as a third country in individual projects under the conditions set out in Council Decision (CFSP) 2017/2315[74] on an exceptional basis, or in any other form of cooperation to the extent allowed and under the conditions set out by future Union acts adopted on the basis of those Articles 42(6) and 46 TEU[75] – the latter still to be determined. Therefore, even if such rules of the Agreement also clearly indicate that the participation of the UK as a third State in PESCO project is admissible by both parties in a longer term perspective, the conditions under which the UK may participate are not yet fully determined.[76]

In addition, and despite the above mentioned derogations, concerning financial support of CFSP/CSDP, the Agreement foresees that until the end of the transition period (31/12/2020) the UK shall continue to contribute to the financing of the European Defence Agency (and of the EU

73 Art 129 (7) foresees that during the transition period, the UK shall not provide commanders of civilian operations, heads of mission, operation commanders or force commanders for missions or operations conducted under Arts 42, 43 and 44 TEU, nor shall it provide the operational headquarters for such missions or operations or serve as framework nation for Union battlegroups and also that during that period the UK shall not provide the head of any operational actions under Art 28 TEU.

74 Arts 4 (2) (g) and 9 (1) of Council Decision (CFSP) 2017/2315 of 11 December 2017 establishing permanent structured cooperation (PESCO) and determining the list of participating Member States, and Council Recommendation of 6 March 2018 concerning a roadmap for the implementation of PESCO, no 13.

75 Art 127 (7) (a) of the Withdrawal Agreement.

76 According to the Council Conclusions on Security and Defence in the context of the EU Global Strategy (Conclusions of 19 November 2018, 1378/18 of 19 November 2018), no 12, a Council decision on the general conditions under which third States could exceptionally participate was expected to be adopted by the end of 2018. However, the Conclusions already indicate some general rules in this respect: a third State would need to provide substantial added value to the PESCO projects, contribute to strengthening PESCO and the CSDP and meet more demanding commitments, while fully respecting the principle of decision-making autonomy of the EU and its Member States. – From the UK perspective see House of Commons, Briefing Paper No 8149, Updated December 2018, EU Defence: the realisation of Permanent Structured Cooperation (PESCO), no 5.

Institute for Security Studies and the EU Satellite Centre) as well as to the costs of CSDP operations, on the basis of the same contribution key, namely in accordance with its Article 5[77].

Finally, although the Agreement on the Withdrawal of the UK does not ignore the issue of CFSP/CSDP and the role of the UK during the transition period, it does not bring much light on the future EU-UK relationship in that field: not only because none of the terms of the (future) agreement is addressed but also because in the only area in which a future UK participation is foreseen as it was already a third State (PESCO), the rules of such participation are still uncertain since not yet determined by EU secondary law. Therefore, the terms of the EU-UK relationship and possible main issues and forms of cooperation in the fields of CFSP/CSDP after the transitional period are still rather uncertain and do not exclude a differentiated third State status.

B. The Political Declaration and Foreign Policy, security and defence

However, the *Political Declaration* setting out the framework for the future relationship between the EU and the UK on 25 November 2018 (foreseen in Article 184 of the Withdrawal Agreement) may, to a certain extent, contribute to clarify the general features of the future EU-UK relationship regarding CFSP/CSDP beyond the transitional period.

Considering its contents on 'Foreign Policy, security and defence', as mentioned above, some of its features are particularly relevant to shape the terms of that future relationship after the end of the transition period. Three of such features should be underlined.

Firstly, the text of the Political Declaration indicates that both parties accept common general grounds for their future relationship based in common core values and rights, identification of areas of shared interests

77 Within the financial provisions of Part Five, Art 156 (The United Kingdom's obligations from the date of entry into force of this agreement) of Chapter 7 (Agencies of the Council and Common and Security Defence Policy operations) foresees as follows: *Until 31 December 2020, the United Kingdom shall contribute to the financing of the European Defence Agency*, the European Union Institute for Security Studies and the European Union Satellite Centre, *as well as to the costs of Common Security and Defence Policy operations on the basis of the same contribution key set out in point (a) of Article 14(9) of the Council Decision (EU) 2016/1353, in Article 10(3) of Council Decision 2014/75/CFSP, in Article 10(3) of Council Decision 2014/401/CFSP and in the second paragraph of Article 41(2) of the TEU, respectively, and in accordance to Article 5 of the Agreement.*

in which participation in Union programmes and dialogues are envisaged.[78] These common general grounds are subsequently detailed in the text of the Political Declaration regarding each area of the EU-UK future partnership, namely in Part III: Security partnership within which the area of 'Foreign policy, security and defence' is addressed (as mentioned above).

Secondly, within the EU-UK Security Partnership, the guidelines on 'Foreign policy, security and defence' foresee general guidelines and instruments regarding dialogue, consultation, coordination and cooperation in this area: (i) structured consultation and regular thematic dialogues identifying areas and activities where closer cooperation could contribute to the attainment of common objectives, namely the Political Dialogue on CFSP and CSDP as well as sectorial dialogues at different levels (ministerial, senior office, working), including invitation of the UK to informal Ministerial meetings of EU Member States; (ii) seeking to cooperation in third countries (including in security consular provision and protection and development projects) as well as in international organisations and fora, notably the UN, allowing the Parties to support each other's positions, deliver external action and manage global challenges in a coherent manner, included through agreed statements, demarches and shared positions. The latter may implicitly refer to the permanent seat of the UK and France in the UN Security Council and cooperation within that organ but may as well refer to the rules of coordination between Member States in international organisations and conferences, including the Security Council, foreseen in Art. 34 TEU; to the rules on cooperation between the external delegations of the EEAS and the diplomatic and consular missions of the EU Member States laid down in Art. 221, 2 TEU – so that after the end of transition period similar coordination and cooperation may continue. However, the concrete terms of both mentioned consultation and cooperation are not foreseen except for the level of consultation and dialogue, the case by case invitation to the informal Ministerial meetings – and still have to be determined in future agreements to be negotiated and signed on the basis of Article 148 of the Withdrawal Agreement.

Thirdly, CSDP is specifically addressed within the concrete areas where EU-UK cooperation is already envisaged (Part III, III, B. to G.) despite their strategic autonomy and freedom of action. In this respect, three of the areas of CSDP already addressed in the Withdrawal Agreement are also men-

78 See Political Declaration, Part I: Initial provisions, I. Basis for cooperation, A. Core values and rights, 6–7 and II. Areas of shared interests, A. Participation in Union programmes and B. Dialogues, 11–15.

tioned: EU operations and missions, PESCO, and financing of CSDP projects – either through the UK collaboration on existing and future projects of the EDA or the participation of eligible UK entities in collaborative defence projects bringing together Union entities supported by the EDF.

Regarding PESCO, the Political Declaration merely assumes the UK's collaboration in projects in the framework of PESCO 'where invited to participate on an exceptional basis' by the Council of the EU in PESCO format and no further rules are foreseen (Part III, III, D., 104 (c)).

Concerning EU's missions and operations (Articles 42 (1) and 43 (1) TEU), the Political Declarations foresees close cooperation in EU-led 'crisis management missions and operations' enabling the UK to participate on a case by case basis in CSDP missions and operations – opened to third countries – through a Framework Participation Agreement (FPA). In this respect some specific rules are already laid down (Part III, III, C. 101–103): the UK may indicate its intention to contribute to a planned CSDP mission or operation (open to third countries); in this case the parties should intensify interaction and exchange of information at relevant stages of the planning process and proportionately to the level of the UK's contribution; and as a contributor to a specific CSDP mission or operation the UK would participate in several relevant bodies meeting (Force Generation, Call for Contributions and the Committee of Contributors meeting) and would have the possibility, in case of CSDP military operations, to second staff to the designated Operations Headquarters proportionate to the level of its contribution. This outline for the future UK participation in EU-led crisis management and operations, does not however envisages neither any form of a differentiated statute of the UK (i.e., according to which the UK could be envisaged as more than a third State) nor (apparently) a participation in all possible missions and tasks foreseen in Articles. 42 (1) and 43 (1) TEU since it refers specifically (to 'Union-led crisis management missions and operations' Part III, III, C., par. 101, first sentence) – which are referred to, among other tasks, in Article 43 (1) TEU ('tasks of combat forces in crisis management, including peace-making and post-conflict stabilisation').

From the contents of both the texts of the Withdrawal Agreement and the Political Declaration regarding the area of CFSP/CSDP in particular some general conclusions can be drawn: 1) EU and UK foreign policies (including security and defence areas) are autonomous despite common values and objectives; 2) on the grounds of *shared* security and defence interests close – 'flexible and scalable' – cooperation may exist; 3) a few general guidelines for consultation and dialogue regarding foreign policy, security and defence are foreseen but those still need to be further detailed; 4) some specific areas of close cooperation are already identified, namely sanctions, intelligence exchanges, space and development cooperation; 5) in the concrete field of EU CSDP, the participation of the UK in PESCO projects and in EU-led crisis management missions and operations both civilian and military is admitted to be tough and exceptional, on a case to case basis and apparently in the capacity of a (mere) third State; 6) in the concrete field of defence capabilities development the UK and its eligible entities may collaborate in relevant projects of the EDA through an Administrative Arrangement and in collaborative defence projects supported by the EDF – so that both parties may benefit from research and industrial cooperation in order to facilitate inter operability and to promote joint effectiveness of Armed Forces. Those conclusions may indicate that the future EU-UK relationship in the area of CFSP/CSDP, on one hand is rather programmatic and modest and that the concrete terms of the participation are rather narrow and still need to be detailed (in future agreements) and that no specific ex-EU Member State statute is envisaged; and, on the other hand, that some of the concrete areas in which closer cooperation is envisaged (in particular PESCO and defence capabilities development) relate to the sub-area of CSDP in which EU policy post-EU Global Strategy has more quickly evolved.

However, the guidelines laid down in the Withdrawal Agreement and the Political Declaration appears to still leave room to shape a differentiated third State status in the field of CFSP/CSDP. Even in areas where the status of third State is clearly mentioned – PESCO and EU missions and operations – neither the rules of third States participation are definitively defined nor is the envisaged FPA necessarily bound to follow a single model.

IV. Shaping a (possible) differentiated third state status in the field of CFSP, including CSDP

A. Common grounds as a basis of the future EU-UK relationship

Addressing the issue of the future of EU's CFSP, including CSDP, after Brexit cannot ignore the possibility of different scenarios, despite the intentions of cooperation of both involved parties – the EU and its Member States on one hand, and the UK as a (future) third State on the other side –, including a more radical scenario in which the UK, once having left the EU, would simply be treated as another third State that would only be able to participate in the EU's CFSP and CSDP to the extent that the EU allows it and under the model and forms of participation that already exists today regarding current third States. This scenario would mean basically none or very weak involvement in the EU's CFSP and CSDP decision-making process and implementation of such policies – even if the EU would have to relate to the UK as an autonomous international actor within several formal international organisations and informal groups participating in the global governance in the area (or related-areas) in question. However, and being the first time that Article 50 clause is activated, it is arguable that in the particular areas of CFSP and CSDP a stronger link between the EU and its Member States and the UK may (and should) exist – although in terms that are not yet completely clear. In fact, the EU's CFSP and CSDP can undoubtedly proceed in its current course based on the EU Global Strategy and the defined 'three pillars' strategy without the UK, but it is questionable that it would be advisable to do so. And if that is not the case, common grounds for a future (different) relationship should exist.

Considering the contents of both the texts of the Withdrawal Agreement (Article 184) and the Political Declaration it can be assumed that such common grounds for the EU-UK future relationship in the field of CFSP/CSDP do exist, despite possible divergent views regarding strategic interests and specific issues. These common grounds can be found either in the axiological basis of the European integration (democracy, rule of law and fundamental rights values) as well as in the UN values and principles, or in shared objectives or shared need to address common threats and increasing challenges to European foreign policy, security and defence – especially those that a single State or States in a bilateral relationship are not able to cope with. Such common grounds can concretely be found, as mentioned above, in the Political Declaration where common values and shared objectives, are foreseen[79]. These shared objectives in respect of foreign policy, security and defence can be listed as follows (as enounced in Part III, III, pars. 92–95): protect citizens from external threats, prevent conflicts, strengthen international peace and security, including through the UN and NATO; address the root causes of global challenges such as terrorism or illegal migration, champion a rules-based international order and project (their) common values worldwide; promote sustainable devel-

79 See Part I: Initial Provisions, I. Basis for cooperation, A. Core values and rights and II. Areas of shared interest and in particular Part III: Security Partnership, I. Objectives and principles (80–81) and III. Foreign policy, security and defence (92–93).

opment and the eradication of poverty and support the implementation of the UN Sustainable Development Goals and the European Consensus on Development. The shared objectives are in line with the EU CFSP objectives foreseen in the TEU as well as with the broad priorities established by the EU Global Strategy.

Moreover, even if autonomous EU and UK foreign policies and therefore different approaches and strategic and security interests (either by geographical, historical or political reasons) may (and do) exist, cross-spheres of interest and activities may still be of interest for both parties allowing each other to act on specific issues and matters but contributing to the overall relevance of Europe within international scene. The Political Declaration indicates that current areas of shared interests are already identified (sanctions, operations and missions, defence capabilities development, intelligence exchanges, space and development cooperation) and new areas of shared interests and close cooperation may be identified in order to attain common objectives, namely through structured consultation and thematic dialogues.

In the field of CFSP and in particular in the field of CSDP the role and contribution of the UK to the implementation of EU objectives up to the present cannot be ignored, either because of its capabilities or different forms of contribution, namely financial (mainly through the EU budget), to the CSDP.

However the way in which the EU will deal with the UK desire to participate, to some extent, in the field of CFSP and CSDP also depends on the development of the implementation of the Global Strategy, the EU new level of ambition and an eventual future decision on a common defence policy (more autonomy vs deeper collaboration with relevant partners in key areas, such as NATO) – and where is the razor's edge in both the perspective of the EU and UK (vg no common defence policy and European army).

In the scenario in which the UK would be a third State, a close relationship with the EU would still be possible by shaping a differentiated third State status in the field of CFSP, including CSDP.

B. Possible issues and forms of cooperation to be addressed

The consideration of the wider context, the EU trends, concerns expressed on both sides[80] and doctrine proposals[81] allow to identify a wide range of both, political and juridical issues regarding the post Brexit and post transitional period future relationship between the EU and the UK, specifically in the field of CFSP and CDSP.

Some of those issues, although not foreseen in the Withdrawal Agreement, were further addressed in general terms and partially clarified in the Political Declaration on 25 November 2018. According to that text: foreign policy, security and defence are addressed together, as a part of a EU-UK security partnership, based on common objectives; the UK may collaborate to some extent in CFSP and CSDP; no other status than the status of third State is expressly envisaged, in particular in respect of the participation of the UK in EU missions and operations and PESCO projects; the envisaged collaboration reveals – besides general structured consultation and thematic consultation – a selective thematic approach in six identified areas; participation of the UK in decision making and EU institutions and organs is only foreseen to the extent that the UK can be invited by the High Representative to informal Ministerial meetings (defence) and may participate in certain EU missions and operations (crisis management) and therefore in their respective structures and organs, although in proportion to the level of its contribution; the mechanisms foreseen to ensure the EU-UK relation-

80 See also House of Lords European Union Committee, *Europe in the World: Towards a More Effective EU Foreign and Security Strategy*, 16 February 2016, HL paper 97 of session 2015–16; House of Lords Commons Affairs Committee, *Implications of the Referendum on EU membership for the UK's Role in the World*, 26 April 2016, HL 545 session 2015–16.

81 See M Chalmers, 'UK Foreign and Security Policy after Brexit' (2017), RUSI Briefing Paper, January 2017; H Dijkstra, 'UK and EU Foreign Policy Cooperation after Brexit' (2016), RUSI *Newsbrief*, 5 September 2016; N Witney, 'Brexit and Defence: Time to Dust Off the 'Letter of Intent'?' (2016), European Council of Foreign Relations, 14 July 2016; S Peers, 'The EU's New Defence Plans Don't Amount to an Army – So the UK Can't Veto Them' (2016), London School of Economics and Political Science Brexit Blog, 28 September 2016; I Bond, 'Brexit and Foreign Policy: Divorce? (2016), Centre for European Reform, 18 July 2016; G Van der Loo and S Blockmans, 'The Impact of Brexit on the EU's International Agreements', 15 July 2016 (available at www.ceps.eu); C Major and A von Voss, 'European Defence in View of Brexit', SWP Comments 2017/C 10, April 2017, 4 p (available at swp-berlin.org); as well as James Black et al., *Defence and Security after Brexit. Understanding the possible implications of the UK's Decision to Leave the EU, Compendium Report* (Cambridge, Rand Europe, 2017, available at www.rand.org).

ship and the model of (closer) cooperation regarding EU missions and operations (Framework Participation Agreement) and EDA (Administrative Arrangement), are not innovative since collaboration with third States through those instruments already exist;[82] participation in international organisations and international bodies is foreseen in terms of consultation, coordination and mutual support of each other's positions in such fora; financial participation of the UK seems to be rather weak and relates mainly to the financing of EU-led missions and operations as well as PESCO projects.

It is therefore now certain that certain forms of cooperation between the EU and the UK in the field of CFSP/CSDP after the end of the transition period have already been addressed in general terms by the Political Declaration as mentioned above – namely common objectives, general provisions of consultation and cooperation in order to achieve them, areas of (current) shared interests and instruments (dialogue, consultation, coordination, exchange of information and cooperation mechanisms).

However, those terms must still be further detailed in the text of the treaty that will apply to the EU-UK relationship after the transitional period in order to translate such general guidance rules into more concrete ways of EU-UK collaboration in the area of CFSP/CSDP (especially when the guidelines are not detailed,vg Space and Development cooperation).

This next step – negotiating and agreeing on more detailed rules – appears to be an opportunity to envisage the features of a possible differentiated third State status in the field of CFSP/CSDP.

In this respect, three points should be underlined in particular that may require further reflection from both involved parties.

First, detailed rules still have to be negotiated and agreed between both parties regarding the points addressed in the Declaration in general terms, which is especially the case of the consultation and cooperation and the establishment of a structured consultation and regular thematic dialogues – which seems to be the main instrument for EU-UK consultation and coop-

82 The participation of third States in EU operations was institutionalized through the signing of FPA since 2004 (see Thierry Tardy, CSDP: getting third States on board, EU Institute for Security Studies, Brief Issue, 6, 2014 (available in www.iss.europa.eu) – vg Framework Agreement between the United States of America (USA) and the EU on the participation of the USA in EU crisis management operations, [2011] OJ l143/2. Administrative Arrangements have already been concluded with third States – Norway (2006), Switzerland (2012) Republic of Serbia (2013) and Ukraine (2015) – enabling them to participate in EDA's projects and programs (see www.eda.europa.eu).

eration in foreign policy and security. It is not yet quite clear whether the mentioned closer cooperation will rely completely on a flexible and scalable cooperation built on a mere case by case approach, according to their strategic and security interests eventually shared at a certain time, or whether both parties want to build a medium and long term stronger partnership based on a continuous and effective cooperation on common grounds enabling them to act together in foreign policy issues. The translation of the general prevision of the Political Declaration regarding the future structured consultation and thematic dialogue into more concrete procedures and rules (as vg those proposed in the DExEU Policy paper of 24 May 2018 above mentioned in II., B.) may be the opportunity to design a status of UK that may clearly differ from the current status of a mere third State. Also in this respect, the shaping of the concrete rules regarding structured and thematic dialogue may lead to the regular contribution of the UK if not to decision making (which is not probable since autonomy of both parties is also foreseen) at least, to some extent, to decision shaping in those topics of clear shared interest where a collective response to external threats and problems is more effective (vg sanctions policy as an instrument of CFSP or crisis management). This could be achieved by the regular (or even permanent) presence of UK representatives in EU EEAS and in particular CFSP structures, such as the EUMS and crisis management structures, or even on some EU delegations in third States. Moreover, the consultation and cooperation at bilateral level and within international organisations could be further elaborated in order to envisage the alignment of the UK with EU foreign policy positions and the possible establishment of procedures to adopt in that respect to ensure coordination of positions on a regular basis and even an *actio pro communitate*.

Second, and in particular in respect of PCSD, one may question why the EU and the UK have not gone further and tried to envisage and design a different status for the UK, 'half-way' between a full EU Member State and a mere third Member State – even if such approach depends on the political will of both parties. However weak the UK contribution (financial or in civil and military capacity) to the CFSP/CSDP may be, and even recognising the lack of consensus on some foreign policy topics, a relationship of decades as an EU 'insider', who participates in most of the post-Global Strategy developments, should not be completely thrown away. In this respect, some more detailed guidelines are foreseen in two of the (current) areas of shared interests: EU missions and operations and defence capabilities development, including PESCO. However, such guidelines included in the Political Declaration must still be further detailed – in particular in the text of the treaty that will apply to the EU-UK relationship after the transitional period. Moreover, further formal agreements – such as the mentioned Framework Participation Agreement regarding EU CSDP missions and operations or Administrative arrangement regarding the participation in the EDA – as well as secondary EU law rules – at least regarding the requisites of participation in PESCO projects – still have to be, respectively, agreed upon by both parties and approved, as a *sine qua non* condition of a concrete and effective collaboration between the EU and the UK beyond the term of the transitional period (31 December 2020) foreseen in the Withdrawal Agreement. In this respect, the elaboration on the concrete terms of such agreements (old instruments with new contents) and of secondary rules regarding the participation of third States in PESCO projects will be an opportunity to further deepen the terms of the future relationship foreseen in the Political Declaration and maybe not (completely) close the door to the possibility of having a different status and model of cooperation (more and differentiated rights of participation in CFSP and more financial and other duties), regarding the participation of a (not mere, since ex-Member State) third State.

Finally, the possible differentiated third State status on a basis that overcomes a simply case by case cooperation (vg on thematic block or even geographical approach basis) could also be achieved – if the political will allows – through the agreement on a formal (or informal) observer status, with some rights of participation in EU institutions, bodies and structures (decision shaping) with financial EU counterparty ('value for money') that could be agreed namely through a contribution to the financing of the most relevant CFSP financial instruments besides the EU budget.

List of Authors:

Giacinto della Cananea : Professor of Administrative Law and EU Administrative Law, University of Rome "*Tor Vergata*"; Principal investigator, ERC advanced grant for the research project on the "Common Core of European Administrative Laws" (COCEAL).

Tom Eijsbouts, Emeritus professor of European Constitutional Law, Universities of Amsterdam and Leiden.

Paula Vaz Freire, Associate Professor Faculty of Law, University of Lisbon

Stefan Griller, Professor of European Law, University of Salzburg, vice Director of Salzburg Centre of European Union Studies

Rui Lanceiro, Assistant Professor at the University of Lisbon School of Law; Senior Research Fellow at Centro de Investigação de Direito Público (CIDP – Lisbon Centre for Research in Public Law); Assessor (Law Clerk) at the Portuguese Constitutional Court.

Jean-Victor Louis, Professor of *European* Law (ret.), Institut d'Etudes européennes de l'Université libre de Bruxelles, fmr. General Counsel of the National Bank of Belgium

Ana Maria Guerra Martins, Associate Professor (with Aggregation) at the Law School of Lisbon University, Researcher at the Lisbon Centre for Research in Public Law (CIDP), former Justice at the Portuguese Constitutional Court, and former General Inspector of Justice

Maria José Rangel de Mesquita, Associate Professor (Professora associada com agregação) Faculty of Law – University of Lisbon; Senior Research Fellow at Centro de Investigação de Direito Público (CIDP – Lisbon Centre for Research in Public Law); Justice at the Constitutional Court of Portugal

List of Authors:

Ingolf Pernice, Professor of Public, European and Public International Law (ret.), Humboldt Universität zu Berlin, Director of the Alexander von Humboldt Institute for Internet and Society, Berlin.

Daniel Thym, Professor for Public, European and International Law and Director of the Research Centre Immigration & Asylum Law, University of Konstanz, Member of the German Expert Council on Integration and Migration

Mattias Wendel, Professor for Public, European and International Law, University of Bielefeld

Jiří Zemánek, Judge of the Constitutional Court of Czech Republic, Jean Monnet Professor of European Law at Charles University in Prague